P9-BTX-976

FORSYTH LIBRARY
FORT HAYS STATE UNIVERSITY

HENRY JAMES AND THE REAL THING

A MODERN READER'S GUIDE

Also by Virginia Llewellyn Smith

ANTON CHEKHOV AND THE LADY WITH THE DOG

Henry James and the Real Thing

A Modern Reader's Guide

Virginia Llewellyn Smith

St. Martin's Press

© Virginia Llewellyn Smith 1994

All rights reserved. No reproduction, copy or transmission of
this publication may be made without written permission.

No paragraph of this publication may be reproduced, copied or
transmitted save with written permission or in accordance with
the provisions of the Copyright, Designs and Patents Act 1988,
or under the terms of any licence permitting limited copying
issued by the Copyright Licensing Agency, 90 Tottenham Court
Road, London W1P 9HE.

Any person who does any unauthorised act in relation to this
publication may be liable to criminal prosecution and civil
claims for damages.

First published in Great Britain 1994 by
THE MACMILLAN PRESS LTD
Houndmills, Basingstoke, Hampshire RG21 2XS
and London
Companies and representatives
throughout the world

A catalogue record for this book is available
from the British Library.

ISBN 0–333–61139–X

Printed in Great Britain by
Antony Rowe Ltd
Chippenham, Wiltshire

First published in the United States of America 1994 by
Scholarly and Reference Division,
ST. MARTIN'S PRESS, INC.,
175 Fifth Avenue,
New York, N.Y. 10010

ISBN 0–312–12313–2

Library of Congress Cataloging-in-Publication Data
Llewellyn Smith, Virginia.
Henry James and the real thing : a modern reader's guide /
Virginia Llewellyn Smith.
p.   cm.
Includes bibliographical references (p.   ).
ISBN 0–312–12313–2
1. James, Henry, 1843–1916—Handbooks, manuals, etc.   I. Title.
PS2124.L54 1994
813′ .4—dc20   94–20523
                                                          CIP

For Chris, Julia and Cas

Contents

'But how does he know?'
  'Know it's the real thing? Oh, I'm sure
when you see it you do know. *Vera incessu patuit dea!*'

'The Figure in the Carpet'

Preface

Does the reader James wrote for still exist? Has an unbridgeable gap opened up between the academic interest he continues to excite and the popular success he always wanted? Are we losing, under the sheer weight of his reputation and of critical comment, the sense of what we read him *for* – the wit, the excitement, the moments of truth?

This book is written in the belief that James's genius easily surmounts these considerations, but that there *are* people who remain unconvinced of this – and that not all of them will read this book. It is written, therefore, for friends who share my enthusiasm for James, without having had my opportunity to indulge it; but it is also intended to be useful to those of their pupils who may feel they haven't the time or the background knowledge to tackle more specialised or theoretical critical texts. And it is aimed, ultimately, at those persons under no obligation to read novels, let alone criticism, who have tactfully said to me that they might become James enthusiasts if they had some idea where to start. If they find this book to have been worth reading in that respect, I shall feel it was well worth writing it.

I have tried in it to strike a balance between two broad views of James: (1) that his work is about (alternatively, not *enough* about) real human dilemmas; and (2) that it is 'about' fictional processes. These views might be categorised as 'ancient' and 'modern'; but that 'modern' in my subtitle is there as an acknowledgement that critical fashions change, not an assertion that the newest model is necessarily the best. It has the function also of distinguishing my book from, and of conscious reference to, the work of S. Gorley Putt, who in calling his 1966 survey of James 'a reader's guide' has already made by implication two important points.

First, that our prime concern with James must be as readers not critics, and not with what he was, but with what he wrote; not to establish his place in the literary canon (or to demote him from it), but to find in him whatever pleasure and interest we can. For that is what's assumed under the term 'guide' (and this is the second point): that we are where we are because we want to be, and being there, intend to make the most of it.

This book, then, adopts a text-centred approach which, while it takes account of different critical viewpoints, is not 'coming from' any particular angle – the feminist, say, or the Freudian. The focus is, rather, as in a guide-book it should be, on what I have tried to get *to*: a sense of the authentic James, on the level that the reader can be expected to absorb it – on a level of awareness, that is, between 'what happens to the characters' and James's manipulation of our reactions.

I have made no attempt to outline the theoretical background of modern critical assumptions or comprehensively to examine the received wisdoms of less recent approaches. That has already been done more than adequately by, for example, Oscar Cargill and Millicent Bell. I have not wanted to write a bigger book – wouldn't indeed have been allowed to: I'm afraid that as it is my 'real thing' will prove – to echo Sir Claude in *What Maisie Knew* – 'impossibly dear'. Far be it from me though to imply (as he goes on to say) that 'anything else is a waste of money'. My greatest debt is to the very many critics whose writing has inspired and edified me and sometimes made me laugh out loud – as James himself, more often, does.

Debts of another kind are less quantifiable, and on the personal level it would be still more invidious to name names. Those who have helped me to see this project through know who they are, and how much I have needed and valued their advice, assistance and support. I would in addition like to thank two anonymous publisher's readers who gave me at the right time encouragement to keep going. And I am lucky to have found in Margaret Cannon and Charmian Hearne the most efficient and considerate of editors.

V. Ll. S.

References and Abbreviations

In quoting from James's fiction I have used the revised New York Edition text, where there is a choice.

The figures in parentheses that follow displayed quotations are page references. In the case of the novels, these refer to the current paperback editions in Oxford University Press's World's Classics series, easily found in libraries and bookshops. The exception is *The Princess Casamassima*, not yet available in The World's Classics; here I have had to refer to the 1987 Penguin edition, which prints the New York text. In the case of the short stories (and I have followed James's own distinction between 'tales' and novels), references citing volume and page number are to the twelve-volume Hart-Davis edition, *The Complete Tales of Henry James* (London, 1962–4), edited by Leon Edel. All page references to James's Prefaces are to the collected edition edited by R. P. Blackmur, *The Art of the Novel* (AN, see below).

All italics in quotations from James's text are his, unless otherwise indicated.

The dates given for James's novels are those of the first book (non-serial) publication.

Places and dates of publication of non-fictional works cited in the notes are those of the editions I have used.

The following abbreviations have been used in both text and notes:

AN *The Art of the Novel*, ed. with an introduction by R. P. Blackmur (New York and London, 1934).

HF *The House of Fiction. Henry James: Essays on the novel*, ed. Leon Edel (London, 1957).

HJL *The Letters of Henry James*, ed. Leon Edel, 4 vols (Cambridge, Mass., 1974–84).

Ntbks *The Notebooks of Henry James*, ed. and annotated by F. O. Matthiessen and Kenneth B. Murdock (Oxford, 1947, repr. Chicago and London, 1981).

Introduction

'The real thing' has always struck me as the quintessentially Jamesian phrase. It asserts the existence of an ideal; it invokes the discerning professional eye; it presupposes some solid basis to judgement. And yet, thrown off as it tends to be in James with gay abandon, it can have an extravagant and even a spurious ring: it is the sound-bite of an unreflective enthusiasm, a means of actually avoiding the reality it assumes, a catch-phrase used by characters who as we shall see cannot be disassociated from pretensions, or pretence, of one kind or another. Yet it is more than a mere rhetorical flourish. It always carries the implication both of reverence, and of some risk well worth running.

From the quintessential phrase to the quintessential James is not a straightforward step, but one which leads into a world where fakes and copies proliferate, and signposts are notoriously unreliable. I should therefore make it clear at the outset, lest the signpost of my title prove misleading, that I am not trying to suggest there exists one single point where all study of James ought to converge, or any final, exemplary statement to be made about him. Least of all am I attempting a philosophical or theoretical enquiry into the nature of reality. This book is about what we read into words, and words that conjure meaning out of the air. It is about flashy appearances and sturdier realities, about refinement of perception and vitality of expression, about methods sophisticated and unsophisticated of communication, promotion and evasion. It is about the confidence of narrative authority and its insidious subversion, about attempting to reconcile feeling safe with feeling free. These are, I believe, the fundamental concerns of James's fiction: they constitute the real James in whose footsteps it is the critic's business to tread. Which is why in what follows I have sometimes appropriated the idea of the real thing to use like a flag stuck in the map, or a banner on a battlefield, indicating that what I am looking for is close at hand.

For a preliminary marker of authentic James territory we need look no further than his short tale entitled 'The Real Thing' (1892). It tells the story of the Monarchs, a good-looking, well-dressed middle-aged couple, and of the young painter to whom in financial desperation they offer their services as models. I call him 'the painter', distinguishing him from the unspecific 'artist' who figures in

James's arguments and mine, for he takes a high view of his calling; but although he would prefer to do portraits, he makes a (bare) living by illustrating popular novels of society. In this connection, their selling-point, as the Monarchs see it, is that they are what they look like, a gentleman and a lady, or true thoroughbreds; 'the real thing' as used by them is a kind of code-word which admits the painter to the camp of the upper middle classes, while excluding his regular models, one Miss Churm, a 'freckled cockney', and Oreste, an undersized Italian or 'bankrupt orange-monger'. It is clear from this – the painter's terminology – and from much else, that he shares the same social perspective as the Monarchs, and within that context he takes them entirely at their own valuation; but the context of art is a different matter. The 'ruling passion' of the painter's life is his 'detestation of the amateur', and

> another perversity – an innate preference for the represented subject over the real one: the defect of the real one was so apt to be a lack of representation. I liked things that appeared; then one was sure. Whether they *were* or not was a subordinate and almost always a profitless question. (8.237)

And while the Monarchs are discreetly attempting to establish a relationship on the basis of cultivated taste, he is mentally relegating them, as an instance of perfect 'type', to the field of advertising: 'I could imagine "We always use it" pinned on their bosoms with the greatest effect.'

He tries them, but it doesn't work. When Mrs Monarch sits, his drawing

> looked like a photograph or a copy of a photograph. ... She was the real thing, but always the same thing. (8.244)

Major Monarch proves similarly unadaptable. Already impressively tall, he comes out twice the right size. Neither is half as much use as Miss Churm, who spots it at once.

There it is then, an ironic little fable, a confrontation of two worlds, one reflecting 'the deep intellectual repose' of 'twenty years of country-house visiting', the other consecrated to the austere mysteries of art; or a juxtaposition, as some readers may see it, of the frankly comic and the self-consciously hermetic. A lesser writer might have left the story here, at the point where the painter's theories are proved – or left us with the feeling that there is something rather smugly 'arty' in his attitude, a touch in his reiterated claims to 'perversity' of playing to the camera (it is one of the story's ironies, more apparent to the modern reader than perhaps it was to James in 1892, that the painter, while taking his illustrating so seriously, is utterly dismissive of photographic art). But 'The Real Thing' develops into something more interesting and characteristic of James at his best. From the moment that Major Monarch betrays the true state of their affairs, the painter becomes personally involved with them; with the result that his portrait of a pair of stupid swells is re-worked to reveal sentient living beings, the 'real marriage' that props up their brave front, and the shadow of a real life behind it. It is, emphatically, the life of the artless, concerned with 'how to get good claret cheap' and more heat out of the stove, but one ruled by gentler passions of its own, in response to which the painter keeps the Monarchs on out of sympathy, and comes to feel for them a kind of respect.

In the end, of course, they must be sacrificed to 'the perverse and cruel law by virtue of which the real thing could be so much less precious than the unreal'. The Monarchs recognise that it is they, not the cockney and the Italian, who are the wrong thing; the painter recognises that continuing to use them will bring about his own ruin. The artificial narrative structure of reversals and balances is complete, and the Monarchs are consigned to the permanent loose end of life – but not before they have exhibited an insight and a grace which might perhaps be finer qualities than the intelligence they haven't got and the taste they think they have.[1] Attempting to straighten out the painter's domestic chaos, they leave the story's intellectual furniture – its social and aesthetic assumptions – in total disarray. Why is their offer to become his servants one that the painter knows he must refuse? Is it because – unlike the Monarchs – he cannot adapt within the social context, because he believes the laws of life can be bent even less than those of art? Or because he fears the desecration of something that is, after all, as good as it looks? He remembers telling Major Monarch that 'if I were only rich I would offer him a salary to come and teach me how to live.' The painter is of course being indulgent (the Monarchs have made him kind, as he has made them interesting). We are left nonetheless acutely conscious of an awkward gap between everyday and mythical reality, a kind of no-man's-land in which the Monarchs have narrowly escaped extinction; and we are left too – not for the first

time in James, or the last – with the impression of someone less comfortably situated than he had bargained for between the competing
imperatives of art and life.

   This, the painter's situation – the conflict between the artist and
the 'world' – struck James as one of the 'great primary motives' or
themes (AN 79), and was one to which he had continuously to
accommodate himself. As a writer, he shared the painter's fascination with the problems of rendering reality: how was the 'direct relation to life' (the necessary approach) to be reconciled with the
indirect presentation of it (the desirable result)?[2] But as a novelist
who, like the painter and his models, had a living to make, he had to
take account of readers whose concerns were rooted in less esoteric
matters: who might perhaps understand a joke better than a theory
or prefer some little touch of the characteristic to a finely considered
abstraction. We have an excellent example of his adjustments to
popular taste in the figure of the Major, who takes so well to artistic
embellishment without ever losing his human face (and who irresistibly brings to mind, in his penchant for convivial society and for
holding forth to a captive audience, the 'real' – that is, the live,
inveterately party-going – James).[3] It is precisely in suggesting some
such identity of interest on one level or another between author,
character and reader that 'The Real Thing' and similar stories
succeed. In 'Greville Fane' (1892), one of the same period also told
by a 'serious' craftsman (in this case a writer), the conflict between
art and the world gets more robustly dealt with, the theoretical
difficulties of rendering reality which exercise the narrator more
firmly put in their place. 'Oh bother your direct relation to life!' says
Mrs Stormer, alias Greville Fane, the scribbler of lucrative trash who
simply rolls up her sleeves and gets on with it.

   The risk with the significant number of James's shorter fictions
which explore the situation of the artist is that if they fail to strike a
few roots into everyday experience, or are not nailed to some stout
peg such as Greville Fane (pegging away 'only from the elbows
down'), they will lack that vivid sense of life that for many readers
(if not so many critics) is the only point of re-presenting it. Fine writing aside, I find James's least successful works those which, like
'The Middle Years' (1893) and 'The Next Time' (1895), repeatedly
allude to a 'great work', unread, unwritten, at any rate invisible, a
black hole that seems to have sucked into itself all the vitality of
the narrative. In particular, we don't get in 'The Next Time' what
the great writer Ralph Limbert recognises as the basis of literature,

the material of his newspaper articles, the material of life: 'all human and elastic and suggestive'. These are exactly the qualities the painter finds in his Italian and cockney models; but they are also the qualities of 'The Real Thing' itself.

What James's fictions reveal at every turn is his own interest in the human and the elastic and the suggestive; what we observe there is the material of life perpetually prodded (does it laugh? does it cry?), stretched and given ideas above its station (all things the Monarchs would, at the beginning, never have done to Oreste and Miss Churm). This is how, so to speak, the 'real thing' becomes the real thing, or how life interacts with art; the tricky bit is to chart a course between the two without getting trapped at the stage where all you have is a mere imitation of life, or worse, an imitation of art: 'a photograph or a copy of a photograph'. It is that two-way process, as it operates within individual fictions to make them more or less 'work' for the reader, and the points of articulation and animation on which it depends, that this book aims to examine.

There is among James's fictions one that notoriously doesn't 'work' for some readers, who see it as making an indecent exhibition of itself in the wasteland between life and art.[4] Certainly 'The Figure in the Carpet' (1896) flaunts the idea of an imitation or copy in its most alarming form, that of parody. Narrated by another of James's 'serious' writers, it tells the tale of his attempts to track down some obscure 'general intention' in the works of a successful novelist, Hugh Vereker: some 'idea', 'a little trick', which Vereker says is the point of his whole enterprise and 'the thing for the critic to look for'.

Others join in the search for this ultimate meaning, or the 'real thing' as it is inevitably designated. But their considerable activity, promoted in vigorous and portentous terms of the hunt and even of sacrifice, doesn't culminate with the narrator, let alone the reader, learning the secret, or even knowing for certain that it exists: the narrator himself voices the suspicion that Vereker's claim might just be 'a monstrous *pose*'. Some readers and critics, especially those impressed by the notion of looking for just one thing, whether to see it or see through it, may think they recognise the authentic James in this ostensibly unproductive fiction and the titillation of its frustrated narrator; and may then suppose the ultimate meaning of it all to be simply that the art of interpretation is long and difficult and that we have in James a difficult author who is inexcusably smug about it.

If the real thing came down merely to that, reading James, not to say writing about him, would be a dispiriting exercise. But the idea of the story as an endlessly unreeling epistemological thread is only a pseudo-model of 'The Figure in the Carpet'; the *working* model is in fact articulated along a very definite series of points: affirmations, recognitions, terminations. 'Life' – if by life we mean lively incidents like a fatal road-accident or the death of an undesirable mother-in-law – is certainly not a casualty in this story; and though it is the narrator's own little narrative trick to try and shovel the whole lot under the carpet, he can't conceal the very human spectacle of his own insecurity, his jealousies and thwarted ambitions, or control the narrative hares his 'passion' for literature has started.[5]

'The Figure in the Carpet', then, is firmly interwoven with the more random twists and squiggles of experience. There is, however, as James asserts in another context,

> the story of one's hero, and then, thanks to the intimate connexion of things, the story of one's story itself. (AN 313)

It takes no great discernment to see that what 'The Figure in the Carpet' is primarily about is the obsession with Vereker's secret. This passes from one person to the next, and as one by one they die off or are worn out, and the narrator himself grinds to a halt, it is still bouncing along with impunity, a parasite in pursuit of its next host, who will be the breeding-ground of a new story – perhaps one of sex and violence, such as 'The Figure in the Carpet' darkly hints at; or simply of impotent outrage, the mark it has left on the narrator of its invisible passage. One might compare for subtlety James's indirect representational technique here with Vereker's clumsy metaphor for an ultimate meaning that is already escaping from his control: 'The thing's as concrete there as a bird in its cage.' The narrator finds a better image in that of the cat let out of the bag; but the story of this story is, really, the fable of the selfish gene – elusive yet tenacious, endlessly adaptable, self-regenerating and self-perpetuating.[6]

Sometimes regarded as a deliberate send-up of plodding critics, 'The Figure in the Carpet' undeniably cocks a snook at critical attitudes which presuppose the existence of an ultimate meaning, discoverable if only the critic feels passionately enough about it. But it is, I think, more to the point to see this tale as conceived in fascinated respect for the vitality of the 'story', and the energies released as it passes. Any critic who gets anywhere near James enters a world of wildly proliferating fictions: plots, fantasies, romances, visions more or less 'blessed' or demented. These fictions represent the efforts of his protagonists to modify the story-gene to their own system, or – to put it less biologically – to rearrange its various components (sex, violence, money, scandal and so on) into what might be for them a more viable or beautiful or just more entertaining way of life.

In this process is generated a lot of heightened feeling, of the kind naughtily incited by Hugh Vereker, which has to do with the tension and excitement of creation, and the hold the idea of the story exerts. Something is going forward, even if we don't know what it is, and will we be a part of it? Will the story go on its way without us? Or might it, alternatively, take us over completely, and *would we be better off without it*? As later chapters will show, James's more imaginative characters are all infected with concerns of this kind, and to the extent that we identify with them, the story tightens its grip on us too.[7]

James provides a striking metaphor for the way bonds are forged between author, character and reader when he evokes himself descending into the gladiatorial arena of the novel to rub shoulders with his characters, the 'more or less bleeding participants', 'the persons engaged in the struggle that provides for the others in the circling tiers the entertainment of the great game' (AN 328). The field of James studies is a similar battleground (though probably affording the audience less pleasure), in which the knives are often out for the author as they are for fellow-critics, and where one can broadly distinguish those that fight in the name of various orthodoxies from those whose approach is more personal, or mercenary – who will ally themselves to any critical approach that has something in it for them. It is interesting to observe that the choice implicitly posed here between authority or organisation and freedom or anarchy reflects difficulties explicitly described by James as inherent in the artist's attempts to subdue, or at least control, the irrepressible stuff of life. 'The effort really to see and really to represent', he wrote,

> is no idle business in face of the *constant* force that makes for muddlement. The great thing is indeed that the muddled state too is one of the very sharpest of the realities ... (AN 149)

Taking to heart these words (so sharply reminiscent of the narrator's dilemma in 'The Figure in the Carpet' and of his terminally muddled exhaustion), I have taken a cautious middle way. On the one hand I have drawn on and been influenced by many other critics; on the other, I have frequently had recourse to James himself as an exponent, through his critical writing, of what fiction in general is. That said, my interpretations are my own, and I march under certain assumptions: first that (as asserted in 'The Real Right Thing', 1899) 'The artist was what he did – he was nothing else'; and second that, as demonstrated in 'The Real Thing', where art is concerned, everything comes back to the studio and what the artist has managed to make of his raw materials.

This is not to deny the intrinsic interest or possible validity of approaches that seek to place James in a different perspective – biographical, psychoanalytical, socio-historical or even commercial (switching perspectives is indeed a very Jamesian way of proceeding). But I am wary of the sort of criticism which in attempting to relate James to some external system of reference can so easily prove reductive. What strikes me as misguided in certain critics who approach James in terms of his personal psychological needs or through strict theoretical analysis is that they can appear to leave out of account the will of the story to survive one way or another, whatever system it's connected to, and the right of the spectator in the arena to enthusiastic, not necessarily respectable, participation. Readers in hot pursuit of their own story can be impatient of abstract ground-rules or the confines of the James family plot; yet such readers may well possess 'the sense of life and the penetrating imagination' without which, James contested, no approach to fiction is competent (AN 78). And if fiction, especially fiction as ambiguous as James's, has any function it is surely to encourage the idiosyncratic response. Otherwise it might as well be propaganda.

I believe James to have been a supremely intelligent, perceptive and complex writer, much more self-aware than critics sometimes give him credit for, and certainly capable of outwitting the reader, but fully cognizant and appreciative of the part he or she plays. He offers us a consummately finished product, one that we can take to pieces and are unlikely to find diminished; and we for our part, in mutual respect, must not fail to consider it and to judge it as a whole.

It follows that I am also not terribly in sympathy with the view that 'all intelligent criticism of James is resolved inevitably into a discussion of plot', when by 'plot' is meant certain characters faced with certain situations – a view that appears to regard the novel as a kind of flow-chart, or series of right–wrong choices leading to an assessment of the protagonist's (ultimately, of the author's) moral viability.[8] Important though they are – indispensable yardsticks, indeed, by which we gauge James's sense of 'life' – character and situation, as is evident from the notebooks where James elaborated his plots, only constitute one element in the complete picture that we can see James in his notebooks striving towards (and see him in the Prefaces retrospectively admiring). I want to see that picture composing as a whole, and the shape it finally took.

I am concerned, therefore, with technique as much as with subject-matter, with stories observed in the course of their development rather than examined as stationary vehicles of preconceived ideas; not with extratextual points of reference, but with what we see on and infer from the printed page, and with the impact of these elements in combination: with 'what actually happens to us as we read'[9] (which is what I believe all intelligent criticism of James inevitably becomes).

This approach for the most part avoids the sort of analysis into discrete compartments whereby, for instance, individual features of James's technique have been thoroughly and repeatedly examined. It demands rather that I 'tell the story', and in so far as I do so it is for two reasons: first, to attempt to convey the dynamics of it, to deploy 'the rope of the *direction and march of the subject*, the action', as James once put it; to feel slacken and grow taut again what he said should be a 'tense cord' pulling it together – 'on which to string the pearls of detail' (HJL iv.131); second, because James's readers can't keep permanently in mind what actually happens – and virtually all of it matters. Hence the details themselves need to be considered – the echo of a phrase, the role of a minor character – small things that are seldom in James gratuitous – and this can involve close textual analysis. But my approach also emphasises James's 'handling' on a larger scale: the importance, for example, of those 'big' scenes which are surprisingly often underestimated. How many critics give due weight to the deathbed scene in *The Portrait of a Lady*, compared with the number of readers who remember it when they have forgotten the rest? To write it off as merely sentimental is wilfully to ignore its key part in the novel and to deny its undoubted effect. It is vital not to make the mistake Mrs Monarch made at first with Miss Churm – not to ask what she *is*, but to ask instead what does she *do* for the story? This is the consideration often overlooked by criticism with a psychological, moral or political basis, which sometimes seems like Mrs Monarch unaware that

> in the deceptive atmosphere of art, even the highest respectability may fail of being plastic. (8.256)

The painter in 'The Real Thing', who knows that the achieved picture, the total effect, is what counts, also knows that the ideal model has, like Miss Churm, 'no positive stamp', only 'a curious and inexplicable talent for imitation', and that that adaptability is there for him to exploit. He discovers too that one cannot easily or profitably make a distinction between style and essence: he sees that the Major is all wrong for his picture, and yet his trousers are all right: 'They *were* the real thing, even if he did come out colossal.' Similarly we as readers have to accommodate our own sense of the solidly authentic to an integrated compositional effect. The painter, who understands the process of adjustment, adaptation and revision involved, might be *our* ideal model; and Mrs Monarch, who finally recognises the real thing in Miss Churm (as marginally adjusted by herself) demonstrates that we can all be connoisseurs.

In expanding these arguments I have followed James's faith in the validity of the 'illustration, the concrete example' (HF 139); so that this book is basically an account of six novels. Three of them – *Washington Square* (1880), *The Portrait of a Lady* (1881) and *What Maisie Knew* (1897) – are generally considered masterpieces; to the remaining three – *The Princess Casamassima* (1886), *The Spoils of Poynton* (1897) and *The Wings of the Dove* (1902) – the critical response is more uncertain. Something of the range of these novels is suggested by the very different circumstances (not to say sizes) of their respective protagonists; and compositely they represent a wide field in which the real thing – the thing that impresses us as ultimately significant – assumes by implication or allusion a variety of guises. Are we being prompted to recognise it somewhere in the solid integrity of New England principle, or the pristine condition of childhood? Is it some quality of the human spirit, the unassuming stoicism for instance exhibited by Catherine Sloper in *Washington Square* – or is it the durability, the unimpugnable *style* of a great work of art like Poynton? Is it something to be tracked down in the labyrinthine workings of the mind, or to be trapped suddenly in some striking image? Is it connected with the kind of reality addressed by painting, or by politics?

Our uncertainty has to do with the fact that all these novels have plots that hinge on the seductive power of beautiful appearances and the difficulty of distinguishing essence from style; all raise questions about the relation, and relative value, of art to life. There are other James novels treating the same matters which I have not considered at length, or at all. *The Tragic Muse* (1890) for instance is omitted because it is too uncharacteristically schematic a representation of the conflict between art and life. It could be said that the same is true of *The Princess Casamassima*, but that is a more complex work, and one which I believe has lost out critically from the misapprehension that politics has nothing to do with style. *The Ambassadors* (1903) has not been singled out, though its hero Lambert Strether, gets a look in here and there, and nor has *The Golden Bowl* (1904). Given that both novels are intensely concerned with the apparent obverse of the real thing, in the shape of blatant false appearances, and that they are also among James's masterpieces, the incidental reference made to them here may seem odd. But my intention has been to give some general indication of the sort of thing James's readers should look for, rather than, like one of those in pursuit of Vereker's secret, 'to trace the figure in the carpet through every convolution, to reproduce it in every tint'. I have written about *The Golden Bowl* elsewhere in terms that relate to what I say here.[10] It continues nevertheless to exert on me a pull that will be evident, if intermittent.

I begin with an account of *Washington Square*, that foretaste of the Jamesian world which reluctant readers like Catherine Sloper herself may subsequently turn their backs on. Then in an introductory section to *The Portrait of a Lady* (pp. 31–42) I take advantage of that novel's wider spaces and more representative context to explain my themes more fully, dealing in particular with the relation of James's heroine or hero to the author and to the story. There follow chapters on *The Princess Casamassima* and *The Spoils of Poynton*, novels which exhibit the protagonist as a perfect model of Jamesian 'type' – and which demonstrate how he or she (like Major and Mrs Monarch) can despite the artist's best efforts remain a misfit. I end with *What Maisie Knew* and *The Wings of the Dove*, stories of misfits who learn to adapt, in which art and life are no longer manifestly in confrontation; and yet we can still sense here (as we shall in *The Golden Bowl*) something of the atmosphere of that conflict. There is a fighting spirit in the air, and also the smell of sacrifice – which has made its presence felt in James's earlier novels, and with which the idea of the 'real thing' has a peculiar affinity. But what, or who, is sacrificed? And is the offering made to appease a vicious world, or, more inspiringly, in the name of art?

In *The Wings of the Dove*, after her first encounter with Milly Theale, Susan Stringham, writer of short stories for the 'best' Boston magazines, goes sedulously about her business:

> But the real thing all the while was elsewhere; the real thing had gone back to New York, leaving behind it the two unsolved questions, quite distinct, of why it *was* real, and whether she should ever be so near it again. (77)

It is a passage which might be haunting if it wasn't so sensibly reined in, and it perfectly captures the fascinating, slightly suspect fly-by-night quality of the real thing. Can we ever hope to pin it down, to distinguish its possibly illusory presence from its mysterious potential? We can make a start, at least, by following it, as Susie will, into that enclave of more ponderable values which is old New York.

1

Washington Square

1.

Retreating from the commercial hubbub of downtown New York, Doctor Austin Sloper finds in Washington Square the 'ideal of quiet and genteel retirement'. The fiction for which this is the setting is one of James's liveliest, yet it is one that repeatedly reverts to the idea of a life left behind. In subject-matter, style and scope it is reminiscent of Jane Austen; but its young woman in quest of a husband remains unmarried, left on the shelf, a relic of the past, and James seemed to wish to consign her story to a similar fate when he eventually excluded it from the New York Edition of his collected works.[1] Written in Europe early in his career, the novel self-consciously evokes in all its (relative) distance and difference the world of James's childhood – a childhood largely spent in the neighbourhood of Washington Square:

> it was here that your grandmother lived, in venerable solitude, and dispensed a hospitality which commended itself alike to the infant imagination and the infant palate; it was here that you took your first walks abroad, following the nursery-maid with unequal step, and sniffing up the strange odour of the ailanthus-trees which at that time formed the principal umbrage of the Square, and diffused an aroma that you were not yet critical enough to dislike as it deserved; it was here, finally, that your first school, kept by a broad-bosomed, broad-based old lady with a ferrule, who was always having tea in a blue cup, with a saucer that didn't match, enlarged the circle both of your observations and your sensations. It was here, at any rate, that my heroine spent many years of her life; which is my excuse for this topographical parenthesis. (14)

Coming at a point in *Washington Square* where the story of widowed Dr Sloper, of his sister Lavinia and his only daughter

13

Catherine ('my heroine') has been running smoothly for a dozen pages, this plainly autobiographical parenthesis, with its abrupt switch to the second person, is curiously, almost awkwardly obtrusive. But the cool transition into it and out again gives no impression of a lapse into irresistible nostalgia. On the contrary. The infant seen here stomping after its nursemaid is precociously intent on marking out the novel as its own territory, and there is nothing faltering, *ingénu* or cosily sentimental in the story that will follow. James starts this novel from a position of confidence and authority: *Washington Square* is a deliberately circumscribed 'circle of observations and sensations', and within it, as we shall see, the author is perfectly in control.

The first intimation of this is his manner of letting us know that perfect control has conspicuously deserted Dr Sloper within his own professional sphere. All his experience notwithstanding, the Doctor has failed to prevent the deaths of his little son and his beautiful young wife. But this misfortune, it is pointed out, has not adversely affected the growth of his medical practice: Catherine, his remaining child, will inherit a great deal of money. James was to return more than once to the theme of a motherless girl wrapped in substantial material assets. It makes a good cradle for a story – and here, with a delicate jab of the pen, he sets the cradle rocking:

> She grew up a very robust and healthy child, and her father, as he looked at her, often said to himself that, such as she was, he at least need have no fear of losing her. I say 'such as she was', because, to tell the truth – But this is a truth of which I will defer the telling. (4)

There follow swiftly nonetheless several items of the 'truth' about Catherine. She is, we are told, much addicted to speaking it. And she is 'imperturbably good', 'affectionate, docile, obedient'; but also addicted to cream-cakes and 'something of a glutton' – 'an awkward confession to make about one's heroine'. An earlier Jamesian heroine, Nora in *Watch and Ward* (1878), was made delectable by the flakes of pastry on her lips. But Catherine Sloper is no *mille-feuille*. 'People who expressed themselves roughly called her stolid,' records the narrator, setting against such crudity an elegantly turned antithesis of his own:

A dull, plain girl she was called by rigorous critics – a quiet, lady-like girl by those of the more imaginative sort, but by neither class was she very elaborately discussed. (11)

Yet Catherine *is* discussed, and in memorable terms, by those more directly concerned with her fate – her father and his two sisters, the elder of whom, also widowed, shares the house in Washington Square. The silly and sentimental Lavinia Penniman would seem to share little else with Austin Sloper: the incongruity in their personalities and in their view of Catherine's destiny provides the basis of the novel's plot and its comic aspect. What they do have in common is that both consider themselves persuasive talkers and both would like to polish Catherine up into a reflection of their own aspirations. When the child is twelve years old the Doctor says to his sister:

'Try and make a clever woman of her, Lavinia; I should like her to be a clever woman.'
    Mrs Penniman, at this, looked thoughtful a moment. 'My dear Austin,' she then inquired, 'do you think it is better to be clever than to be good?'
    'Good for what?' asked the Doctor. 'You are good for nothing unless you are clever.' (7)

Next day, he restates his position in terms moderated by Catherine's congenital propensity to disappoint him:

'... I am not afraid of her being wicked; she will never have the salt of malice in her character. She is "as good as good bread", as the French say; but six years hence I don't want to have to compare her to good bread-and-butter.' (7)

Just at this point, where the reader might reflect that good bread-and-butter is not after all so out of place in the genteel ambience of the Square, the Doctor is quick to make clear that, presented in the right way, even stodge can make a story:

'When Catherine is about seventeen,' he said to himself, 'Lavinia will try and persuade her that some young man with a moustache is in love with her. It will be quite untrue; no young man, with a moustache or without, will ever be in love with Catherine. But Lavinia will take it up, and talk to her about it ... Catherine won't see it, and won't believe it, fortunately for her peace of mind; poor Catherine isn't romantic.' (8)

Undeniably, Catherine lacks the successful romantic's talent for self-expression. In a later novel, James would write of another heiress from New York, one who dons her pearls and a 'wonderful white dress' and becomes a dove. Catherine's wardrobe is also impressive in its own way and 'she sought to be eloquent in her garments'; but 'her anxiety, when she put them on, was as to whether they, and not she, would look well'. What she is and what she appears to be are things Catherine can't quite get to fasten together. It is not at any rate in any conscious attempt to express the solid wealth of her father's house that she acquires 'a red satin gown trimmed with gold fringe', in which the narrator says she looks about thirty.

Catherine is twenty when she attends a party given by her father's other sister, Mrs Almond, to celebrate her daughter Marian's engagement to Arthur Townsend, a stockbroker. Conspicuous in her red gown, or 'royal raiment', Catherine catches the eye of Townsend's cousin Morris, an impecunious bachelor looking out for a snug marital berth. Thus Catherine's romantic destiny stands in a similar relation to her shiny bulk as does her first polka with Morris to the little sofa into which she sinks, red-faced, beside him at the end of it; and the ensuing courtship will always be accompanied by our feeling that the lovers would be more comfortable with their dancing shoes off. James conveys its lameness perfectly in their first leave-taking:

'We shall meet again,' he said to Catherine as he left her, and Catherine thought it a very original speech. (19)

Here, evidently, the narrator's anxiety is that he, not Catherine, should 'look well', or present himself, at her expense, as a wit and man of the world. These are the terms in which Austin Sloper is described in the preamble to the story, and the narrator's tone is often indistinguishable from the Doctor's. The latter's excesses of sarcasm, however, can be seen as the fruit of his bitter disappointment in Catherine, whose bad luck it is to stand for his present substance, not for the disembodied romance of his past. The reader has the option of supposing that the Doctor's composed exterior hides an aching heart, and if having a psychological 'excuse' for treating Catherine as he does has the benefit for the Doctor that it increases his interest as a character, the narrator has the compensating advantage that his cruelties, being gratuitous, are both funnier and more alarming. His preliminary sketch of Catherine fills us with a wholly enjoyable trepidation. 'He is in love with this regal creature, then?' inquires the Doctor 'humorously' in respect of the handsome newcomer, as he drives home from the party with his daughter and sister; and in so doing raises the question really at issue: whether the reader will fall in love with so unlikely a heroine. Mrs Penniman's cautious admission that Morris admired the red dress prompts in her niece a ludicrously naïve reaction:

> Catherine did not say to herself in the dark, 'My dress only?' Mrs Penniman's announcement struck her by its richness, not by its meagreness. (22)

Their carriage-ride marks the point where the story really gets rolling, and the Doctor recognises it: 'The hour has come! ... Lavinia is going to get up a romance for Catherine ...'. *Washington Square* is full of these blatant signposts, and the one that now follows is the first unmistakable indication that the Doctor's standpoint is not the narrator's. In the dark and glad of it, sensing that there's safety in silence, Catherine pretends ignorance of Morris's name; and 'with all his irony, her father believed her'. It is a tiny step on the narrator's part towards Catherine, who from this moment is the Doctor's adversary; unwittingly, too, she has guaranteed the tension of the story – a tension like that in a piece of elastic causing a ball to bounce and circle round a fixed point.

2.

'It's a great secret, my dear child; but he is coming a-courting!' Mrs Penniman's every breath is now directed into the sails of Catherine's romance; and it gets a further boost from her father's breezy remarks ('Well, my dear, did he propose to you today?'), remarks which he intends to have the opposite effect. These are strange siren sounds in Catherine's ears. She is bemused, but the reader is in on the joke, as the narrative now moves swiftly through the medium of lively talk. The Doctor prides himself on his clear sight ('Catherine is not unmarriageable, but she is absolutely unattractive'), and to him the rocks ahead are clearly visible. He must talk to his daughter, to his sisters, and to Morris's sister, in order to demonstrate incontrovertibly that Morris is a shiftless opportunist. Morris must talk to Catherine in order that she may bring her father round, and Mrs Penniman must talk to Morris, simply because she must talk. Catherine, the object of discussion, talks rather little.

The effect of all this talk is to establish a clear opposition between the stern masculine logic which deals with Catherine like a commodity on the market and a feminine warmth and empathy which sees her as a sentient being; for even Mrs Penniman is genuinely fond of Catherine, though she becomes fonder of Morris. Her other aunt speaks of Catherine more like the appreciative mother the girl never had, though it is not obviously on this account that, unlike her niece and sister, Mrs Almond enjoys the Doctor's respect. She meets the Doctor as an equal, albeit not on his own ground. His reference to Arthur Townsend, Morris's stockbroker cousin, as the 'little boy' who is going to marry her 'little girl', gets a firm, if not strictly logical response: 'Arthur is not a little boy; he is a very old man; you and I will never be so old!'

Her comment illuminates from an unexpected angle both Austin Sloper and the value of material respectability, the matter at issue between the Doctor and Morris. Their duel, conducted for the most part in terms of 'rational, dry discourse', is ostensibly over Catherine, but reveals on both sides a concern with more serious things – property, employment, and masculine self-esteem – things whose intimate connection is cleverly laid bare in the occasional thrusts that go near the bone.

From the rational point of view, the force of the Doctor's arguments is self-evident, liable to win him the sympathy of other middle-aged parents and of everybody who doesn't see the real thing coming along in a shape like Morris at a party. Morris has no money, no job, Catherine barely knows him and he doesn't care a straw for her. But the function of the Doctor's arguments is not to convince the reader of this. The reader has known all along what Morris is, has witnessed him drop his guard in the presence of Mrs Penniman, whose romantic glosses he corrects with weary pedantry ('I *do* like the money!'). The function of the Doctor's arguments is to show what the Doctor is; they continue a process of self-revelation that began with his first comment on the prospect of his daughter's being wooed: 'Catherine won't see it and won't believe it, fortunately for her peace of mind; poor Catherine isn't romantic.'

Catherine initially doesn't see or believe it because she doesn't imagine herself as the heroine of a story. 'She was not', we are told, 'particularly fond of literature', and although she recognises heroic features in Morris – his smile of respectful devotion makes her think of 'a young knight in a poem' – literature has not left much mark on her powers of expression:

> Catherine thought he looked like a statue. But a statue would not talk like that, or, above all, have eyes of so rare a colour. (18)

This plodding inventory of physical attractions may be compared with the Doctor's evaluation of Morris on brief acquaintance:

> '... a very good head if he chooses to use it .... He has the assurance of the devil himself! ... And his powers of invention are most remarkable. He is very knowing; they were not so knowing as that in my time. And a good head, did I say? I should think so – after a bottle of Madeira, and a bottle and a half of claret!' (38)

The play on Morris's 'head' makes it a very much more interesting item than the barber's block which holds Catherine mesmerised (her falling for Morris comes over in fact as something almost as absurd as the young man's passion for a hairdresser's dummy in James's slight short story of 1878, 'Rose-Agathe'). What the Doctor gives us is an insight into Morris's *literary* potential, or capacity to adapt to the requirements of the story. Catherine's failure to recognise this quality in herself or others is implicit in her father's remark that she 'isn't romantic'. The Doctor recognises his own literary potential, to the extent that he sees the romantic hero of the story as none other than himself.

Secure in his Byronic attributes – sex-appeal, self-confidence and sarcasm – the Doctor dominates Catherine and Mrs Penniman (or, as he puts it, inspires them with 'salutary terror'); and the pursuit of respectability for his daughter enlarges his opportunities for domination. His saving mission takes him to the humble home of Morris's sister, Mrs Montgomery. The Doctor notes her to be 'a brave little person' who keeps 'her pretty eyes, which were illumined by a sort of brilliant modesty, attached to his own countenance' while he

brutally breaks down her defence of Morris, reducing her eventually
to tears. The incident brings up in perhaps its sharpest form the
question of the truth about the Doctor. Is he vain, cruel and manipulative? Or is he really wise and just, only lapsing occasionally from
civility under the pressure of hidden sorrows? Obviously, the reader's response may have to do with age, sex or circumstances; but few
could deny that the novel would be a non-starter without the Doctor,
or fail to recognise in Mrs Penniman's appraisal of Morris as 'a wonderful character, full of passion and energy' a more accurate description of her brother. The Doctor is a 'wonderful character', an actor
conscious always of his audience. If he seeks to rescue Catherine
with passion and energy, it is because he is offended at having in
Morris, with his devilish assurance and his knowingness, a bad
stand-in for himself; and because the role of 'ladies' doctor' in old
New York offers too little scope for the expansion of his superior personality. The Doctor is looking for a wider stage; meanwhile, his
withered emotions and thwarted ambition find an eloquent symbol
in the 'fountain sheeted with dead leaves' which Mrs Penniman considers the appropriate venue for a lovers' tryst.

There is a clear illustration of the difference between the Doctor
and Morris in their attitude to Catherine's being, as she guilelessly
puts it, 'ugly and stupid'. This galling half-truth makes her father
grimace with distaste, whereas Morris swallows it down and comes
up with an 'ardent murmur'. Love's bitter-sweet draughts are not
his cup of tea. When Catherine is taken abroad he will spend many
hours, at the risk of Mrs Penniman's company, in the Doctor's 'well-
stuffed arm-chairs', recovering from the strain of his amorous
advances -- which have retained a perceptible limp ('after all ... you
are irresistible ...'). Morris operates in two dimensions, the intellectual and the physical. In a third dimension, that of the emotions, he
simply isn't there, although Catherine believes he is. That 'this brilliant stranger – this sudden apparition who had barely heard the
sound of her voice' – could be in love with her had struck her at first
as a figment of Mrs Penniman's 'powerful imagination'; but shortly
afterwards she is able to tell her father 'I don't know why it is, but
he *does* like me. I am sure of that.'

The reader knows this sturdy assertion to be baseless, and the
path by which Catherine comes to it remains obscure – which indicates that the emotional dimension into which she has ventured is
not intended to bear much weight of analysis. One feels Catherine
to be on firmer ground when her attempts at conjunction are con-

fined to the one dimension she shares with Morris, in the drawing-room where the upholstery is 'chaste' and where the 'volumes which she had exhibited one day to her lover' disappointingly turn out to be only her copy-books. Catherine is 'extremely fond of copying'. So suppose she were to take her line from Morris, with his predilection for sitting comfortably, and settle for a prosaic domestic life, passionless, unperplexing? Catherine, we are told,

> would have made a wife of the gentle, old-fashioned pattern – regarding reasons as favours and windfalls, but no more expecting one every day than she would have expected a bouquet of camellias. (154–5)

Might the Doctor's previsions of her future pain be wildly off the mark? When her father is treating her particularly badly, Catherine states gently of Morris: 'He will never be rude to me.' And indeed so feeble is Morris's way with words and so dull her ear that she probably wouldn't notice if he was. So on the one hand we have the narrator, exploiting his standpoint of omniscience, inviting us to regard Catherine's as a real-life story which might have turned out quite differently; on the other hand we have the sneaking suspicion that this sort of interpretation is a soft option which should attract only reluctant readers like Catherine and Morris. But there again, Moris's agreement with Catherine that 'books were tiresome things' emphasises the distinction between those who regard Catherine's situation as the raw stuff of drama and entertainment and those who think that she would be better off outside the story altogether.

As the Doctor foresaw, being a heroine is bad for her peace of mind. Catherine is baffled by witty repartee and made uneasy by an atmosphere of plotting. 'Why do you push me so?' she demands of her aunt, displaying the obstructiveness, much deplored by Mrs Penniman, that constantly threatens to impede the forward rush of the narrative. The story that Morris has in his head is of the simplest, but it does require that the lovers take a line, and Catherine is at first incapable of arguing with her father ('I would rather not ask him … I never contradict him … I couldn't say that!'). For all his smooth talk, Morris can't move if his partner won't even get her skates on. Catherine is stuck, her loyalties divided between the father whom she adores and Morris who says he loves, 'or rather', adores her:

> She put off deciding and choosing; before the vision of a conflict
> with her father she dropped her eyes and sat motionless, holding
> her breath and waiting. It made her heart beat; it was intensely
> painful. When Morris kissed her and said these things – that also
> made her heart beat; but this was worse, and it frightened her. (54)

Harbouring the memory of Morris's kisses like so many cream-
cakes, she retreats into the shell of day-to-day existence, as if willing
the wit, the plot, the narrative, all those elements that comprise the
novel, to sweep over her head.

Nothing, however, can shake her position at its centre; and
repeated reference to her physical presence and physical sensations
ensures that Catherine makes herself *felt*. When Dr Sloper takes his
daughter on the Grand Tour of Europe, we learn that 'Catherine was
always at her post, and had a firm and ample seat.' She maintains
her place in the novel like someone unfamiliar with the game of
musical chairs, who has grasped nonetheless that the idea is to sit,
and sit tight. It is characteristic of the novel's insidious ironies that
our interest in Catherine, as she lies low, should be quickened by a
rather striking passage:

> Catherine meanwhile had made a discovery ... it had become
> vivid to her that there was a great excitement in trying to be a
> good daughter. ... She watched herself as she would have
> watched another person, and wondered what she would do. (80)

This is as close as Catherine gets to reading her life like a book or
spotting her own literary potential in the assumption of a distinct
identity and role. The irony of course is that, in her book, playing
the part of a good daughter can only mean remaining as self-
effacing and inactive as possible.[2] The narrator can be observed here
helping Catherine to sound interesting, but the effect is to remind us
that as the heroine of a novel she is going to need all the help she
can get. Which makes her the worst daughter her father could have
had. Dr Sloper is almost a figure of pathos at this point, especially as
his latest discovery – that 'paternity was, after all, not an exciting
vocation' – only makes him sound rather stale too.

'I know not', says the narrator knowingly, 'whether he had hoped
for a little more resistance ...'. It is in fact clear that the Doctor wants
Catherine to resist, precisely because the excitement he seeks in his
relations with her, as with other women, consists in having the whip

hand. To control a situation, there must *be* a situation; and though
we learn that, as Catherine grew up, the Doctor was 'in no haste to
conclude' concerning her deficiencies, it is thereafter on the basis of
having concluded – Catherine to be a weakling, Morris a scoundrel
– that Dr Sloper operates. Having once established the situation, he
can prove himself to be the master of it. 'And shall you not relent?'
asks Mrs Almond, to which her brother replies: 'Shall a geometrical
proposition relent?' – an answer betraying that satisfaction in the
steady progression of events towards a definite conclusion which is
also one of the satisfactions that novelists seek to provide. When
Mrs Montgomery, questioned on the subject of her brother, at last
cries out, 'Don't let her marry him!' the Doctor learns nothing he
didn't know already: what seems to gratify him is that with this
emotional outburst he has forced matters to a *conclusion*.

Catherine, however, develops a resistance to this form of verbal
intercourse: her response to her father's polite requests for information defy definition and conclusion: she has 'nothing particular to
say', she and Morris 'can wait a long time'. 'Of course; you can wait
till I die, if you like,' replies her father grimly. His remark provokes
in the good daughter a 'cry of natural horror', but hurts him more
than it hurts her; for he can't stand the idea that after his death
events will be quite beyond his control.

As if in mockery of the Doctor's slipping grasp, the narrator's
prompts to Catherine from the wings are now wholly audible:

> Suddenly ... she had an inspiration – she almost knew it to be an
> inspiration.
> 'If I don't marry before your death, I will not after,' she
> said. (99)

Since the Doctor's mind is focused on controlling the present situation, not on Catherine's distant future, he is unable to interpret this
statement except as an inappropriate epigram. Just as he found it
shocking that the cat – 'at her age?' – had had kittens, so he is astonished at 'this wanton play of a fixed idea', at the notion of Catherine
disporting herself on his own verbal terrain. It is a sort of anarchy,
which, like the kittens, requires suppression. This is the Doctor's
consolation as, feeling a little sorry for her, he coldly rejects his
daughter and shows her out. 'I believe she will stick!' he tells himself – 'stick', that is, to her guns; and he anticipates with pleasure the
dramatic possibilities this will bring. But Catherine sticks in the

reader's memory as the silence on the other side of the door, and as the creak of the stairs which reminds us that

> The idea of a struggle with her father, of setting up her will against his own, was heavy on her soul, and it kept her quiet, as a great physical weight keeps us motionless. (81)

Made almost palpable here is a sense of foreboding that the Doctor's lurid predictions can neither express nor explain. This is the heavy stuff of the novel; and it finds its shape and definition as it settles over Catherine's still hulk.

3.

The pressure lifts a bit as the second phase of the novel opens on a note of light relief. The Doctor and Mrs Penniman work through a well-worn comedy routine, assaulting the problem, and one another, in terms of 'high treason' and 'murdering' one's child; the weight on Catherine becomes a matter of her 'plumping down into the paternal presence' (like some character from P. G. Wodehouse), having refused, to her aunt's disappointment, to miss breakfast. And yet it is through her physicality that we are made to feel, increasingly, the poignancy of Catherine's predicament. The large, dignified creature sobbing soundlessly in her aunt's embrace, or extending her hands to grasp 'her refuge' in Morris's person, is disconcertingly pathetic, like a beached whale. Catherine can at this point neither advance nor retreat, because the Doctor has threatened to disinherit her and Morris is no longer urging marriage. The stalemate that results gives the Doctor the chance to take Catherine to Europe; his idea is to get Morris out of her head, but also to get something into it.

Europe was the home, as James's fictions repeatedly seek to demonstrate, of history, art and culture, but also of things taken less account of in New England philosophy: sophistication and guile such as Mrs Penniman's wildest dreams are made of, only practised with quiet professionalism. The effect of the Old World on the inhabitants of the New was of 'being exposed to peculiar influences', as the old Puritan Mr Wentworth puts it in *The Europeans* (1878) – a little sugared pill of a novel which perfectly encapsulates the theme. As its title implies, Europe is not the theme of *Washington*

Square, but its influence is everywhere in the novel: it is present, for instance, in the manner of the narrator's describing how Catherine reacts to 'Europe', and reacts in particular to Morris's suggestion that she might cleverly take advantage of a different ambience to soften the Doctor's heart:

> The idea of being 'clever' in a gondola by moonlight appeared to her to involve elements of which her grasp was not active. (124)

The narrator's subsequent reference to the itinerant Catherine's 'ample seat' is a dig at her narrow mind, for she appears indifferent to the cultural experience of Continental travel. At the same time, she has 'completely divested herself of the characteristics of a victim'.

Six months of her infuriating unresponsiveness prompts the Doctor to stage a showdown. He and Catherine have climbed to a lonely Alpine valley (James will use a similar romantic and portentous setting in *The Wings of the Dove*). She is taking a breather, looking about her 'at the hard-featured rocks and the glowing sky', when her father approaches with a meaningful air:

> He stopped in front of her, and stood looking at her with eyes that had kept the light of the flushing snow-summits on which they had been fixed. Then, abruptly, in a low tone, he asked her an unexpected question:
> 'Have you given him up?' (129)

At last the Doctor has found the amphitheatre for which he has been saving his best lines:

> '... you ought to know what I am. I am not a very good man. Though I am very smooth externally, at bottom I am very passionate; and I assure you I can be very hard.' (129)

Catherine could not be more taken aback if some old mountain goat had suddenly turned satyr. Her father not a good man! She 'hardly went so far' as to imagine him about to murder her – it is left to the narrator to supply a sketch of him doing so, with his 'neat, fine, supple' surgeon's hand. 'I am sure you can be anything you please,' she replies, reminding us that her father is under no Lucifer-like obligation to be proud and evil. The Doctor's passion and violence splatter about a bit more: it was to have been his finest hour; but Catherine's wonderfully literal responses have stolen the show.

On the eve of their return to America, the Doctor has his revenge. In the 'great, dim, musty sitting-room' of their Liverpool hotel Catherine risks being mistaken for some warehouse commodity made more valuable to Morris by the stamp of 'Europe'. The Doctor makes the point more crudely: 'We have fattened the sheep for him before he kills it.' It is the most disturbing moment in the novel, one that drives the reader, as Catherine is repeatedly driven, into a corner, forcing us to choose between the rival claims of common humanity and artistic licence, daring us not to appreciate the Doctor's wit and the authority of his logic, demanding that we identify with his victim's vulnerability and primitive strategies of evasion as she turns away and stands 'staring at the blank door'. The Catherine her father calls 'as good as good bread' invites comparison with Mrs Bread, housekeeper to the wicked Bellegarde family in *The American* (1877), who epitomises the virtues of decent thinking and plain speaking, yet in her innocence and insularity is a figure of fun. There is no denying the ambivalence of James's attitude to Catherine, no way round the suspicion that with her he is having his bread and scoffing his cream-cake. Europe in *Washington Square* is represented by that most 'European' characteristic in the narrator, which is to attempt to get the better, and the best, of everything.

'I have been as good as I could, but he doesn't care. Now I don't care either. ... I am come home to be married. That's all I know.' The Doctor's words have cut the bond between father and daughter, and Catherine at last moves with the current of the narrative as it makes swiftly towards a dénouement. Morris, though he would prefer not to hurt Catherine, having none of the Doctor's taste for blood, walks out on her. In this distressing scene, when her imagination 'at a single bound' comes near the 'awful truth', it is again Catherine's physical presence that asserts itself, as she tries with both hands to hold Morris fast: 'All her being, for the moment, was centred in the wish to keep him in the room.' She is shaken off and as her father predicted, 'sent tumbling into the dust'. Mrs Penniman, whose loyalties have slithered from Catherine to Morris, accepts that Catherine disinherited can only be a candidate for 'the sacrificial knife'. In an ensuing scene between aunt and niece, as if in belated compensation for her earlier inarticulacy, the narrator makes free with melodramatic terminology: Catherine speaks 'fiercely', she 'flamed up', she utters 'a sudden, imploring cry'; reference is made to her 'bitterness' and 'vehemence', even to the 'clairvoyance of her passion'; but the words that the reader remembers are those that purport directly to convey Catherine's thought:

> A consummate sense of her aunt's meddlesome folly had come over her during the last five minutes, and she was sickened at the thought that Mrs Penniman had been let loose, as it were, upon her happiness. (168)

Note the precision of 'the last five minutes': it is the characteristic note of Catherine's true voice, which she has found since her return from Europe – not a European voice indeed, but plain, literal speech, after the manner of Mrs Almond's, but without the salt. Catherine 'enjoys it as people enjoy getting rid of a leg that has been crushed': thus, effectively, her aunt Almond counters the Doctor's nasty suggestion that jilted Catherine may be enjoying a rest 'after her little dance'.

His nastiness gets its deserts, for in fact Catherine's 'little dance' is the one she leads her father after Morris has left her. By pretending that she, not Morris, broke the engagement, and concealing her grief from him, she robs her father of 'a little triumph that he had rather counted on'. He is naturally sceptical of Catherine's version, but all he can claim to be able to see is that

> '... She is perfectly comfortable and blooming; she eats and sleeps, takes her usual exercise, and overloads herself, as usual, with finery. She is always knitting some purse or embroidering some handkerchief, and it seems to me she turns these articles out about as fast as ever. ...' (177)

He suspects it may be a false front; 'but it was his punishment that he never knew.' Unable to feel sure that the lovers have not merely agreed to separate until after his death, he tries, even after the passage of years, to extract from Catherine a promise that she will never think of Morris again. But Catherine, now middle-aged, has too solid a sense of herself to be pushed around any more. Her earlier inertia, which had such a restricting effect on the bouncier fictions invented around her, has developed into a quasi-creative obstinacy – for it is in obstinacy, not cruelty, that Catherine denies her father what he always wanted – the sense of an ending. And it is she herself who has the last word where the Doctor is concerned. To cut her out of his will is a futile gesture, since she has her mother's money and no longer cares about his goodwill; but the Doctor does it anyway, with sarcastic reference to 'those unscrupulous adventurers whom she has given me reason to believe that she persists in regarding as an interesting class'. It is the Doctor's doom that his final rhetorical flourish should be confined *in perpetuum* to an ineffectual legal document. 'I wish it had been expressed a little differently!' Catherine's comment perfectly acknowledges the indignity of it.

So she triumphs over her father; and it only remains for her to triumph over Morris who after many years returns to New York. Because her niece has had offers but has never married, Mrs Penniman thinks she cherishes an undying passion. She tips Morris the wink and he reappears in Washington Square. Catherine, gravely polite, turns him away. 'Why the deuce then would she never marry?' he wonders. But James has not left gaps in the text inviting speculation, as he was hereafter increasingly to do. If *Washington Square* had been written twenty years later, we might like the Doctor never know what passed between the couple when Morris left Catherine, or when he returned; nor would we have been offered the precise description of Catherine's state of mind which anticipates, and explains, her final rejection of Morris:

> From her own point of view the great facts of her career were that Morris Townsend had trifled with her affection, and that her father had broken its spring. Nothing could ever alter these facts; they were always there, like her name, her age, her plain face. Nothing could ever undo the wrong or cure the pain that Morris had inflicted on her, and nothing could ever make her feel towards her father as she felt in her younger years. (180)

The power of Catherine's narrative voice lies in this strong, inflexible tone. It seems to tell us firmly that there is nothing left to say which could be more effectively said.

'Such as she was', it was stated as the story began, her father 'need have no fear of losing her'. But now he *has* lost her; so that we may feel entitled, as the story ends, to demand a new portrait of Catherine, such as she is. Ever obliging, the narrator, having left to Catherine the last word on her *vie intérieure*, turns to her public persona as she stands kitted out in the inalterable facts of her name, her age and her plain face. She

> went generally, with an even and noiseless step, about the rigid business of her life ... her habits, once formed, were rather stiffly maintained; her opinions, on all moral and social matters, were extremely conservative; and before she was forty she was regarded as an old-fashioned person, and an authority on customs that had passed away. (179–80)

The picture is uninspiring: it isn't even witty, as it would be if James intended it as an ironical comment on the rapidly changing values of New York society. Why doesn't he let Catherine keep in her middle age the palpable physical individuality she once had, like the 'broad-based' schoolmistress in his opening flashback? (Does *Catherine's* teacup match its saucer now, or doesn't she care about keeping up appearances any more?) Instead, that vivid, barely relevant digression is left like the calling-card of a talent that has been and seen but isn't interested in hanging around any more; and Catherine is left a prototypical, admirable old maid. She even takes up charitable interests, which had never impinged on Washington Square as we knew it.

But she also appears in places more familiar to the reader, 'respectable entertainments' at which she is liked by the young men and confided in by the young girls. The reader is bound to register some unease at this. Can Catherine's heart really be in the part once acted with such relish by Mrs Penniman and which has become, through her, so firmly discredited? Equally unconvincing is the assertion of the narrator, now expatiating on Catherine's suitors, that one John Ludlow, a bachelor not intent on making a marriage of convenience, 'spoken of always as a young man who might have his "pick", was seriously in love with her.' *Seriously*? Are we to suppose that Mr Ludlow, who sounds suspiciously like Catherine's 'young knight in a poem' or a legacy of Jane Austen, a hand-me-down Mr Knightley, has seen some 'truth' about Catherine that inspires him with romantic passion and is heavily concealed from the rest of us? If so, the narrator is being unfair to his reader; but one feels, rather, he is being unfair to Catherine, draping her in such implausible fictions just as she is about to retreat from the novel altogether.

As Morris beats *his* retreat,

Catherine, meanwhile, in the parlour, picking up her morsel of
fancy-work, had seated herself with it again – for life, as it were.
(196)

Has Catherine's 'firm and ample seat' finally pinned down here at
the close of the novel, that truth about her which the narrator
deferred telling? Certainly her solitary, composed figure suggests
both stoic endurance and the achievement of personal freedom;
and, confronted with her silent dignity, we may wonder whether
the narrator's needles of wit and neatly turned phrases are anything
more than the 'morsel of fancy-work' in Catherine's lap – the frivolous ornament of a sober theme. But just as Catherine, according to
her father's observation, is not to be parted from her finery, so there
is built into *Washington Square* a central disparity between its comic
features and the gravity of Catherine's experience. The resultant
slightly *louche* combination recalls that initial image of Catherine in
her red gown, the sense that the one didn't quite express the other,
that Catherine might be something different from what she
appeared to be.

Nor was she, in fact, what her father, Morris and Mrs Penniman
believed her to be; her stout resistance to the drift of their fictions
surprised them all. But now, when Catherine makes her last stand, it
is on ground prepared by a story-teller whose manipulative charm
has more staying-power than any amateur's, and whose spadework
is responsible for what is perhaps, our final, lasting impression: that
the stolid placidity which the Doctor suspected as a false front rises
now from the foundations of Catherine's being; that the gap has
closed between appearance and reality, the dignified façade fused
with the solid brick at the core. Such as she is, settled 'for life',
Catherine no longer holds any surprises for the reader.

Why then 'for life, *as it were*'? The last phrase of the novel is the
narrator's reminder that the story remains his, not Catherine's, that
he might, if he wished, deny us the sense of an ending. In this complex hint of impermanence there is the faintest mockery of Catherine's permanent incomplexity, as she is left behind in one of the
'very solid and honourable dwellings' of Washington Square. The
infant who enlarged there the circle of his observations and sensations moves on, in pursuit of a truth whose telling will be an affair
more complicated than even Mrs Penniman could conceive of.

2

The Portrait of a Lady

1.

'... What shall we call our "self"? Where does it begin? where does it end?...' (216)

Gardencourt, where Madame Merle puts this question to Isabel Archer, is a larger, more immediately impressive house of fiction than Catherine Sloper's, as the philosophical reach of such a question manages to imply; and Catherine, were she to overhear the conversation of these two sophisticates, might be impressed by several aspects of it. Madame Merle denies that a person's essential being can be separated from the 'envelope of circumstances', the society and the artefacts that surround us: 'I know a large part of myself is in the clothes I choose to wear. I've a great respect for *things*! One's self – for other people – is one's expression of oneself...'.

Catherine too liked dressing up, and we remember how she 'sought to be eloquent in her garments', though she was, mercifully, more conscious of the way they looked than of what they said about her. But in Isabel Archer we have a heroine who is both self-confident and articulate, especially when talking about herself, and she argues:

'... I think just the other way. I don't know whether I succeed in expressing myself, but I know that nothing else expresses me. Nothing that belongs to me is any measure of me; everything's on the contrary a limit, a barrier, and a perfectly arbitrary one. Certainly the clothes which, as you say, I choose to wear, don't express me ... To begin with it's not my own choice that I wear them; they're imposed upon me by society.' (216)

'Should you prefer to go without them?' Madame Merle's sharp answer is the sort of response that Isabel's headlong rushes into

31

rhetoric positively invite. Catherine would recognise the sensation of being tripped up; what she might not see is that the Jamesian narrator mocks Isabel's exaggerated self-regard as systematically, if more subtly, as he made fun of Catherine's own clumsier attempts at the heroic style.

The conversation between Isabel and Madame Merle raises, rather more self-consciously than the novel does as a whole, two principal concerns of *The Portrait of a Lady* (1881). The first is the discrepancy between style and essence, the relation of image to reality, which is the problem implicit in the concept of portraiture, and raised, more or less explicitly, throughout James's fiction. The second, also inseparable from any artistic endeavour, is what Madame Merle calls the 'expression of oneself', which Isabel interprets as involving not 'things' (a portrait of herself would presumably come into this category), but noble ideals and the attempt to realise them.

This again makes her very different from the heroine of *Washington Square*. Yet Catherine would instantly identify with Isabel in the insistence on choice. For it is in making her choice that Catherine eventually finds a satisfactory means of self-expression. She does it with less talk but equal determination. And both start by making a bad choice, fooled by an image that doesn't correspond with reality.

A rich young woman is deceived by a fortune-hunter, and suffers for her mistake: Isabel's story is simple enough in essence, and very similar to Catherine's. But *The Portrait of a Lady* is built in the grand style. James called it 'constructionally speaking, a literary monument' (AN 52), and Graham Greene's comparison with a cathedral[1] aptly conveys both its physical and metaphysical dimensions: its spaces are vaster, its purposes loftier, its illuminations profounder and more searing than those of *Washington Square*. The very scale of the enterprise encourages the expectation that Isabel, as its focal point, will represent the great and the good.

But the image the novel projects is very different from the reality it represents. It promotes, in the person of Isabel, the notion of an irresistible vitality, the attraction of the unconventional, the allure of the broader horizon, the value of travel and culture and art. Above all, it promotes the exhilaration, particularly as discovered by a woman in the latter half of the nineteenth century, of freedom and independence. Yet what we read about in its pages is a knowledge of the world that is severely limited, an attitude to life that is almost one of fear, marriage to a man who is 'convention itself', the cultivation of an art that is merely artifice, a constant returning to a past of lost hopes, the attrition of advancing years, a journey that ends in a 'dead wall' and in a posture of renunciation and submission. And for all the transparency of the writing (which exhibits none of the complexities of later James) *The Portrait of a Lady* concludes, notoriously, in an enigma. We look for Isabel at the end and she isn't there.

'The one thing which the book is not, is what it calls itself,' wrote a contemporary reviewer,[2] reflecting the exasperation felt by many readers who consider Isabel to act inconsistently with her (lengthily described) character, especially at the end, when she refuses to leave her husband for a better man (it is the term 'portrait' that is being objected to, for Isabel is undeniably behaving like a *lady* here). More than one critic has indeed suggested that we have in Isabel an emblematic figure rather than a psychological study. But emblematic of what? It is legitimate to ask whether Isabel ultimately represents anything other than disappointment – and I mean not just her own but, more significantly, the reader's disappointment in *her*. Disappointment, together with advancing age and opportunities lost, is after all only the sort of reality in which novelists like to steep their protagonists: compare *Washington Square*. But if Catherine failed, Isabel, we feel, ought to have made these commonplace sadnesses reflect some arresting image, tragic or triumphant, of a proper heroine. Or might she not, at the very least, represent the stability and traditional values of Gardencourt and old New York without the reader reading inertia into stability, and dull resignation into those values?

Instead, Isabel must be held responsible for the fact that *The Portrait of a Lady* is, as cathedrals go, oddly uninspiring. It is not a tragedy in the classical tradition, because although Isabel's downfall is largely the result of her own hubris, the heroic scale by which we are inclined to measure her is partly of her own making. It isn't clear that Isabel is innately grand, but it is clear that she assumes grandeur, for example in the conversation with Madame Merle about one's self, or in her response to her cousin Ralph's hesitant criticism of her husband-to-be:

> 'I can't get over the sense that Osmond is somehow – well, small.' ...
> 'Small?' She made it sound immense. (373)

Later, when proved right, Ralph will tell Isabel that she has been 'ground in the very mill of the conventional'. He means it sympathetically: but what if the reader suspects her to have emerged from the mill, well, *small*?

Yet if Isabel may be accounted a disappointment, *The Portrait of a Lady* as a whole cannot. It is the 'big' novel James had planned for years to write, one that in the judgement of many critics guarantees his stature, and almost certainly the most widely read of his longer works. The book's popular success is easily explained. In a story of a basically familiar kind, it offers the excitement of romance, wickedness, mystery and melodrama; also the direct appeal of vividly drawn peripheral characters, and a degree of satisfaction, partly compensating for any disappointment, in the diminishment of the heroine who considers herself above them. These are conventional elements of the nineteenth-century novel, and James knew how to capitalise on them.[3]

At the same time, he clearly regarded Isabel as something special, and central to his ambitious conception of the book: writing his big novel became a question of 'positively organising an ado about Isabel Archer' (AN 48). It is generally accepted, on extra-textual evidence, that he was inspired by memories of his cousin Minny Temple, for whom he felt affection and admiration, and who had died at the age of 24 in 1870. James insisted, however, that 'the thing [was] not a portrait' of Minny (HJL ii. 324).[4] His predilection for Isabel Archer is arguably most apparent in his Preface to the novel, written decades later; and what is striking in all the Prefaces to the New York Edition is how comparatively little James reveals there of the actual sources of his inspiration, and how much he revealed himself charmed and fascinated by the *idea* of certain key characters. In the case of *The Portrait*, having cited Turgenev's account of how for him the image of 'a particular person or persons' preceded the book, James identified 'the conception of a certain young woman affronting her destiny' as the 'single small corner-stone' of his own edifice (AN 48). The contrast with the notebooks is interesting: there (allowing for the fact that their record is incomplete) he can be seen to be almost wholly preoccupied with the mechanics of plot and overall effect.

This is not to say that the James who wrote the Prefaces ever saw Isabel, or any other character, as an entity detachable from the fiction. On the contrary. The very nub of the problem with Isabel was, as he put it:

> By what process of logical accretion was this slight 'personality',
> the mere slim shade of an intelligent but presumptuous girl, to
> find itself endowed with the high attributes of a Subject? (AN 48)

Somewhat disingenuously, he makes much here of the difficulty
involved in making young women 'as a class' interesting. Scott,
Dickens and Stevenson may have shirked it, but in the course of
argument James draws attention to the fact that Shakespeare and
George Eliot managed it pretty well. It might be supposed that
Catherine Sloper, not intelligent, presumptuous or even slim, might
have presented more of a challenge, and yet one feels sure that
James would not have written about Catherine Sloper quite like
this. Some kind of personal magnetism quite distinct from
Catherine's gravity is exerting its pull on him across the years.

The James of the Prefaces is like the elderly head of a family firm,
justifiably pleased with himself as its originator and still absorbed in
the technical side (the actual processes of writing), but whose survey of the past is perhaps slightly distorted by his now being a little
out of touch (we may remember the transactions between writer,
protagonist and reader rather differently).[5] Some employees whom
the reader may consider to have done quite a lot of the work, like
Henrietta Stackpole in *The Portrait of a Lady*, are summarily dismissed; others are the sons and daughters of the house, who bear a
family likeness, the mark of an intimate connection with their pro-
genitor and his enterprise. It is they who are worthy of promotion,
they who are treated virtually as partners in the business; James
speaks in the Preface to *The Portrait* of enjoying a 'relation of confidence with the actors in my drama who *were*, unlike Miss Stackpole,
true agents' (AN 55).

Those of his brainchildren who belong to this category occupy a
privileged position in James's imaginative world. He characterised
his 'agents' elsewhere as 'interesting only in proportion as they feel
their respective situations' (AN 62); and, being loaded with 'feeling'
(the Jamesian heritage of acuteness of perception and heightened
sensibility), they possess in common what one might call, with reference to the passage cited above, 'accretability' – a special property
in which inevitably (or in James's gloss, 'logically') the story finds
its point of departure.

Isabel is but one of a number of his major characters (Catherine
Sloper is not among them) who are described by James as 'mirrors',
polished and 'pre-eminently' polished, of life. But for him the

crucial point is that 'Their being finely aware ... *makes* absolutely the intensity of their adventure' (AN 62, 70). In other words, these characters are not *passive* reflectors, but generate an energy of their own, as a mirror concentrating the rays of the sun produces fire.

James claimed in his Preface to *The Portrait* that he was barely able to conceive of a 'fable' that 'didn't need its agents positively to launch it'; and the review of agent Isabel that follows makes clear the distinction between her and the presumptuous heroines of other writers whose inadequacies are 'eked out' by other characters, subplots, and 'the great mutations of the world'. Isabel, like her kin, is 'of the essence' of the work of fiction, ensconced in the body of the coach, as James puts it (whereas Henrietta merely runs alongside it); she exemplifies the notion of a particular personality, 'the stray figure, the unattached character' who hangs about soliciting the author's attention, demanding that a narrative vehicle be constructed for his or her benefit. But Isabel isn't in James's conception merely instrumental in getting the coach on the road: it is her energy that helps to propel it, for if, as James suggests, her adventures are 'mild', it is *her* 'sense of them, her sense *for* them' that he wanted to render, and what he delights in is the 'mystic conversion [of her adventures] by that sense, conversion into the stuff of drama or ... of "story"' (AN 44–56).

If by some such process of conversion – a kind of instinctive transmission of the possibilities of life into those of fiction – Isabel seeks, as Gilbert Osmond will put it, to make her life a work of art, what for James always came first was the story, the 'prime and precious thing' (AN 314). The reader recognises a 'story' in the structure towards which the conventional elements of James's novel tend; and Isabel, who has read a great many novels, sees herself in a heroic part, and sometimes seems to see a narrative in which she plays it. And yet she will prove an unconventional heroine, who denies the reader the expected satisfactions; who, when she acts at all, doesn't act as a heroine should, who appropriates to herself ways of self-expression which don't fit the pattern of, even seem inappropriate to, the conventional novel; who presents us with what at times seem less like a portrait than fragments of a life.

Obviously there is some element of conflict here. It is hard to accept what Isabel 'lets' finally happen to her, even when we can see a number of reasons why it was bound to happen. But of course the more we think of Isabel in this way, as 'real', or independent of

James's general intention, then the more the novel as a whole can be said to have made an indelible impression.[6] To that extent the relationship between James and Isabel is indeed a partnership, or a conspiracy: they are working together, in the pursuit of self-expression, and it seems likely that what James at the time of writing his Preface most fondly associated with Isabel was this joint endeavour, retrospectively reviewed.

James's ideal, as his critical writing makes plain, was to make the English novel a better thing; and in the Preface to *The Portrait of a Lady* there is a central discussion of what that involved. He emphasises there that every window in the house of fiction 'has been pierced, or is still pierceable ... by the need of the individual vision and by the pressure of the individual will' (AN 46). Without the sense of intensely subjective experience, or real life, locked up in it, the novel would be an empty form; and its very essence, James suggests, lies in the tension that is produced between the author's assumption of control and his assertion of individuality, as projected in the individuality, or freedom, of his characters:

> Here we get exactly the high price of the novel as a literary form – its power not only, while preserving that form with closeness, to range through all the differences of the individual relation to its general subject-matter, all the varieties of outlook on life, of disposition to reflect and project, created by conditions that are never the same from man to man (or, so far as that goes, from man to woman), but positively to appear more true to its character in proportion as it strains, or tends to burst, with a latent extravagance, its mould. (AN 45–6)

It is other novelists, James has implied, with substandard experience (or capacity for translating it), whose efforts are likely to collapse in this pressurised processing-system. But, as we shall see, the delicate adjustment between fitting in and bursting out that James seems to be trying for in the person of Isabel (who fits and yet doesn't fit the form) entails a risk of malfunction, in so far as it deals in packets of imaginative energy, intensely compressed, that may or may not be harnessed in the direction James originally intended. In this way, the Jamesian novel subverts our expectations of nineteenth-century fiction; and its mould was cast – to adopt James's analogy – in *The Portrait of a Lady*.

2.

Its celebrated opening scene, set in 'the perfect middle of a splendid summer afternoon (and written, by coincidence, close to the mid-point of James's life), rather strikingly evokes the scope, and the serene self-confidence, of James's mature fiction. That is the domain of which Isabel might be taking possession as she advances purposefully across the vast lawn at Gardencourt. Three men, idly enjoying afternoon tea in the open air, watch her approach. They are Isabel's cousin Ralph, a young man but a chronic invalid; his father Daniel Touchett, an expatriate American businessman and a millionaire, now also in feeble health; and their neighbour and friend Lord Warburton, an English peer. Possessing greater wealth and higher social position than anything encountered in Washington Square, they represent James's grandest manner, which, discarding the crude clash of money and mores depicted in *The American*, allies an aristocracy of wealth and taste with an aristocracy of breeding. But more significantly, they represent the bonds of friendship, the ties of blood, romantic love, and mortality. These familiar elements constitute James's real subject-matter: the stuff of life, which naturally includes death.

Isabel is wearing black, in mourning for her father. Though *The Portrait of a Lady* contains his greatest deathbed scene, death in the Jamesian drama most commonly makes its presence felt offstage. A remarkably large number of James's protagonists have lost father or mother or both – and according to well-worn fictional convention this always has some bearing on the plot. It means in Isabel's case that she feels free – free to leave America, free to make her own choices and invent her own future, and the spaciousness of the scene at Gardencourt suggests her sense of boundless opportunity. Yet being an orphan can also have a more mundane significance. It tends to mean being very poor, like Hyacinth Robinson, or Charlotte Stant in *The Golden Bowl*; or very rich, like Milly Theale. Isabel is left poor, but then Daniel Touchett, a sort of surrogate father, leaves her a fortune. This transforms her into the 'American princess', a figure who is both innocent of the new commercial world and inextricably tangled in the old, sophisticated and relatively corrupt world of European society.

Isabel, like Milly Theale after her, is James's 'international theme' writ large – written, that is, in large amounts of dollars. For his 'international theme' – the meeting of cultures facilitated in the second half of the nineteenth century by rapid transatlantic steamer – is of course generally written small, on an intimate, domestic scale; which is why the tea-table at the end of the lawn which Isabel is heading for is also metaphorically appropriate. The international theme was the perfect vehicle – as the success of 'Daisy Miller' had demonstrated – for James's expertise in drawing-room comedy, or, what raised eyebrows in Rome or Mayfair. The enormous attraction of the international theme for James (and he perhaps overdid it, in that there are more expatriate Americans among his characters than thematic necessity dictated) was, clearly, that it combined the reality of social experience with the poetic resonance inherent in the idea of the Old World versus the New.

On the lawn at Gardencourt 'the flood of summer light had begun to ebb', the first sign of the darkness to come. James's 'international theme' is always associated with the notion of innocence deceived, but the converse doesn't hold. (Innocence deceived was also the subject-matter of *Washington Square*, where the international theme was firmly squashed by Catherine's 'ample seat'.) Deception goes far deeper in James than the portrayal of false expectations excited by cultural change. It is the central theme of James's fiction, and the backbone of the plot in nearly all his novels.

Why deception, or to give it its more melodramatic name, betrayal, should exercise such a hold over James's imagination is not my concern here. The point is that it is there, not just as a theme incidental to James's fiction, but deeply embedded in it and ineradicable. It infects relations between lovers and friends, between the author and his characters, even between the author and his reader, as language itself becomes treacherous. What does 'saving the children' mean in *What Maisie Knew* or 'The Turn of the Screw'? What does Osmond mean by suggesting to Isabel that 'one ought to make one's life a work of art' and that it was 'exactly' what she seemed to be doing with her own?

Osmond's remarks, made in the context of her incipient global travels, correctly identify the high seriousness of Isabel's desire for the world, her Emersonian need to assimilate the whole of it to a personal sense of integrity and search for meaning.[7] But Osmond says this because he wants Isabel to desire, exclusively, him, and to identify him as a prime exemplar of the aesthetic of the Old World; which has further sinister implications, should Isabel become his, for the reader knows by this time that Osmond's understanding of this aesthetic, with its emphasis on style and tradition, is sterile and restrictive: a work of art, in his conception, is merely something to be criticised, collected or copied.

James on the other hand positively parades in his initial presentation of Isabel a passionate belief in freedom, vitality, individualism and the capacity for intense feeling, revivifying qualities which, if not the exclusive property of the New World, might reasonably be regarded by Americans in the century of Emerson, Thoreau and Whitman as their contribution to art and aesthetic debate. What James felt that contribution should be was set down in very general but emphatic terms in a letter to aspiring American novelists at the Deerfield summer school in 1889:

> Oh, do something from your point of view ... do something with life. Any point of view is interesting that is a direct impression of life. You each have an impression colored by your individual conditions; make that into a picture, a picture framed by your own personal wisdom ... I have only two little words for the matter remotely approaching to rule or doctrine: one is life and the other freedom. (HF 46–7 ; HJL iii.257)

The critic Richard Poirier has shown how closely Isabel's 'large and imaginative view of human experience' corresponds to James's ideals as expressed in the Deerfield letter.[8] That this is so may well explain whatever emblematic significance she may have had for James. But, as I have suggested, this significance is not clear to us as, actually reading, we feel that Isabel's special qualities have not been altogether assimilated to the form and direction of the narrative vehicle. James may have conceived her as having the 'intellectual grace' and 'moral spontaneity' he saw in American women, and specifically in his cousin Minny (HJL i.208); but Catherine Sloper, with all her lack of these characteristics, seems to survive James's handling in rather better shape than Isabel. Catherine at least preserves a solid integrity; Isabel's virtues are not so conspicuous, and her 'large view', or freedom from narrowness of vision, when translated into the artist's freedom to experiment, extends the view beyond the edges of the picture, so that even at the end of the novel we never really get her into focus. Isabel *would* like her life to be a work of art: and in so far as she stands for and voices ideals that James associated with the art of the novel, she is rather exceptional among his protagonists. But in her complex relation to the novel he actually wrote, and through her experience of being *in* the novel,

Isabel is, I would suggest, a paradigm of the Jamesian heroine or hero.

The Jamesian heroine (we are usually, though not always, concerned with a female) doesn't have to be rich or beautiful (as will be demonstrated by the failure of the glamorous Princess Casamassima and the success of the child Maisie); her heroic potential lies in her imagination. Peculiarly receptive to the variety of experience, she is required to make sense of it, in social, sexual, ethical or aesthetic terms. She must discover, like Maisie, what her position is in a network of relationships; or – this is harder – how to do what is right (like Fleda Vetch); or, harder still, how to do what is fine (Isabel Archer and Hyacinth Robinson must discover all these things): she must discern structures in the random agglomerations of life and find out where she fits in (the problem hauntingly conveyed in *The Golden Bowl* by Maggie's vision of the pagoda from which she is excluded). The concerns of the Jamesian heroine, in other words, are remarkably like those of a novelist; her task is to find her own story, and take control of it.

And she must be free. Free from the claims of what is vulgar and mercenary in society? That is one aspect of the quest for liberty in which the heroine, who is often like Isabel an idealist, may be overtly, even eloquently engaged. But, since there are tighter grips than that of society, the struggle to be free can take a more compelling form: in the story, for instance, of Hyacinth Robinson, whose destiny appears to be mapped in the genes of dead parents, or of Maisie Farange, whose destiny appears dictated by a proliferation of live ones. The paternal and maternal images that haunt James's world can pose a risk. The orphan Isabel assures her cousin: 'I'm not a candidate for adoption.'

To be free is to create one's own image, yet the heroine must not be so free as entirely to escape from the social, conventional and literary terms whereby the novelist gives her a recognisable shape. James defines his protagonist in a great variety of ways: from the ironic perspective (Catherine and Isabel); from the perspective of the past (Hyacinth as the product of his history); from a pictorial perspective (Maisie as an image in miniature of her mother). These are all frames, or traps, from which it may be impossible to escape, and the most obvious frame, or trap, is the plot of James's novel.

The plot can be a plot in the sense of 'intrigue' but, except in *The Portrait of a Lady* and *The Wings of the Dove*, 'intrigue' is too melodramatic a name for the way in which other characters seek to use and manipulate the heroine; it is more a case of their having their own stories in mind, with a prescribed role for her. The adults who surround Maisie Farange, for example, find it convenient to relegate her to the position of the child who 'knows' or who is, finally, 'too good for us'; and so nearly trapped is she in these images that critics still promote them at the expense of her real achievement. It is dangerous to be part of someone else's story, or 'to be seen in a light', to put it the Jamesian way – even when the light in question is indistinguishable from the glow of an affection that promises security. It is that kind of safety which Mrs Gereth holds out to Fleda Vetch, and Mrs Wix to Maisie and Susie Stringham to Milly Theale; but it goes hand-in-hand with being forced into a particular role.

Yet role-playing in itself offers its own brand of security, and the recognisable identity it gives the heroine may be the only thing she has to hold on to (Catherine Sloper could see herself as a dutiful daughter when her father saw her as nothing). In particular, role-playing may provide cover in which to survive a threatening environment until the heroine can see how to exploit her situation. Milly Theale becomes the dove, for it was she who had seen that 'The case was the case of escape ...'. To escape from other people's plots – really to *be* the heroine – means to carry the novel with you, and make it different from the story that the other characters – and perhaps James himself – intended it to be. It means to make *your* life the work of art. We shall see how Fleda Vetch fails in this because she is only capable of appreciating works of art, not of making them. She lacks, furthermore, one signal advantage that Isabel Archer has – someone who can recognise beauty and value and meaning in her. Ultimately, though, the Jamesian heroine must rely on herself. Which is why Isabel's story – her voyage of self-expression – ends somewhere between life and art, like a portrait left incomplete.

3.

Unlike Catherine and several of those that come after her, Isabel has no difficulty in establishing herself from the outset at the centre of the picture. Although one of her suitors, Lord Warburton, is distinguished for his enlightened views, and the other, Caspar Goodwood, for his entrepreneurial drive, their function will not be to bring the realities of the English political or the American industrial scene into the novel, but to offer Isabel the leading role in two different types of narrative.

The first derives from the fictional world of Jane Austen, where social position, values, motives and the satire that examines them are all clearly marked. It is easy to see why Lord Warburton, with his radical politics, his bunch of dim sisters and need of an heir should want to marry Isabel, who is so attractively representative of the New World and flatteringly appreciative of the Old ('I adore a moat,' she tells him to smooth an awkward moment). It is also easy to see an irritating superiority in her firmly held but narrow attitudes to the aristocracy and in her immense self-satisfaction when she rejects him. Isabel, like Austen's Emma Woodhouse, is unambiguously designated an opinionated young woman headed for a fall, and the narrator unambiguously predicts it.

The part that Caspar Goodwood, on the other hand, offers Isabel suggests a literature yet to be written, in a wilder western context, the irresistible imposition of order on inchoate nature. Caspar himself, who claims not to be conventional, who certainly lacks Warburton's urbanity and is 'not romantically ... much rather obscurely handsome', is nevertheless not made after the pattern of Heathcliff or Mr Rochester. He is too reasonable, too analytical, too grimly civilised. Hence his *tête-à-têtes* with Isabel are superficially rather dull, yet also vaguely portentous and increasingly charged with repressed sexuality (Isabel is both impatient of and disturbed by them). The background to their courtship is opaque, and what specifically they see in one another is never very clear, although we learn that Isabel feels for Caspar 'a sentiment of high, of rare respect', while he admires her independence, and doesn't 'wince' (as the narrator implies one might) at the 'large air' and the 'grandeur' with which she proclaims her liberty. There are, however, two aspects of their relationship which are obvious. The first is that Caspar sees Isabel and himself in quasi-mythological terms, representing together the hero and heroine of the American story, no less. The second – and this is where James's emphasis lies – is that Isabel feels Caspar to have some indelible claim on her, which she persistently tries to evade. She is always running away from him, in what is sometimes regarded as a flight from her own sexuality but which may also be interpreted simply as a flight from America and from the past.

Despite the opportunities that Lord Warburton and Caspar Goodwood offer her – not just different ways to see the world, but different ways of being seen *by* the world – their relations with her will produce a rather negative picture of Isabel. It is left to her third admirer, Ralph, to create a flattering portrait, one that puts Isabel in a realistic perspective without sacrificing the mythological dimension.

Her attractive side has been reflected from the beginning in her affection for all three Touchetts. This domestic loyalty, which extends to old friends, indicates (as in the case of Emma Woodhouse) that the heroine is intrinsically good and valuable. Paternal, maternal or fraternal warmth, wherever his orphans can find it, is an important source of heat in James's bleaker houses of fiction. As Isabel basks in the glow of Ralph's love and admiration, the reader warms to her too, despite her faults.

Ralph sees these faults, and likes to tease Isabel about them, lightly underscoring the narrator's irony. In his affection for Isabel, which is as acutely perceptive as it is imaginatively sympathetic, he is virtually identifiable with the novelist himself. It is he who coins the metaphors that most vividly define her experience, and he who urges the greatness of her claim on the reader's imagination:

> 'A character like that,' he said to himself, 'a real little passionate force to see at play is the finest thing in nature. It's finer than the finest work of art – than a Greek bas-relief, than a great Titian, than a Gothic cathedral. ... Suddenly, I receive a Titian, by the post, to hang on my wall – a Greek bas-relief to stick over my chimney-piece.' (65)

This is no mean endorsement, and one that clearly recognises Isabel as both powerful and independent. It is a mistake to assume that Ralph, like Gilbert Osmond, reifies Isabel – regards her, that is, merely as a desirable thing to have about the house.[9] He envisages for Isabel some destiny more interesting than ending up with the right man, that fate whereby the nineteenth-century novel tended to dispose of its opinionated heroines (Emma Woodhouse, Natasha Rostova, Dorothea Casaubon). Certainly Ralph is self-interested: Isabel is to be his 'entertainment'; but the essence of it is to be his enjoyment of the freedom and uncertainty that his own circumstances deny him. Observing Isabel's life as a dynamic process – how will she act, what will she become? – beats contemplating a painting on the wall. That sort of activity is put in its place by Lord Warburton's sister's comment on picture galleries: 'They're so very pleasant when it rains.'

Picture galleries are of course one abode of what is called in a later novel the 'larger life', the life of the expanded mind and senses, which embraces both the visitable past and further, less apprehensible dimensions. It is the life to which every Jamesian heroine worth her transatlantic fare aspires; and Isabel shares Ralph's liberating vision of her destiny while 'affronting' it with the rigid singleness of purpose often associated, in James's day and since, with American tourists. She has 'a fixed determination to regard the world as a place of brightness, of free expansion, of irresistible action', and a very definite view of what she intends to represent within it. She will be independent, true to herself and she will be good. These are plainly the values of her native culture, as variously exhibited in Catherine Sloper and Daisy Miller, but only Isabel is distinguished by the Transcendentalist inheritance of an intense and idealistic preoccupation with her self:

> Her life should always be in harmony with the most pleasing impression she should produce; she would be what she appeared, and she would appear what she was. Sometimes she went so far as to wish that she might find herself some day in a difficult position, so that she should have the pleasure of being as heroic as the occasion demanded. (53)

There could be no more explicit statement of the intention to be a heroine. Isabel is as conscious as any portrait-painter of the desirability of complete identification between essence and image (things, it will be remembered, that Catherine Sloper had conspicuous difficulty in getting together). She even *wants* to find herself in a difficult position (the last thing Catherine would have wanted). Such fixity of purpose has in itself a heroic aspect (if Catherine is fixed in the reader's memory, it is largely for being admirably obstinate). But Ralph advises Isabel: 'Don't try so much to form your character – it's like trying to pull open a tight, tender young rose.' Too resolute a streak may pervert that natural spontaneity which makes Daisy Miller, for example, a more obviously attractive heroine than Catherine Sloper.

Daisy perfectly exemplifies the importance for the Jamesian heroine of catching the right tone. She fails spectacularly to catch the tone of Roman society, yet it is precisely her spontaneity that makes social convention look wrong: no reader could suppose the heroic part belongs to the inhibited Winterbourne. It is a question of finding a particular style that puts its stamp on the narrative. (Daisy is too bright for tragedy, not robust enough for farce.) The infinitely more self-conscious Isabel has difficulty with this. Trying to be grand, she often appears gauche. When Madame Merle at their first encounter enquires politely if she is 'the niece – the young American?', Isabel replies, 'I'm my aunt's niece.' Said 'with simplicity', this is clearly intended by Isabel to have a certain style, but Madame Merle's reaction suggests that she is not impressed. At other times Isabel's grandeur almost comes off, as when, retrieved by Mrs Touchett from the solecism of remaining with the gentlemen after dinner, she declares:

> '... I always want to know the things one shouldn't do.'
> 'So as to do them?' asked her aunt.
> 'So as to choose,' said Isabel. (71)

This last remark is left to resonate unchallenged in the ensuing break between chapters. Isabel speaks as if she were independent of the structures of society, yet it is plain that she has enormous respect for them. Her concern for what is 'right' – socially acceptable – is remarked on by Ralph and criticised by her friend Henrietta, who tells her she is too ready to please other people. It is also evident in her deference to the Touchetts, and, above all, in her attitude to Madame Merle, who represents after all nothing more than the high degree of social competence evinced in her capacity to live entirely at the expense of other people. Isabel doesn't admire Lord Warburton for being a radical, and finds some satisfaction in turning him down precisely because she shares society's view that he remains an ideal match despite his aberrant politics.

Having placed Lord Warburton in the social structure as 'a personage', she finds it hard to see him, in the more worthy context of hero to her heroine, as having 'character' like herself. But this, from the reader's point of view, places Isabel as a conventional rebel, a person of unformed character whose attitudes are shaped in automatic reaction to established forms, and who, if she is going to be interestingly different, must find other terms in which to define herself – some more striking way of capturing the reader's imagination. She could do this, perhaps, by being simply the American (like Christopher Newman or Daisy Miller), but we have seen that she objected to Madame Merle's calling her that, as not individual enough.

The grasp of 'form' that Isabel likes to display is not allowed to conceal her inner uncertainties about what and where she is. There is a marked discrepancy between her socially impeccable behaviour towards the rejected Lord Warburton and her secret sense of having acted recklessly; between the way she imagines him proposing in terms of an attractive, conventional picture, and the deep unease she feels about the scene even weeks after the event; between the irreproachability of her formal written refusal ('We see our lives from our own point of view ...') and the incoherent, almost bizarre explanations she gives him to his face:

'That reason that I wouldn't tell you .... It's that I can't escape my fate. I should try to escape it if I were to marry you. ... it's giving up other chances. ... I don't mean chances to marry ... I can't escape unhappiness. ... In marrying you I shall be trying to.' (140)

Mystery and sinister foreboding: if Catherine Sloper, at least in her father's eyes, had no literary potential, Isabel here assumes it to an almost embarrassing extent. How much more complicated life is for someone like her who reads books, and how much more complicated our response to her, who is so clearly in a book. After all, if she can so impressively 'choose', why can't she escape her fate? Isn't this stuff about her destiny merely a romantic pose? Isabel parodies it herself when she tells her friend Henrietta that her conception of happiness involves a swift carriage rattling to an unknown destination in the dark. This invites Henrietta's cross response that she sounds 'like the heroine of some immoral novel', and invites the reader to observe that the 'fate' deemed inevitable is now, apparently, open-ended.

Isabel, evidently, has no clear idea about what will constitute her happiness or unhappiness, or the kind of novel she wants to be in.[10] She seems simply to say the first thing that comes into her head, which often happens to be some melodramatic image. When Ralph asks her what she 'had in mind' in refusing Lord Warburton, she disingenuously denies having had anything in mind and goes on, more puzzlingly, to say that a life of opportunities wider than those Lord Warburton offered is not what she wants:

'No, I don't wish to touch the cup of experience! It's a poisoned drink! ... I don't know what you're trying to fasten upon me, for I'm not in the least an adventurous spirit. Women are not like men.' (160)

What is this? Silliness? Perversity? A knee-jerk response to unwelcome pressure (which for Isabel means the pressure of any idea that isn't hers to start with)? Isabel's behaviour – her inconsistencies, her evasive tactics and the final retreat into cliché – can be interpreted in several different ways. It can be regarded simply as evidence that her character is, as Ralph observes, not nearly as developed as she likes to think. Or if we prefer, it can be taken as articulating, in sociohistoric terms, the dilemma of the new woman who on the threshold of a different age hesitates finally to abandon the dogmas of a restricted female upbringing. But it is perhaps more interesting to see Isabel as caught in the grip of psychological conflict between an innate craving for a safe, structured existence and a yearning for the wider, uncharted world and ill-defined opportunities.

Such a conflict is discernible everywhere in James's fiction. It is expressed in *The Portrait of a Lady* not only in Isabel's attitude to experience but in the ambivalent presentation of, for example, convents, art-collecting, filial piety – things which seem at times admirable, at others sinister. In *The Princess Casamassima* it is embodied in the person of the hero, Hyacinth Robinson; in *The Wings of the Dove* it takes the form of direct confrontation between the hazards of life and the safe haven of death. But – taking our cue from Isabel's acute literary self-consciousness – it is also possible to see this conflict reflected in James's work on a deeper level, as the conflict between 'safe' traditional fiction – fiction that is firmly pinned to established social and narrative structures – and 'unsafe' or experimental fiction, where changing narrative methods and possibly even some fundamental shift in values render familiar terrain increasingly unfamiliar.

Rejecting the 'splendid security' that Lord Warburton offers her, Isabel takes refuge in a curious simile in which escape cannot be distinguished from retreat:

> though she was lost in admiration of her opportunity she managed to move back into the deepest shade of it, even as some wild, caught creature in a vast cage. (115)

The cage is a recurrent figure in James's fiction, which, if it suggests the imprisoned imagination, can also be a place of safety. A cage has structure: it posits a controlling authority, and its significance for those whose problem is one of self-definition and self-expression, as well as the difference between safe and unsafe stories, is illustrated, not unexpectedly, in James's short story 'In the Cage' (1898).

A young woman of indeterminate social class and not identified by so much as a name, sits all day in an enclosure at the back of a grocer's shop, handling telegrams. Having a vivid imagination, she finds an outlet for it in composing stories around the messages she reads and the people who send them. At first these are safe stories, reflecting fairly obvious realities: if a wire has, for example, details of a meeting-place, she reads an intriguing liaison into it. But just as life influences fiction, stories influence life, so that the telegraphist begins to put fantastic constructions on reality, finding *her* story, *her* tale of intrigue, in the nice gentleman involved in a liaison who seems to take a particular interest in *her*.

At the same time, with a brilliant facility for making imaginative connections, she seems able to conjure meaning out of muddled, encoded telegrams, where no one else, including the reader, can (this is how she impresses the nice gentleman). The reader, then, discovers two stories in it. One is an unsafe one, because it implies meanings that are beyond our grasp: what on earth are the telegrams, a teasing puzzle of cross-references, trying to say? The other, easily recognisable story is that the poor girl will be disappointed in her dashing admirer. This is a safe, traditional story, though not a good one for the telegraphist to be in: as she eventually realises, the only safety for her in fact lies outside of it all, with her fiancé Mr Mudge – who presumably at least knows her name.

'In the Cage', with its unsafe story held inside the safe one, mirrors the tensions of Isabel's uneasy relation to Lord Warburton. He offers her a way to fit in, a part in a recognisable fiction, the traditional happy ending of a good marriage. She refuses, and the anxiety underlining her refusal seems already like a nostalgia for old securities irretrievably lost, which in a world becoming increasingly insecure will achieve its most poignant expression in that revised version of Isabel's story which is *The Wings of the Dove*. Milly Theale, the ailing American heiress who has Isabel's thirst for life and Ralph's physical incapacity for it, is acutely conscious of 'not having had from the beginning anything firm': her 'queer little history' lacks definition: all it has been is a 'sense of loosely rattling'. Yet if the physical extinction that Milly faces is the ultimate loss of definition, death is as firm as a full stop: as the recognised terminal point of many stories, it knocks whatever queer little history it precedes into a final shape. And the same is true of any traditional fictional ending – including the unspecified unhappy fate to which Isabel makes hesitant allusion. It is as if, possessed by the same desire for meaning, or 'firmness', as Milly, Isabel were trying to catch the echo of her own story; just as the responsive reader (one conditioned by fictions) catches behind her romantic pose something oddly like the echo of a real tragedy.

Without her knowledge Ralph waives his inheritance in Isabel's favour, so that she becomes, like Milly Theale, very rich. He intends his gift to spell not the ending of some traditional fairytale but a new beginning. Yet Isabel is troubled and self-absorbed, concerned not with the good she might do with the money, but with whether it will be good for her:

'...A large fortune means freedom, and I'm afraid of that.' (241)

4.

We are almost at the mid-point of the novel, and the question of whom Isabel will marry, which has determined the (relatively few) narrative developments so far, looms larger and larger. The money makes her twice as interesting in this respect, vulnerable to the fortune-hunters lurking near every heiress, but at the same time truly independent: no longer needing the support of a husband, she is free to marry for love.

Isabel has always considered, and chooses publicly to prefer, the further option of not marrying at all: 'I shall probably never do it – no, never,' she informs Caspar Goodwood. He doesn't believe her, and nor do we, for the same reason: we already know Isabel too well. We know her because so much of the earlier part of the book is devoted to the exploration of her personality, or what she figures, fancifully, as 'the garden of her soul'. Isabel's garden is filled with 'perfume', 'shady bowers', 'lengthening vistas' and so on. It is a place for dreaming, reflecting, and gathering stray impressions, a 'maze of visions', many of them indeterminate, which acknowledge but distantly a world beyond and 'places which were not gardens at all'. It is, however, also a place of intensive cogitation on the subject of her immediate position. We know Isabel will marry, because we have seen how persistently her thoughts dwell on herself in relation to her various suitors.

At the risk, foreseen by James in his notebook draft, of it all becoming 'too psychological' (Ntbks 15), Isabel's garden provides the solid groundwork of her story, necessary to understanding it.

We identify the idealism, the self-regard and insecurity which will explain her choice of husband. We also see the way her mind works, and that despite its frequently fuddled expression it has its fine discriminations and sharp images. Her habit of seeing in terms of pictures and confusing style with substance has led to her being accused of a 'fatal aestheticism'.[11] It is undeniably the case that it does her no good to choose the particular aesthete she does, and furthermore that her representations of reality sometimes look less like the truth than an evasion of it. But it is also fair to say that in the first half of the novel Isabel needs the pictures she sees and the occasional image of herself she comes up with to retain her grip on the reader's imagination. She has not established herself as a wit like Dr Sloper; nor has she Catherine's memorable bulk, and unlike Catherine she cannot surprise us by a sudden move, because she is constantly fidgeting. So that any little flash of a particular vision or a particular style helps to stave off a feeling of impatience – are we *getting* anywhere? – during the long preliminary perambulation of her garden and of the marriage question.

The Portrait of a Lady marks a stage in that attempt to transfer the focus of interest from external events to a single central consciousness which James had essayed in his first novel, *Roderick Hudson* (1875), and which would be most perfectly achieved in *The Ambassadors* (1903). The consciousness of the hero, Lambert Strether, functions there as a kind of kaleidoscope: a mirror that makes a pattern, or a story, from the reflected interplay of three separate entities – fragments of Strether's own past and present, the Parisian setting, and the plot, or hidden intrigue not quite sufficiently hidden which got him sent to Paris in the first place. *The Portrait of a Lady* operates rather differently. Here, the purpose of the viewfinder appears simply to be to get a better look at Isabel. The sense of a story anywhere else is only fleeting, as when Isabel registers, in connection with Madame Merle, the impression that the reality of friendship doesn't quite match up to her ideal of it. Suddenly, outside the garden and threatening to overshadow it, there stands a wholly different construction. This is the version of Isabel's story conceived by Madame Merle.

There is now a marked switch to a faster tempo and to plainer indicators of the narrative's direction. The existence of a conspiracy against Isabel and the nature of the conspirators is made very clear very quickly, from Madame Merle's first betrayal of contempt for the Touchetts (touchstones of decency) to the sight of her in collusion with Gilbert Osmond, and having 'ambitions for him', just before she tells him about Isabel and about her money. However, Madame Merle's advancement into the spotlight is not entirely to Isabel's disadvantage. Within a few pages of their discussion on the self which laid bare all Isabel's naïve self-absorption, the balance has altered sufficiently to consign Madame Merle to the ranks of the superficial and confirm Isabel as a serious person.

It is Osmond who really does threaten to put Isabel in the shade. James's portrait of him, achieved unlike Isabel's with great economy, is a marvellously pointed and controlled exposé of implacable vanity expressing itself in a peculiarly negative and petty nastiness. It is characteristic of Osmond, who 'had never forgiven his star for not appointing him to an English dukedom', that he finds Isabel attractive for having disappointed a lord; characteristic that he tells her he finds St Peter's 'too large', without even pretending, fabled aesthete as he is, that this is an aesthetic judgement. At the same time, he admits he would like to have been the pope. *Faute de mieux*, all Osmond does is paint on a modest scale and collect modest *objets d'art*. As his sister the Countess Gemini points out, he has plenty to be modest about; only Isabel wrongly identifies modesty as integral to his style, which mesmerises her as it obsesses him.

What *is* integral to his style is a kind of transparency. Osmond is very frank: frank when he tells others about their shortcomings, frank when he chooses to tell Isabel about his own ('I'm not conventional: I'm convention itself'). This quality does not make him likeable as in James other, more devious betrayers of innocent faith are likeable. Osmond's simplicity reflects his brutality as clearly as his daughter Pansy's austere Florentine home reflects her convent-prison in Rome. He wants Isabel to 'publish his "style" to the world' with the *éclat* that money confers; and in a metaphor memorable for the light it sheds on art-collecting far ahead into this and the later novels, he envisages an Isabel lending herself to this purpose 'as smooth to his general need of her as handled ivory to the palm'. In fact it is Osmond in his patent villainy who lends himself to James's purpose, representing the tide of evil advancing step by visible step, while Isabel flounders on the shoreline of experience.

A dramatic counterpoint is set up between the crude danger of her situation and the delicate handling of Isabel seen at its best in the masterly scene preceding her departure from Rome where Osmond first presses his suit, playing expertly on Isabel's imagination with his graceful speeches: 'Don't you remember my telling you that one ought to make one's life a work of art?' He denies making light of her plans to embrace the world in her travels. He claims that he *would* like to visit Japan – for the 'old lacquer' – which might be a synonym for the highly polished Osmond himself.

It is a quintessentially Jamesian moment, one which invokes – without using the phrase – all the ambiguous reference of 'the real thing': a moment when the allure of brilliant appearances and the authority of the connoisseur make an irresistible combination, and yet they engender almost by virtue of that brilliance and that authority a fundamental distrust. We know that Osmond is a fake (even Isabel perceives that he isn't really interested in her travels), yet at the same time we recognise how badly she needs – how she has been designed by James *for* – the portentous significance that Osmond articulates on her behalf.

One might compare how in *The Golden Bowl* Charlotte, like Isabel, is seduced by the aesthetic, the semblance of the perfect artefact; and yet how she also needs, and is designed for, what the *antiquario*'s connoisseurship seems to guarantee: that she and the Prince, objects of beauty themselves, belong together, that their (secret) life is also a work of art, that it makes a story.[12] The Prince, on the other hand, rejects the bowl, suspecting its gilt to conceal a flaw, and that it prefigures another story – that of a damaged marriage – which he definitely doesn't want to hear.

Ultimately, in *The Portrait of a Lady* as in *The Golden Bowl*, we shall have to consider where the *real* story lies. If we define it as the one packing the maximum punch, what strikes us most forcefully at this critical point of Isabel's falling in love is not (as was the case in *Washington Square*) the heroine's capacity to be deceived, but her capacity to conceive her experience in imaginative terms. In an image of great beauty and resonance her imminent embarkation is equated with the end of her Roman adventure and what she expects to be the loss of Osmond:

> Happy things don't repeat themselves, and her adventure wore already the changed, the seaward face of some romantic island from which, after feasting on purple grapes, she was putting off while the breeze rose. (333)

Isabel's perplexed perception of some gain inextricable from sacrifice anticipates Susan Stringham's anxiety in *The Wings of the Dove* about 'the real thing' that had gone away: would she ever find it

again? (see above, p. 12). It anticipates too the way that Milly
Theale's own story will be told in extravagant images of the ship,
the adventurer, and of lushness and decay which represent a safe
haven from the perils of exploration. Yearning 'Ah never to go
down!' from the security of her Venetian palazzo, Milly will be
about to fall victim to the plot; and Isabel now, upon Osmond's declaration of love, can't distinguish the sensation of imprisonment
from that of release – feeling 'a pang that suggested to her somehow
the slipping of a fine bolt – backward, forward, she couldn't have
said which'. Further images – among them the banal and the frankly
bizarre – flood her consciousness. The end of the chapter sees Isabel
go down waving metaphors like a drowning man: it is a flamboyant
capitulation of the individual imagination to the more stringent
demands of narrative.

Returning from her travels (of which we hear nothing), Isabel is
plunged into a series of rows provoked by her choice of Osmond.
The process of her marrying, by now looking to become intermina-
ble, is revitalised by the objections of her friends, expressed without
inhibition. ('You're going to be put in a cage,' Ralph warns her.)
Isabel, though hurt by the barrage of criticism, is not to be moved.
Her position as she makes it out is thoroughly reasonable: she isn't
marrying to please her friends, and finds the values of those who
prefer Lord Warburton deplorably materialistic. If she herself is, as
she assures Mrs Touchett, well aware of the value of money, then
'that's why I wish Mr Osmond to have a little.'

Her attitude here, undeniably fine and delicate and honest, makes
the accumulating warnings seem in comparison a little exaggerated
and melodramatic – as if Isabel truly belonged, in her refinement
and integrity, to a higher order of fiction. Yet she never shakes off
her social conditioning to prove herself independent of those values
that underpin the novel of society. She wants to offer Osmond
money, and she herself feels 'worth more' – just as Dr Sloper esti-
mated Catherine – as the result of her foreign travels. By this
implicit acceptance of the currency of the marriage market she is
drawn into a world where money and culture are grossly equated
with power and repression. And at her supreme moment of choice,
when Isabel is supremely conscious of living up to her ideal, of
'being what she appeared to be'– transparently independent, rational, and in the right – the 'irresistible action' that beckoned to her
from infinite horizons takes the form of marrying Osmond, who is
exactly what he appears to be – to everyone except Isabel. If the

warning signals were blatant, the irony of this outcome is crude enough to match them.

The narrative makes at this point an abrupt leap forward, to find Isabel three years later in wretched spiritual isolation in the Palazzo Roccanera, the 'dark and massive structure' where she and Osmond are living in Rome. In the interim, she has had a child and lost it – but where we look to see Isabel's experience of motherhood, there is a blank. She keeps that story to herself, as if she recognised it as irrelevant to James's story, and knew what was expected of her.

She does not speak of her baby even to Ralph, who is in Italy for his health, and anxious about his cousin. But since her marriage Isabel is no longer frank with him, and Ralph feels that from now on 'for him she would always wear a mask.' He finds her spirit, her curiosity, her pleasure in argument dulled, as her surroundings and personal appearance increase in brilliance. The truth of his observations is confirmed by Isabel's relation to Madame Merle, which is no longer intimate but remains one of admiration. She envies Madame Merle the 'sort of corselet of silver' which appears to shield her friend from the possibility of hurt, or even happiness: 'It was ... as if the art of life were some clever trick she had guessed.' The trick, it appears, is to make your life not a work of art but a copy of one: copies are the safest form of art there is. Isabel, so quick to pick up any social manner that reinforces the protective image of a lady (knowing, sophisticated and in command of any situation), herself now assumes a glittering, if brittle carapace, which resembles but isn't the intellectual grace Ralph misses in her: indeed her new, coldly critical attitudes display something of Osmond's cruel verbal facility. The grim palazzo's comfortable interior is, as she tells Lord Warburton, to Osmond's credit: 'He has a genius for upholstery.' Pansy's 'very limited' admirer Ned Rosier 'has about the extent of one's pocket-handkerchief – the small ones with lace borders'.

Isabel's barbed remarks betray the depths of her disillusionment, but they also show that she has got to grips with the new plot involving Pansy and her suitors which is now developing. Osmond wants to marry his daughter to Lord Warburton, who is Ralph's companion in Rome. Warburton finds Pansy charming, but is still attracted to Isabel, who makes no attempt to encourage him, although as we have seen no attempt either to disguise her contempt for Osmond. Meanwhile, Pansy is in love with Ned Rosier, a collector like Osmond of old china, but without money enough left over to buy his 'Dresden shepherdess'. The young couple have

Isabel's somewhat detached sympathy, but if she sticks up for Pansy, Osmond will think she wants Warburton for herself.

Adapting to this conflict, Isabel gives it the sharp tone and the sharp focus needed to balance the book's discursiveness. She strikes sparks from Madame Merle, she wounds Osmond, she boldly targets the real issues: who, she asks Warburton, is he really pursuing? This is one of two questions that are kept dangling before us, in an atmosphere of thickening speculation. The other concerns Madame Merle's part in it all. The enigma of this woman and the peculiar interest she takes in the Osmond household is underlined by obvious clues, dropped by the narrator and by Madame Merle herself, who now becomes for the reader the object of fascination she has always been for Isabel, particularly as we see her begin to crack under the strain of her ambitions for Pansy.

This half-hidden but increasingly intriguing story, of which Isabel catches only an occasional glimpse, threatens to leave our heroine behind. She catches up with it as she broods alone one evening before the dying fire in the celebrated and conspicuous scene which James claimed 'is obviously the best thing in the book'. Isabel's meditation far into the night moves from the problem of Lord Warburton and Pansy to a wide retrospective review of the relationship with Osmond, to the point where she confronts the extent of her error, Osmond's true nature, and the fact that he now hates her. Some five thousand words of uninterrupted free indirect style, taking us into the deepest depths of Isabel's garden, it was a bold gamble for the reader's interest which James himself regarded from a technical point of view as an important triumph of 'lucidity' over action, of Isabel's 'motionlessly *seeing*' (AN 57). From the reader's point of view, what Isabel sees restores to her a measure of life and freedom, first through the illusion of a past recaptured on her terms (it is an illusion because her analysis of her faults and Osmond's yields nothing we haven't seen for ourselves); secondly, in a series of vivid images:

> she had suddenly found the infinite vista of a multiplied life to be a dark, narrow alley with a dead wall at the end. ... the shadows had begun to gather; it was as if Osmond deliberately, almost malignantly, had put the lights out one by one. ... It was the house of darkness, the house of dumbness, the house of suffocation. ... Osmond's beautiful mind indeed seemed to peep down from a small high window and mock at her. ... his egotism lay hidden like

a serpent in a bank of flowers. ... Her mind was to be his – attached to his own like a small garden-plot to a deer-park. (461–2, 466, 469)

The images represent of course restriction and imprisonment. But in their extravagance, their haphazard accumulation, their disregard for measure and, almost, taste, representing everything Osmond loathes, they contrive to establish a territory beyond his reach.

5.

Not invited to stay at the Palazzo Roccanera because Osmond finds the idea of such a guest preposterous, Henrietta comes to Rome nevertheless, prompted by her anxiety for Isabel; and with her re-appearance, James readjusts the balance between Isabel's solipsistic picture-painting and that engagement with the novel's more famil-iar concerns needed to satisfy readers who, like Carroll's Alice, want a book with conversations in it. Isabel drops the barriers, admitting the failure of her marriage; and, as they talk, the scent of freedom grows powerful on the air. It isn't simply that Isabel had always identified her friend with the 'strong, sweet, fresh odour' of 'the great country stretching beyond the rivers and across the prairies'; nor even that Henrietta, with her independent career and scorn of Pansy's compliance, is the prototype of the modern liberated woman, and advises Isabel bluntly to leave Osmond. It is that, embodying warmth unaffected by self-interest, curiosity uninhib-ited by good taste, and perception uncomplicated by niceties of expression, Henrietta is the antithesis of Osmond, and as such insist-ently asserts the life Osmond would deny to his wife and daughter.

Henrietta is a journalist, who produces (as James did) sketches of her travels for the transatlantic readership. As staunchly supportive of American ways ('I don't care much for these European potatoes') as she is fascinated by foreign exotica, she represents the interna-tional theme in its most literal (and entertaining) form, and repre-sents also, in a self-consciously literary context, the most direct and unsophisticated relation to reality. Henrietta is not like Isabel 'a kind of novelist of her own experience';[13] nor is she like Pansy, whom Isabel regards with condescending affection as 'a sheet of blank paper – the ideal *jeune fille* of foreign fiction'. She is, the narrator observes with affectionate condescension, 'a strictly veracious reporter'; and as such risks appearing as out of place in James's stylish house of fiction as Osmond deems her to be in the Palazzo Roccanera. Henrietta, we recall, was not cited as one of James's 'true agents' in the Preface to *The Portrait of a Lady*, where he is apologetic about the 'overtreated' and 'almost inexplicably' pervasive Miss Stackpole, who 'must have been at that time a part of my wonderful notion of the lively' (AN 57). It is tempting to observe, faced with this air of weary retrospection which positively parodies Isabel's, that his energetic, eclectic reporter, with her fascination for people, places, customs, titles, must have something in common with the James who wrote dozens of competent, lively short stories for the commercial market.

Henrietta is not ashamed to represent the ephemeral. 'I consider', she declares, irritated by Pansy's deference to her, 'that my conversation refers only to the moment, like the morning papers.' But it takes Ralph to recognise her quality, 'crisp and new and comprehensive as a first issue before the folding', and with 'probably no misprint'. It is typical of *The Portrait of a Lady*'s tone that Ralph's elaborate metaphor, like Isabel's earlier one, lends Henrietta a certain cachet, and that a straightforward comment by the narrator on her devotion to the Correggio Virgin ('she thought it the most beautiful picture in the world') should sound like a sneer. As an outsider in a world complacently *au fait* with higher conceptions of art, Henrietta, with her concern for the actual and immediate, her common touch and her pragmatic decency, is irresistibly sympathetic.

The same is true of the Countess Gemini, who with her flashy glamour makes a comic foil to the well-scrubbed Henrietta. But she comes as clean as Henrietta in her contempt for 'poor old Osmond, with his curtains and his crucifixes!' and her pity for Isabel: though 'If she has simply allowed him to trample upon her I don't know that I shall even pity her.' The Countess might very well be speaking for the reader here, as that other sophisticate Madame Merle, lacking passion and honesty, seldom does.

Isabel's attitude to the Countess is significant. Like Madame Merle, she strikes Isabel as having a 'polished surface', but Isabel assumes there is nothing behind it; she thinks the Countess doesn't count. 'She was not indifferent to her husband's sister, however; she was rather a little afraid of her.' This fear is not the same as the disquiet aroused in her by Madame Merle, that 'bright, strong, definite, worldly woman' whom Isabel is at last to recognise as 'a powerful agent in her destiny'. Here Isabel has defined the scope of a threat which has long been clear to the reader, even if the nature of the danger remains obscure. It is not so easy to put a name to what frightens her in the Countess, but we perhaps get a sense of it in the wonderfully plastic and accommodating manner in which the Countess lets Isabel cart her off on cultural excursions, exhibiting a sort of blithe receptivity apparently facilitated by inner emptiness. This is the quality in the Countess that makes her so lively; but it also signals the chaos and disorganisation inherent in life, out of which comes the random element, the danger from the least expected quarter; and it is this that threatens Isabel.

Urged by Henrietta to leave Osmond, Isabel replies:

'I can't change that way ... I can't publish my mistake. I don't think that's decent. I'd much rather die. ... One must accept one's deeds.' (531–2)

Earlier, we were told that Isabel had found an idiosyncratic satisfaction in keeping the truth from Ralph. Now, she regards speaking it as tantamount to indecent exposure, directly contradicting her previous principled stand on the importance of essence *vis-à-vis* appearances. The Isabel who confronted life so boldly then is now in patent retreat from it. 'You're like the stricken deer, seeking the innermost shade,' Henrietta informs her (foraying briefly into the grand manner). Isabel tells Henrietta, 'I want to be alone.'

Towards Caspar Goodwood, also brought to Rome by reports of her misery, Isabel's attitude is more equivocal. Apparently in preparation for some kind of leave-taking, she wishes 'to put her spiritual affairs in order', and counts him as among those things with which she wants to 'set herself right'. She can't see herself married to Caspar, but 'would have been glad to have been in some way nearer to him'. She discovers him to be 'the only person with an unsatisfied claim on her. She had made him unhappy, she couldn't help it; and his unhappiness was a grim reality.'

Ralph, and indeed Osmond, might challenge this, for she has made them unhappy too (the grimmest reality, in fact, is Osmond's unhappiness). Isabel's view of Caspar is romantically self-indulgent, and noticeably at odds with the reader's view, which is directed by the strong erotic undertone of their encounters. Isabel is afraid that he will discover 'the intimate disarray of her affairs', and this will result in the bitter frustration of his eventual departure from Rome, when he tells her, 'I can't understand, I can't penetrate

you!' His claim on Isabel, clearly, is that of a lover. But she sees him
very differently. She isn't looking for developments in her story, but
winding it up with that summary disposition of characters endings
often impose. Asking Caspar to take care of Ralph takes care of both
of them:

> It seemed to Isabel that she had been very clever; she had artfully
> disposed of the superfluous Caspar. ... she had converted him
> into a caretaker of Ralph. (540)

Later, Isabel will accuse Madame Merle of having 'made a convenience' of her. Here, she blatantly makes a convenience of Caspar.
Her 'artfulness', and the smooth hard façade of which he accuses
her, indicate that Isabel has now mastered Madame Merle's 'trick' of
the 'art of life' – at the cost, it seems, of spiritual death.

But at this point the reader's attention is claimed by Ralph's physical dying, promoted by Henrietta as the business of conveying him
back to England. His decision to leave Rome opens the last phase of
the novel, which is constructed in terms basically as simple, melodramatic and primitive in their appeal as a tabloid newspaper.
Henrietta and Caspar are converted from caretakers into angels of
mercy, performing the office of Ralph's devoted friends, while Isabel
remains chillingly aloof, and very far from making the 'pleasing
impression' she hoped always to produce. Instead of visiting him,
she pictures Ralph 'sinking to his last rest' at Gardencourt; the
others meanwhile take responsibility for the practical problem of
getting him there. 'The great thing is that he shouldn't die in the
cars,' declares Henrietta, whose eyes, elsewhere described as
'lighted like great glazed railway stations' reflect what Osmond at
least would regard as the indecent exposure of public transport.
Henrietta and Caspar are both experienced train-travellers. But if
the speed with which they get about, and Henrietta's habit of fraternising with her fellow-passengers suggest brash American ways,
these things also represent the energy, and the contact with humanity, that Isabel has lost.

Meanwhile Osmond, disappointed in his hopes of Lord Warburton,
is behaving spectacularly badly towards everyone who has dis-
pleased him. When the call comes from Ralph, back in England and
finally at the point of death – the one call that Isabel had promised to
answer – Osmond forbids her to go. Her duty to him is set in the balance against her debt to Ralph, manipulating our sense of proportion

and our readerly expectations in the way a situation is blown up by the popular press. What is Osmond to Isabel against our desire to see him brought low and to see her and Ralph finally reunited? The tension is relieved by the Countess Gemini's revelation of Pansy's parentage. At the convent, where Osmond has shut the child away, Isabel comes upon Madame Merle. There is a confrontation, Madame Merle declares she will leave for America, and Isabel leaves for England, where she is met by the unexpected alliance of Henrietta with Mr Bantling. Marrying an English gentleman, a baron's brother-in-law and a fine specimen 'of "type" ': it's a genteel newspaper-woman's dream come true.

Among the crudely striking antitheses presented in this sequence of events – good and evil, imprisonment and escape, banal satisfactions and unspoken griefs – Isabel becomes a shifting locus of complexity that refuses to engage with a recognisable plot-structure in the obvious ways and at the obvious places. She has the chance splendidly to defy Osmond, but is loath to do so. It isn't, so we are told, because she is afraid of being judged by him or having misjudged her own moral position: it is the 'violence' of a rupture she fears. Violence signifies the disruptive, the dark and uncontrollable, something we catch a glimpse of in Isabel's final dialogue with Osmond when he speaks 'with a quick, barely audible tremor in his voice' of Ralph's 'hating' him. The undercurrent of hysteria which just breaks the surface here will become powerful in later James, and more menacing in proportion as it is suppressed.

James is already starting to manipulate the terror of the things that haven't been or that can't be spoken in his handling of Isabel's reaction to the truth about Madame Merle, and to her treachery. Isabel's first response is to burst into tears of pity – tears that seem to retrieve the lost story of the child that *she* had to give up; her second, to maintain a silence that brings Madame Merle to the verge of breakdown as deliberately as Maggie's silence will deal with Charlotte in *The Golden Bowl*. What James envisaged in his plan (Ntbks 17) as 'the "great scene" between Madame Merle and Isabel' never materialises in the expected terms of anger and catharsis.

Isabel has further chances to play the traditional heroine who is guided by the rightness of her instincts. She might rescue Pansy, and be *her* mother; but Pansy, her spirit broken, refuses Isabel's impulsive offer to take her away to England, and although Isabel prom- ises to come back, it is not clear, here or in a later discussion with Henrietta, whether or with what purpose she will return. Her reaction to

Henrietta's engagement to Mr Bantling is similarly equivocal. At Euston station, Isabel had 'thought of him, extravagantly, as a beautiful blameless knight' – a literary, but also a natural response to Henrietta's gallant, and Ralph's devoted friend, and to being met after a fraught journey. But then her feeling changes to one of disappointment for Henrietta: 'There was a want of originality in her marrying him – there was even a kind of stupidity; and for a moment, to Isabel's sense, the dreariness of the world took on a deeper tinge.' Isabel might have drawn a salutary lesson from Henrietta's artless happiness, which implicitly mocks the inverted snobbery of her own marriage, but instead James draws a state of mind: thoughts aimlessly revolving in the tangle of the garden. As Isabel is borne inexorably onward towards a resolution of the drama, her own story seems uncertain of its direction, striking here and there into new narrative possibilities, but losing momentum and definition; and only with Ralph's death do her purpose and the narrator's appear to coincide, bringing his story to a close with a clarity of vision which seems an end in itself.

6.

Isabel's leave-taking of Ralph is an extraordinarily confident handling of revelation, catharsis, reconciliation and death – dramatic elements popular with Victorian novelists, but which risk offending sophisticated taste. It is a passage in which one has the impression, as one rarely does in later James, that the author's personal emotions and convictions are very close to the surface, and for every reader who finds in it a commonplace sentimentality, there must be many others whom it moves repeatedly to tears. Ralph confesses to having given Isabel the money which he believes ruined her life; Isabel admits that Osmond married her because of it. Both facing extinction of a kind, they acknowledge their love for one another and the terrible pain of loss. In doing so, Isabel 'finally achieves that absolute union of outward expression and inward feeling for which she has laboured'.[14]

Ralph's part has more of spiritual wisdom in it; he comes close here, in his generosity, kindness and courage, to what we may surmise to have been James's own idea of morality. Horrified as he is by Isabel's intention to return to Osmond, which clearly doesn't enter into his idea of the 'right', Ralph offers her consolation. Pain is very deep; but he concedes that it passes:

'... it's passing now. But love remains. I don't know why we should suffer so much. Perhaps I shall find out. There are many things in life. You're very young . ... I don't believe that such a generous mistake as yours can hurt you for more than a little.' [15] (630)

It is open to the reader to see these words simply as evidence of a capacity for hope and comfort peculiar to Ralph and shortly to be extinguished with him. But the claims of life have already been borne in on Isabel during her journey from Italy as, sitting in the train, she has the sense 'that life would be her business for a long time to come'; a conviction so strong that 'it was a proof she should some day be happy again. ... To live only to suffer ... it seemed to her she was too valuable, too capable, for that.' Ralph dies, but his passing is signalled to Isabel by a singularly self-effacing ghost; and the message of a resurrection not after death, but in the midst of life is firmly reasserted by his funeral, which takes place amid the 'splendour of nature' at the end of the 'treacherous May time'.

And now the claims of life, not to say 'the splendour of nature' are urgently and vociferously embodied in Caspar Goodwood, who returns to Gardencourt to assume responsibility for Isabel after Ralph's death and with his permission. Caspar makes a pedantic point about the permission, curiously at odds with the scope of his intentions (wildly exceeding Ralph's brief), and with the romanticism of the scene which begins with his sudden, soundless appearance in the twilight. Isabel is filled with a sense of danger. and feels that 'she had never been loved before'; Caspar makes an appeal to freedom in the trumpet-tones of the Declaration of Independence: 'Were we born to rot in our misery – were we born to be afraid?' He embraces her passionately; she flees from him across the garden. This is pure melodrama, and yet the lines that carry most impact broach a mystery, rather than resolving one in the way generally associated with melodrama:

His kiss was like white lightning ... But when darkness returned she was free. ... She had not known where to turn; but she knew now. There was a very straight path. (644)

Rejecting the liberties that Caspar takes and offers, Isabel sets out for Rome. Her life's destiny was to be a work of art: now, choosing to assume the attitude of a dutiful wife, she becomes the portrait of a lady that Osmond has framed.

How can someone once so concerned that image should correspond to essence let herself be trapped in this imitation of the real
thing? Why does Isabel reject Caspar, and in what sense is this freedom? The ending of *The Portrait of a Lady* puzzles and irritates many
readers, but this is indicative of the different ways there are of looking at the novel rather than of some intrinsic flaw. James's house of
fiction has many windows; and he himself from the start – so the
notebooks suggest – looked on Isabel as a victim of the world's failure to live up to her expectations: 'The idea of the whole thing is
that the poor girl, who has dreamed of freedom and nobleness ...
finds herself in reality ground in the very mill of the conventional'
(Ntbks 15). That is the simplest answer to those who ask 'why?', and
not one to be discounted, although as I shall argue the novel as actually written doesn't frame Isabel as definitively as that.

Many alternative answers are on offer, some of which fit better
than others into the picture that we have seen take shape. Isabel's
behaviour has been explained, by Poirier and others, in terms of her
idealism of the self, with its logical extension into the assumption of
responsibility for one's own errors. Her mistakes are her own, their
consequences hers to deal with alone, and the straight path leads
out of the garden of her dreams into these acknowledged realities.

Interestingly, before she leaves for England, Osmond makes to a
recalcitrant Isabel very much the same case for preserving the status
quo as she makes to herself and to Henrietta. 'One must accept one's
deeds,' she had maintained, and 'Certain obligations were involved
in the very fact of marriage'; and Osmond: 'I take our marriage seriously ... I think we should accept the consequences of our actions.'
If he speaks like Isabel, does she think like him? We are led to consider, not for the first time, the extent to which in James utterance
can be detached from solid conceptions of 'character'. Poirier has
called *The Portrait of a Lady* 'a novel of ideas more than of psychology, an imitation of moral action more than a drama of motive':[16] if
Osmond, who likes copying, is imitating Isabel's moral position
here, he does so literally with a vengeance, for he traps her in the
image of his own rigidity.

It perhaps needs to be emphasised, outside Poirier's context, that
the morality in question is not specifically Christian. Whatever this
novel is about, it is not a glorification of that self-denial and submission to higher authority figured in the closing chapters by Pansy
immured in the convent. Nor can we suppose that what sets Isabel
free in the garden is her recognition of the commandment that pro-

hibits adultery, for the imagery is wrong: the kiss is light, knowledge is darkness.

If her stance is one of principle, Isabel has positive reasons for
rejecting Caspar Goodwood. But elsewhere James will demonstrate
– notably in the case of Hyacinth Robinson, and of Fleda Vetch –
how close a renunciation made on principle can come to neurosis.
There is an obvious negative aspect to Isabel's behaviour too, and
this has its roots in her character as we have observed it. We know
her always to have been obstinate and resistant to pressure; we have
noticed her ambivalent, half-fearful response to opportunities much
less alarming than Caspar offers her. We have watched her as
Osmond's wife gradually lose, as one might lose sight or hearing,
her feeling for liberty; we have seen her grow cynical about marriage, and life in general, and then grow almost afraid of life itself;
we have felt her unease at the lack of inhibition and sexual permis-
siveness exhibited by the Countess, who would certainly react differently to advances from Caspar, were he (unthinkably) to make
them.

Isabel's resistance to Caspar, in conjunction with the sexual imagery of their last encounter, inevitably raises the question of whether
she is afraid of sex itself. It has been suggested that she is, and that
the psychological implications of this could have been made
clearer[17] (we seem to discern some meaning, but the text doesn't
give us enough); and that she isn't, that she is capable 'joyfully' of
'surrender', but only when she has found – or thinks she has – 'the
right person' in Osmond[18] (we read a particular meaning where the
text gives us nothing: James gives us no clue as to the nature, or consequences, of Isabel's sexual surrender to Osmond). We may wish to
sidestep these dark places and the whole question of whether James
left them deliberately obscure, and simply see Isabel's behaviour in
the light of an aversion to male domination, either psychological or
economic. There is one feminist point of view that puts a positive
construction on her action: awful as he is, Osmond is preferable to
the more aggressively masculine Caspar; and Isabel goes back to
him to show solidarity with Pansy, and protect her.[19]

The reader then has two frames, the emblematic or the psychological, in which to see Isabel's rejection of Caspar, and at least three
explanations for it, broadly definable as the moral, the neurotic and
the feminist. These categories may overlap, depending on the point
of view (Isabel's moral stance is not easily separated from her fear of
action), which means that though any one of these explanations is

all right as far as it goes, none completely covers the case. None is able fully to explain, in so far as it assumes an Isabel who is moral or committed or just mixed-up, the reader's feeling of disappointment in the ending, and its overwhelming sense of sadness.

If, for example, one sees Isabel's action as one of resistance to male domination, then there is little essential difference between her rejection of Caspar and her rejection of Lord Warburton (Caspar's may be the more domineering personality, but they are both offering social and economic security). A similar objection applies to the contention that Isabel 'is simply not deeply enough in love with [Caspar] nor has she ever been'.[20] This seems confidently to quantify 'being in love', while leaving out of account what we know always to have been there in Isabel's relation to Caspar – not just the strong sexual element, but the sense of a bond between them which Isabel resents and yet acknowledges: she cannot escape the impression of his having some claim on her. It is wholly characteristic of Isabel that she consciously dissociates Caspar's claim from her own reaction to it. But if there isn't at the crucial moment some unique quality in her feeling for him, her flight from him loses its dramatic perversity and becomes merely the equivalent of her uneasy retreat from Lord Warburton. Yet the second encounter is obviously climactic, and the novel's highly organised structure demands a sense of progression.

Lord Warburton's links with the framework of Isabel's story are looser than Caspar's, and her relations with him partly submerged in the conventions of social comedy. Nothing could be less like the intensity of her relationship with Caspar, whose 'way of rising before her' with 'a disagreeably strong push, a kind of hardness of presence', insistently reasserts the intimacy of their connection and forces Isabel to recognise it:

> Sometimes Caspar Goodwood had seemed to range himself on the side of her destiny, to be the stubbornest fact she knew; she said to herself at such moments that she might evade him for a time, but that she must make terms with him at last – terms which would be certain to be favourable to himself. (122)

If Isabel as defined by Ralph is a sailing ship, an unfolding rose and the 'young lady ... who won't marry Lord Warburton', Caspar is easily recognised as the New World, the lover of the mature woman and Warburton's natural successor. In an emblematic scheme of things, he is so plainly Isabel's destiny that we are not surprised to find Henrietta, who tends to see people (like potatoes) as emblems, promoting Caspar's claim to Isabel. Her interest alone encourages us to expect from it more in the way of riveting reading than a single thrilling kiss (which is why it is so difficult to accept that Isabel might, in the wake of that climax, actually behave as people do in real life, resuming the daily grind as less dangerous, or simply less demanding).

It would be odd if we were expected to take *The Portrait of a Lady* as a series of one-off *tours de force*: to read, that is, the kiss episode as we might read Henrietta's finest article, 'Moors and Moonlight'. But it's precisely in trying to relate the last encounter with Caspar to the design of the whole novel that we see the impossibility of Isabel's running away with Caspar; and see too that it is the thrill of his embrace that clinches the impossibility. For if, after that kiss which is so unmistakably signalled a success (in revision James emphasised its eroticism), Isabel were to throw in her lot with Caspar, that would be as good as having her announce, 'This is it, *this* is the real thing: it was sexual excitement that was missing all along'; and where would that leave, in the league-table of lovers' recognitions, the love-scene with Ralph that immediately precedes it? So much depends in this novel on our appreciating the fine tuning, the capacity for discrimination, of Isabel's consciousness: could she risk letting her destiny appear to resolve itself in terms of primitive sexual competition (Ralph can't have her, but Caspar can)? In his plans for *The Wings of the Dove* we can see James reject on his heroine's behalf any simplistic equation between the experience of sex and the experience of life she would find in love: '"Oh, she's dying without having had it? Give it to her and let her die" – that strikes me as sufficiently second-rate' (Ntbks 170). No more will it do for Isabel to 'have it', and live.

James did, in *The Bostonians* (1886), establish a clear-cut opposition between orthodox sexuality and a 'liberating' love that, overtly at least, makes no sexual claim;[21] and concluded the novel almost literally with a tug-of-war between them. But there, both his intentions and his tone are markedly different. The choice facing Verena Tarrant is made as distinct as that between different-coloured counters at the start of a game, and (it is implied) might be as arbitrary, since the outcome of the game doesn't matter, only the subtlety of the moves. A sardonic distance is maintained between the narrator and characters who are all presented as victims of their assorted delusions.

The problem for Isabel is not Verena's problem of distinction so much as one of accumulation. With Ralph barely buried, she must now take on board a new way of being loved, a new manifestation of her destiny; and at the climactic moment of the kiss, submerged as we are in Isabel's consciousness, we apprehend in images of storm and shipwreck what we can subsequently rationalise as a conflict between the erotic and some obscurer desire of liberty, or even freedom-in-death.[22] If it is all too much for her, the reader also has a sense of incipient overload as Isabel, 'really' drowning in metaphor now, seems about to call up the 'train of images' people see before they sink. For us, the return of darkness has the effect of a fuse blowing: it is not so much a metaphor in itself as a means of escape from the rampant expansion of Isabel's mental garden.

But if the darkness releases us from the grip of a particular narrative method, what, looking from within the same perspective, is *Isabel* escaping from? And in what sense does the darkness set her free? When he comes to Isabel in the garden, making his 'queer grim' point of having as it were inherited her from Ralph, she is struck by a difference in Caspar: his 'aimless, fruitless passion' has been replaced by 'an idea, which she scented in all her being'. His 'idea' consists, evidently, on his having appropriated Isabel's story, grasped its essentials and decided on the desirable outcome:

> '... You're the most unhappy of women, and your husband's the deadliest of fiends. ... I see the whole thing. ... You can't turn anywhere; you know that perfectly. Now it is therefore that I want you to think of *me*.' (641–2)

There is a powerful attraction in Caspar's certainties and in his energy, qualities which, like Doctor Sloper's, are inseparable from his sexuality, but which also, as in *Washington Square*, offer the reader reassurance and the promise of interesting developments. Just as the Doctor was right about Morris (no fortune-hunter should get the girl) and makes an issue, or a story, of his opposition, so Caspar is right about Osmond, and looks set to deliver him the *coup de grâce* (Osmond will be cuckolded by a man he didn't even dislike!).

The sexual impression that Caspar makes on Isabel has, however, never been entirely comfortable:

His jaw was too square and set and his figure too straight and stiff: these things suggested a want of easy consonance with the deeper rhythms of life. (124)

Substitute for the rhythms of life those of story-telling, and we can see how easily clarity and drive become coercion and pressure, forcing the narrative into a rigid mould.[23] An obvious illustration of this is the way the governess tells the story in 'The Turn of the Screw'(1898), but Caspar and Dr Sloper are attempting the same sort of thing. In all three cases the reader feels uneasy, not with the end in view (which is after all to protect the children and Catherine and Isabel), but with the manner in which it is pursued. And we shall feel something similar at the end of *What Maisie Knew*, when her governess Mrs Wix tries to save Maisie by imposing her lively but crude view of things on the child's. If we translate Caspar's claim into terms of his narrative function, we can see that what is wrong with him is his tone. He is too explicit in his demands, too glib in his exhortations, too clumsily penetrating in his analyses of Isabel's situation to appear anything other than embarrassingly uncomplicated in the face of the complexity Isabel now embodies. Earlier, Isabel had in fact been rather like Caspar, with her rigid projects of self-improvement and habit of lecturing Madame Merle, Lord Warburton and others. Even the unhappy fate she dimly foresaw then was as conventionally predictable as the happy ending Caspar now puts forward. Whether Isabel goes with Caspar or returns to Osmond, the story conforms to a pattern in which walking off into the sunset with the former is virtually the equivalent of the latter's 'put[ting] the lights out one by one'. And the message unsubtly conveyed at Ralph's funeral, that springtime inevitably comes round again, belongs to the same familiar set of stylistic templates (the sort hymns tend to be written on). They are templates of safe stories, in which Isabel can choose to play a part: she could be an object of male desire, or simply a plucky little woman in difficult circumstances, or a light burning steadily in the darkness (the governess in 'The Turn of the Screw', who has good reasons to make her story a safe one, sees herself in all three parts).

Or, alternatively, Isabel can evade such obvious typecasting. The issue therefore is again one of safety versus escape; and all we can safely say is that, escaping from the garden, Isabel really chooses not between Caspar and Osmond but between Caspar and Ralph, turning away from the fable that clamours to be written (Henrietta would give it banner headlines) to the fable invented by Ralph, in which she had already arrived with him at the point where fables traditionally, and safely, end, in truth and knowledge:

> nothing mattered now but the only knowledge that was not pure anguish – the knowledge that they were looking at the truth together. (628)

The specific truth referred to is that Osmond married her for her money; but if there is a truth that will set Isabel free, it must go beyond this, beyond Caspar's analysis of her situation which, accurate though it is, suggests a tale told in terms of rigid quality control ('the most unhappy of women ... the deadliest of fiends') and new markets ('The world's all before us, and the world's very big – I know something about that'). What Isabel recognises at Ralph's bedside is a different plane of experience:

> '... In such hours as this what have we to do with pain? That's not the deepest thing; there's something deeper.' (629)

There's love, as Ralph concedes; the love figured in their case not by physical union, but by the single vision that is attained when Isabel finally identifies Ralph as an inseparable strand of her own story, and with her cry 'Oh my brother!' poignantly echoes earlier recognitions of kinship and shared history. As if they were indeed viscerally inseparable, both express the wish that the other shouldn't survive ('I wish it were over for you,' says Ralph, and Isabel: 'I would die myself, not to lose you.'). Yet Ralph, as indicated above, also expresses a belief in Isabel's future and, more persuasively (since we must all have felt this to be true), that the legacy of the dying to the living is 'the sense that we remain'.

This seems to me unmistakably to affirm, among the many other levels of implication contained in the deathbed scene, two things: that Isabel is the heroine of a story which ends with Ralph's death, but that she also exists in some relation to Ralph in a dimension ('there's something deeper') beyond that of the immediate action – not the dimension which produces the 'castle-spectre', or mild hallucination, that Isabel sees at the moment of Ralph's demise, and not the 'America' to which Madame Merle is dispatched: these are simply narrative short-cuts to dead ends. Isabel survives in so far as she is a vision of freedom, a metaphor of becoming, an irreducible imagination. These are the terms in which she is presented to us, and they are not adaptable to the world of tangible goals and quantifiable success that Caspar represents, any more than in *The Ambassadors* Strether's liberated imagination could be reassimilated to the manufacturing milieu of Woollett. And though an Isabel seen in such terms seems readily transferable to that limitless plane of experience which is Caspar's projection of the future, James is writing only a big novel, not a mighty myth: the processing power even of Isabel's consciousness might not be able to cope with the entire harvest of the prairies.[24]

Not surprisingly Henrietta, whose natural elements are the prairies and the future rather than the realm of the imagination, cannot see this. She doesn't quite manage to deliver Isabel to Caspar but, taking his arm, steers him firmly in the direction of that happy outcome. '"Look here, Mr Goodwood," she said; "just you wait!"' The novel originally ended with these words, doubtless calculated to appeal to romantic readers without offending morality; but in the coda he added in revision James has Caspar reject as 'cheap comfort' this popular press you-gotta-believe-it version of his own coercive approach.

Caspar is left facing the long journey of the middle years, the same journey that Isabel faced in the train as she travelled from Rome. And the effect of this conclusion is to leave the reader with that bleak prospect, unable to see any point on the track ahead that marks a new direction, or a spiritual step forward, or even a degree of suffering which holds the guarantee of redemption. There is no arrival: there is only the journey, confronted with a clear-eyed appraisal of the chances of existence and the capacity of the individual to endure. It is as if we had lost the story of a life, and strayed into the process of living; so that Isabel is bound to disappoint us, in so far as she represents an appointment with meaning that will never be kept. Certainly by the last page of *The Portrait of a Lady*, where she seems irretrievable by Caspar and irredeemable in any higher scheme of things, she appears to have gone beyond the scope of the novel to reclaim her.

7.

The resultant void is filled only by what Ralph has left us on the different, more profound level of suggestion that emerges most clearly in his last minutes with Isabel. Ralph doesn't speak of Caspar Good-wood: his hope for the future doesn't take that, or any, specific shape. Yet he is obviously and intensely concerned not to express some general philosophy of life, but to affirm his faith in Isabel's personal value and destiny. It isn't just that pain passes while love remains, it is *she* who will not be hurt for more than a little, and *she* who has been '*adored!*'. The scene has the air of a consecration: there is even a hint of mystic vision in Ralph's 'You'll grow very young again. That's how I see you.'

Isabel has just seen the exact opposite in the gallery at Garden-court. Ostensibly looking at the pictures, but actually looking through them at her own failures, she compares the ravages of life with the immutability of art, envying

> the security of valuable 'pieces' which change by no hair's breadth, only grow in value, while their owners lose inch by inch youth, happiness, beauty ... [25] (602)

It is perhaps only this longing for the security of the inalterable which stiffens Isabel in the attitudes her friends deplore: we remember how she preferred to think of Ralph dying picturesquely at Gardencourt rather than lingering messily in Rome. But Ralph's vision of her was always a more exciting picture than something merely to be contemplated on a rainy day, and he invites us to look at Isabel's situation differently from the way she sees it.

Sitting in the train, she takes a very literal, analytical view. She estimates herself to be worth a certain amount, concludes that she is bound to suffer ('Wasn't all history full of the destruction of precious things?'), and assesses the future ('She should never escape; she should last to the end'). Ralph on the other hand at Gardencourt looks with the eye of the writer. He sees what has been, recognises it as an entity complete in itself: the precious thing *is* destroyed, but there, precisely, is the story. Stories endure, yet they can never be finally evaluated, they are always capable of becoming something else, and Ralph sees in Isabel that potential for change. What he seems to be doing on his deathbed is to confer permanent meaning and value on the botch Isabel feels she has made of her life, and beyond that, to suggest the capacity for change and development, the mysterious protean quality, of great art.

Only Ralph can see Isabel in this light, because no one except him understands what art is: Isabel confuses it with the artificial,

Osmond and Pansy with copying, and Ned with the antique. And only Henrietta, who is all nature and no art, catches in her practical concern a stray reflection of Ralph's crucial hieratical function: 'The great thing is that he shouldn't die in the cars': Ralph must make it to that last meeting at Gardencourt, in order to consecrate his Isabel as a work of art before she is permanently fixed as the lifeless image that Osmond would prefer to have about the place.

At the end of the novel Isabel sets out from Gardencourt for Rome – apparently to trace in reverse the passage from life to art, for she sees that treasure-house of art as fragments of ruins that in a very direct and tangible way link her life to the ruined lives of the past. But we don't know exactly why she goes – to confront Osmond? to rescue Pansy? To be happy again one day, or to endure a living death? We don't see Isabel 'in the cars', and we don't see her reach Rome. Her journey is analogous to the self-imposed absences of Mrs Touchett, who follows her timetable like an automaton but whose mysterious peregrinations suggest another dimension to her existence, and purposes inscrutable to the reader. Isabel leaves us with a similar impression: that whatever *The Portrait of a Lady* may have in the way of firm architecture and neat finish doesn't encompass the whole of her; and if she slips out of the frame, it is perhaps into that haunting darkness of James's fiction where ghosts take the forms of doubles, where the portrait is a copy of the real thing.[26] What after all does the title 'portrait of a lady' guarantee except anonymity? What does it suggest but the possibility of infinite reduplication?

The novel is full of reflections of Isabel, which help us to see, or revise, the structure of her story more effectively than did her own attempts to imitate the social manner of others. In Mrs Touchett we see the enigma that she becomes, in Henrietta her affectionate, human side, in Madame Merle the woman deceived, and in Pansy a conventional miniature of Isabel, in which we would like to see the orphan's tale develop into something original, but fear that it won't. By virtue of mystery, vitality, pathos or potential, each of these women contributes to the *idea* of the heroine. But only Isabel is in a special relation to the story, and seems to know it. The conviction that whatever is going on around one has some intimate and crucial connection with oneself is the mark of the heroine, or hero, by which we can track reduplications of Isabel through James's fiction and sort out the superficial copies, like Daisy Miller, from those like Fleda Vetch in *The Spoils of Poynton* who more closely resemble her.

'Reduplication' is not meant too literally. The portrait of Daisy is actually a preliminary sketch of Isabel, exhibiting some similarity of character; but character is not the point here (Fleda's character is very different from Isabel's), nor is sex, or age: Ralph's assurance, 'You'll grow very young again' doesn't mean that Isabel becomes Maisie. Yet there is an important sense in which *The Portrait of a Lady* develops into *What Maisie Knew* (or what Maisie knew to do with the orphan's tale).

The two novels could scarcely be more dissimilar, and only in the conclusion to Maisie's story does any resemblance become apparent. Like Isabel, Maisie is borne away across the sea and out of the story, supposedly saved from immorality and, more obscurely, set free by what looks on the face of it like a defeat. Yet Maisie's friend Sir Claude, with a tenderness that inarticulately recalls Ralph's consecration of Isabel, claims that in Maisie something 'exquisite' and 'sacred' ('I don't know what to call it') has been produced. But the difference between Maisie and Isabel is that the child's act of creation is all her own work, and she seems to get away with it: the story she leaves behind is one that she has made, and made different from what it purported to be.

James's true agents, from Isabel to Maisie and beyond, are those who consciously or otherwise seek to transform life into art; but it is those with the most imaginative energy and the strongest will to make their story *the* story – those, in other words, that most successfully mimic James's own intense creativity – who induce the reader to see in a light where it seems no longer possible to distinguish which is the real, the essential story. And if we can't distinguish, consequently, whether this involves, as between James and his 'true' agents, complicity or betrayal, then that only makes the case more characteristically Jamesian.

'Nothing is any measure of me,' Isabel had said; 'everything's on the contrary a limit, a barrier, and a perfectly arbitrary one.' But what is the form of the novel if not a limit and a barrier, and what if the heroine is trapped in its frame, as Isabel risks being trapped in the conventional image of a 'lady'? Yet having a novel written about her seemed to provide the ideal vehicle for self-expression. Could she have made it work *for* her? Nothing is any measure of Isabel except, perhaps, the larger arena of James's fiction, in which his heroines and heroes have to assault this problem. How they measure up to the task, and the extent to which the novel's success depends on their efforts, are questions the following chapters aim to consider.

3

The Princess Casamassima

'Certainly, in her position, I should go off easier if I had seen them curls.' It is with this optimistic appeal to maternal sentiment that James begins his novel of radical conspiracy. Mrs Bowerbank, a wardress at Millbank Prison, bears a request from one of the inmates that she should see her child before she dies. The woman in question, a French seamstress, is serving a life-sentence for stabbing her lover, Lord Frederick Purvis, to death. The child's guardian, Miss Pynsent or 'Pinnie', believes the pretty, curly-headed little boy whom she has kept in ignorance of these events to be Lord Frederick's son, and would much rather he were told that than that his mother is a convicted murderess. A bit of a snob, Pinnie takes refuge from the tawdry reality of her cheap dressmaking business in fantasies about the boy's noble lineage. She fears that taking her delicate Hyacinth to see his mother will expose him to a scene upsetting in itself, and which might lead him later to uncover the scandal of his origins. So she consults her friend Mr Vetch, an impoverished musician and a man of culture and intelligence, whose affectionate concern for Hyacinth comprises, unlike Pinnie's, a degree of realism and psychological insight.

More is in question, in the ensuing discussion, than the projected prison-visit. Pinnie's arguments against it are based on what Hyacinth, in her view, *is* – her child now, not his mother's, though definitely also Lord Frederick's. Mr Vetch on the other hand is concerned with what will become of Hyacinth – 'a prostitute's bastard', as he describes him, thin-skinned and introspective, with more imagination than perseverance, 'who'll expect a good deal more of life than he'll find in it. That's why he won't be happy.'

Two different types of narrative make a bid for the reader's attention here. Will the story be about Pinnie's Hyacinth, who is essentially a hero of fairytale, a princeling in disguise concerning whom,

as Pinnie likes to imagine, the 'truth' – the secret of his blue blood – lies waiting to be discovered? Or will it be the story of the other Hyacinth who, as Mr Vetch points out, isn't necessarily his father's son? This Hyacinth will claim our interest not by virtue of his blood-line but, as Isabel Archer did, by affronting his destiny, and in the getting of wisdom: the truth is for him to seek, whether in love or in the ways of the world.

Hyacinth's story is in fact a version of that modern romance which Lionel Trilling has called the novel of 'the young man from the provinces', which comprises elements of fairytale and which is also a kind of *Bildungsroman*.[1] It owes more to the traditional nineteenth-century novel than most of James's fiction, and has, in particular, interesting affinities with two great exemplars of the genre, *Le Rouge et le Noir* (1830) and *Fathers and Sons* (1862), in both of which the question of paternity is crucial. Stendhal's thin-skinned, introspective Julien Sorel, denying his real father, virtually invents his life by recreating himself in the image of powerful father-figures. Turgenev's Arkady Kirsanov, influenced by the nihilist Bazarov who embodies a new rootlessness in society, starts by denying the ideals of his father but finally attains self-knowledge in the context of the conservative institutions and family life his father represents.[2] Imagination, rootlessness, the challenge of the great world and its problems as against the consolations of a loving home – these are also the themes of *The Princess Casamassima*. Hyacinth Robinson is a Julien Sorel without optimism, an Arkady Kirsanov without resilience, unable to sustain confidence in his heroic part or find security in his origins: neither the romantic nor the realistic context will offer him a way of survival.

The initial discussion between Pinnie and Mr Vetch does much to explain why Hyacinth develops as he does, but it also provides a perspective on the wider social and political issues that, like Stendhal and Turgenev, James claimed to be tackling in his novel. It illustrates the difference between atavistic impulses and civilised ones, between conservatism and pragmatism, between the individual as totem and the individual as psychological entity, between certain 'truth' and elusive 'right'. 'If you want the only right you're very particular,' Mr Vetch tells Pinnie; but he sees clearly the right-ness of bringing Hyacinth to his mother's deathbed. The 'truth' – whether Hyacinth is or isn't what Pinnie believes him to be – takes second place to what simple decency dictates must be done in a specific case.

Another author might have played the prison-visit straight, for tears. James makes it also funny and ironic, by giving it over to Mrs Bowerbank, a conscientious *metteur-en-scène* who seems aware that a situation involving such genuine horrors and sentimental traps demands expert theatrical handling, but is lumped with actors that don't come up to scratch. The child duly brought to Millbank is very much Mr Vetch's introspective Hyacinth, who, having tried in vain to discover from Pinnie where *he* comes into it all, holds himself aloof, 'not in sympathy' with the spectacle made by three distressed, excited women. Only at the last minute, prompted by an apparently instinctive delicacy, does he rise suddenly to the occasion, submitting gracefully to his mother's 'terrible, irresistible embrace'. It makes a charming picture, and yet it is also a moment of real pathos: Mrs Bowerbank has got the effect she wanted.

Ten years later, Hyacinth has fulfilled the expectations of both surrogate parents. He believes 'immutably' that he is Lord Frederick's son, and at the same time the knowledge of his origins, gleaned in the aftermath of Millbank, makes him resolutely unhappy. '*He* was the one properly to have been sacrificed: that remark our young man often made to himself.' The crux of his discontent is his sense of being, as a plebeian Frenchman and an English lord, different from everybody else. Consequently, 'he was to go through life in a mask, in a borrowed mantle; he was to be every day and every hour an actor' – but an actor who hasn't even seen the latest popular play, because 'poor devils' like himself can't afford it. Hyacinth is acutely conscious of social circles

> where, in splendid rooms, with smiles and soft voices, distinguished men, with women who were both proud and gentle, talked of art, literature and history. (114)

His exclusion from such circles is the more painful because he seems in nearly every respect eminently fitted for them. For Hyacinth *is* different from other members of his social class. He hates liquor and pubs; he writes, and secretly aspires to literary distinction; he wears his workingman's clothes with unmistakable style; and (as the finishing touch) his features are 'perfect'. Pinnie of course sees in this innate refinement the evidence of Hyacinth's noble blood; and so, presumably, do the astonishing number of critics who do not question his paternity.[3] Hyacinth, to do him justice, ascribes his singularity at least in part to his being French, his

success as a bookbinder to having *la main parisienne*; but one suspects that he wouldn't enjoy being French so much if it weren't, in
the late nineteenth century, a smart thing to be – that he wouldn't
find similar pleasure in being, say, Frisian. French culture means so
much to him that he has learnt to speak the language fluently –
though it is observed that he hates being called 'M. Hyacinthe' , *à la
française*, which reminds him of a hairdresser.

This is the sort of aside critics have in mind when they describe
James's irony in respect to Hyacinth as superficial – which it is,
though there is a lot of it and invariably directed at Hyacinth's superior self-image. But the deeper stratum of irony at the novel's core is,
as we shall see, implicit: dependent not on what the narrator says,
but on what the reader sees. It is broadly speaking true that James's
novels rely increasingly less on the narrator's 'saying' – stating this
or that to be the case – and more on the reader's 'seeing' – developing a personal point of view from material other than the narrator's
gratuitous statement. While it cannot be singled out as the last
refuge of the old authorial regime, one does have the impression in
The Princess Casamassima that certain information is communicated
with peculiar insistency – stridency, even; and that the assembly of
components (dialogue, background information, imagery, and so
on) from which the reader may compose an alternative picture is
correspondingly energetic – a kind of democratic resistance, as it
were, to dictatorial pressure. Some readers may well feel a difficulty
about taking on trust James's effortlessly aristocratic Hyacinth, and
the more so later, when he does gain admittance to high society and
the heavy narratorial hand is clapped on our shoulder, telling us
that he jolly well deserves to be there. It is easy on the other hand to
believe in Hyacinth the bookbinder who visits his French colleague
Poupin, a refugee from the Paris uprising of 1871, and to see why he
appeals as an orphaned 'offshoot of the sacred race' to this self-
dramatising exile and his childless wife. If Hyacinth's romance
began – slightly late on cue – with his noble comportment at
Millbank, the *Bildungsroman* starts in the Poupins' Lisson Grove
apartment, with a solid basis in the plausible detail of their circumstances and those that led Hyacinth there.

His cockney girlfriend, Millicent Henning, might argue that the
Bildungsroman, in so far as that involves a sentimental education,
began earlier, in Lomax 'Plice', where at eight years old she used to
upset Pinnie by kissing him. This precocious beauty, formerly rather
grubby but now cleaned up as befits an assistant in a department

store, represents to Hyacinth 'the eternal feminine', yet he is far from putting her on a pedestal, as later he will put the Princess. It is hard to see how Hyacinth, described by Lionel Trilling as a 'child-man' in a 'novel full of parental figures', is thereby, as Trilling claims, ruled sexually out of court.[4] Millicent is a woman of blatantly sexual charm, and he is 'her personal fancy'. Her consenting to walk out with Hyacinth patently endorses the smartness and swagger which is part of his sexual persona (and her own smartness and swagger alarm Pinnie precisely because she knows they will appeal to him). He deliberately seeks, as a substitute for marriage, 'the soft society of women', and this Milly pre-eminently represents. He deplores her commonplace manners and mind, but likes her because she is beautiful, sympathetic and, up to a point, his (she refuses to tell him in what respects she isn't, which again is not the sign of a platonic relationship). And if at the end of the novel he runs to Millicent as a child to its mother, he doesn't begin like that; outside Millgate Prison he looked at Pinnie with 'eyes which always appeared to her to belong to a person older and stronger than herself', and his bitter reaction when he first suspects Millicent's association with Captain Sholto seems to embody an age-old knowledge of human, and particularly female, frailty. Sexual jealousy is unmistakably involved here, as it is in his friendship with the Princess.

That said, the issue of sexuality is never as intrusive in Hyacinth's case as it becomes, abruptly, in *The Portrait of a Lady* at the climactic moment of the kiss. His relationship with Millicent is clearly designed to exhibit Hyacinth not as a sexual but as a social misfit, imbued like Isabel Archer with a narrow self-absorption which distances him from well-wishers of both sexes, and with a chip on his shoulder that makes him much less attractive. He is irritated by Millicent's suggestion that he might do better than the bookbinding trade, and also irritated by Pinnie's conviction that he might do better than Millicent. When at the Poupins' he meets Paul Muniment, in whom he instantly sees a leader of the people, he feels aggrieved not to have been introduced before; and when he goes home with Paul and meets his crippled sister he suspects he has been brought there merely to amuse the invalid. He takes the chance to envy Rosy her mother, described – like everyone dear to Rosy – in hyperbolic terms, though it appears that he himself has been more comfortably brought up, culturally and materially, by Pinnie and Mr Vetch. James's irony works very much against Hyacinth in the opening chapters of the book, which reveal a marked discrepancy between his determination to feel hard done-by and the goodwill and affection shown him in Audley Court and Lisson Grove, not to speak of Lomax Place.

These are the factors that combine to explain Hyacinth's embrace of the radical cause. It is the inevitable consequence of his friendship with Poupin and Paul, coupled with the idea fostered by Pinnie that he is less a fortunate foundling than a rejected scion of the aristocracy. Hyacinth is astonished to hear Paul Muniment talk with levity of his co-conspirators, for 'he associated bitterness with the revolutionary passion.' The extent to which his own revolutionary passion is subjective is clear:

> When he himself was not letting his imagination wander among the haunts of the aristocracy ... he was occupied with contemplations of a very different kind; he was absorbed in the struggles and sufferings of the millions whose life flowed in the same current as his, and who, though they constantly excited his disgust and made him shrink and turn away, had the power to chain his sympathy, to raise it to passion, to convince him for the time at least that real success in the world would be to do something with them and for them. (129)

Hyacinth finds this vision particularly vivid in the presence of the upwardly mobile Millicent: proof, as the narrator drily comments, of his 'fantastic, erratic way of seeing things'. We have here a Hyacinth who hasn't advanced much in social theory from the little boy who, despite his distaste for the squalid scene, submitted to his mother's embrace as if in a moment of inspiration, a sudden perception of the part he must play. His declaration of commitment to the anarchist cause in the Sun and Moon public house, a gesture made in the face of what he perceives as intellectual squalor, is similarly stagey, and similarly invites the reservation that a serious subject is here being subjected to a theatrical treatment, fantastic and possibly falsifying. Jumping on a chair, taking a vow: is this the stuff of revolution, or is it merely the stylised idea of revolution?

'I cannot congratulate the author too heartily on his escape into fiction,' wrote a contemporary reviewer of *The Princess Casamassima*.[5] He welcomed as new to James's work 'conspirators, and harlots, and stabbings, and jails, and low-lived men and women who drop their h's, and real incidents, and strong emotions' – which made for 'a real story'. Most of this, as the phrase 'real incidents' indicates, is also the stuff of real life. Yet other critics did (and do) feel uncomfortable with the more picturesque elements of this 'real story', taking them as evidence that the book wasn't a real political novel, that its author was writing about affairs of which he knew nothing. This was galling for James, who certainly had intended to follow the example of novelists like Zola and Turgenev in rendering the contemporary socio-political scene. He had done some local research for the book, and was well-informed on political and social issues.[6] It should also be borne in mind that some permanent features of the political scene reflected in *The Princess Casamassima* – the lurking violence, the exploitation of idealism, the power of money, the far-reaching influence of a single individual will – were all typically Jamesian preoccupations, reflected in many of his works.

If, however, as James afterwards claimed, Hyacinth 'sprang up for [him] out of the London pavement' that concealed 'some sinister anarchic underworld' (AN 60, 76), he also springs from the long line, descending from *Roderick Hudson* through *The Portrait of a Lady* to *The Golden Bowl*, of those Jamesian protagonists who symbolise a kind of innocence or pristine value – art, say, or liberty or the faculty of wonder – that lends itself to the melodramatic requirements of a 'real story', but who may also come to assume the function of the 'recording consciousness' whose intellectual and emotional experience gives the novel a competing focus of interest. In *Roderick Hudson*, the symbolic function is assumed by the sculptor Roderick, that of the recording consciousness by his friend Rowland Mallet. In *The Portrait of a Lady*, two pictures are superimposed one upon the other, as if by a careless photographer or a sophisticated painter: the first exhibiting Isabel as the heroine of a romance, the second 'the reflected field of life' (AN 65); and if we attempt to take them apart we risk losing Isabel. But in *The Princess Casamassima* there is a less indulgent, more judicious separation of the ideal from the real, a firmer demarcation drawn between two worlds, one composed of dreams and aspirations and the other of those psychological and social realities which put dreams into heads like Hyacinth's. There is also a much sharper image of the protagonist, caught like some strange bird of passage between these distinct frames of reference. Hyacinth is Roderick Hudson and Rowland Mallett fused in one, poised between the heroic and the neurotic, the picturesque and the analytical, flamboyant action and sophisticated mental stance. His is a precocious scepticism trapped in a 'real story'; and through him James explicitly articulates the question of the real thing – of what it might be, and whether it can ever be entirely distinguished from appearances.

When Hyacinth has jumped down from his chair in the Sun and Moon, Paul asks him with a touch of condescension if he would like to see 'the real thing', by which he means a genuine anarchist, their leader Hoffendahl. The 'real thing' that Hyacinth is ultimately look-ing for – perhaps, like other political activists, in brotherly love – lies somewhere behind gesture or rhetoric like Hyacinth's and charisma like Paul's, and both seem to know it. But as the 'lamb of sacrifice' expresses his first misgiving about his friend's fraternal loyalty – '"Are *you* the real thing, Muniment?" asked Hyacinth' – it is clear that if the 'real thing' isn't rhetoric, gesture and charisma, yet these things are, precisely, politics.

At Paul's lodgings in Audley Court, where Hyacinth finds Rosy's sickbed in place of the expected hotbed of revolution, the question of the real thing is raised in a different form. Here Rosy's blithe acceptance both of the political status quo and her own disability only exacerbates Hyacinth's chronic discontents, and Paul exhibits a devotion to his sister very unlike Hyacinth's offhand treatment of Pinnie and Mr Vetch; while Lady Aurora's practical care is a com-ment on his patrician fastidiousness; he 'wonders' at her 'perform-ing the functions of a housemaid', and one flinches for him, left alone with the garrulous Rosy, lest she tell him that Lady Aurora (like the Monarchs in 'The Real Thing') empties her slops.

There is, then, the implicit suggestion that the cramped theatre of domestic action has its own forms of grace. Is perhaps charity, *noblesse oblige*, the real thing, in the sense of the real solution to the social problem? The Muniments certainly don't see it in that light. Rosy maintains that Lady Aurora's good works are simply a waste of her decency, because the lower classes are incapable of appreciat-ing it; while Paul dismisses her invalid-sitting services, which enable him to go about his solitary business, with 'It's no use trying to buy yourself off. You can't do enough; your sacrifices don't count.'

Lady Aurora shares with Hyacinth the isolation of a social misfit, but embodies rather more convincingly than he does an ideal of sen-sibility and altruism unappreciated by the world of which James's fiction offers numerous exemplars, without always providing the narrative opportunities to display these qualities to advantage. Like Fleda Vetch in *The Spoils of Poynton*, Lady Aurora represents a redundancy of good intentions, an awkward overflow of 'free spirit', an energy never channelled in the direction James's story is taking. But although, unlike Fleda Vetch, she would rather not be a heroine, just as Catherine Sloper inadvertently makes herself felt by flattening the fictions around her, so Lady Aurora, by functioning as the passive reflector, the slightly dull mirror of Hyacinth's situation, has a temporarily steadying effect on the novel's hectic processes of buttonholing, self-promotion and limelight-seeking. 'I've blood in my veins that's not the blood of the people,' Hyacinth tells her in a moment of *rapprochement*. This perfectly illustrates the gracelessness of gratuitous statement, as opposed to letting the truth simply appear, as the evidence of Lady Aurora's good breeding does in the delicacy and restraint of her reply: '"Oh I see," said Lady Aurora sympathetically.' 'Seeing' is subtler than 'saying': Hyacinth, embarrassed, takes note.

Lady Aurora's gentle handling of his sore spot may be compared with Paul's rough handling of hers, when he tells her that her siblings are fortunate not to be 'all *your* size!' Yet this gratuitously graceless remark makes a narrative point. This is a story in which size counts. It counts as the most fundamental – because inalterable – of those personal characteristics which are noted in this novel in terms as specific and meaningful as those dealing with social theory are vague. The cruelty of Paul's comment is precisely that Lady Aurora's large size 'matches' her at least to him – and he isn't interested. Paul makes much of his height to assert superiority over the much smaller Hyacinth, particularly in competition for the Princess; and Sholto's six feet imply an advantage over him with Millicent, who is in Pinnie's snide estimation 'too tall for a woman', but who takes an 'artless pride in her bigness' because it belies her lowly origins. Physical attractiveness is repeatedly weighed against markers of social class: 'Did you twig her good bust?' says Sholto to Hyacinth of a barmaid, 'It's a pity they always have such beastly hands.' Hyacinth, who dislikes Millicent's thick wrists, cheap jewellery and modes of speech, tells her grimly, 'It's a good job you're so lovely.' Lady Aurora, with whom he is in some respects more obviously paired, is not lovely; and the sexual silence between them is as eloquent as Hyacinth's *frisson* when Millicent behaves noisily in the theatre foyer.

Not all of the novelistic capital James makes out of this sort of thing is funny. We share Hyacinth's anxiety about his romantic neckties since they are made by Pinnie, whose taste in fashions has been certified *passé* by Millicent; but Millicent's own preference for good grooming as opposed to radical chic leads to her unfortunate association with Sholto, though it also leads, albeit for the wrong reasons, to her sensible disparagement of 'that dirty young man, Mr Muniment'. The dirty young man himself, though he has no idea what tone to adopt in polite society, knows enough to smarten himself up for the Princess as Rosy observes he never did for Lady Aurora. It may be felt that points made in terms of feet and inches, neckties and gloves fail to lend *gravitas* to the revolutionary theme. What they effectively do is suggest that the novel's centre of gravity lies deeper perhaps even than anarchic impulses, in the atavistic rituals of courtship; and in these, as James tellingly indicates, outward display is at least as important as inner conviction. It is a point which by extension also has a bearing on politics.

Reality, then, in this novel, the reality that Hyacinth and the others come up against, is very largely constructed from and seen to be a matter of social circumstances and physical characteristics: however human nature may duck and dodge them, these are the factors that inexorably shape individual experience. Physical characteristics are in general inalterable; social circumstances, on the other hand, are not, and the bridge to social advancement is style, or image, as Millicent's success with Sholto and Hyacinth's with the Princess demonstrate. But if reality is translated into style, or image, does it somehow cease to be the real thing?

James gives the question of the relation between reality and image a peculiarly arresting form in the shape of Paul's invalid sister. Crippled and confined, Rosy Muniment doesn't rate on the novel's sexual-social scale at all; and yet her 'recumbency appeared not in the least to interfere with her universal participation'. Rosy claims to see everything in the world, and Paul asserts that 'It's very wonderful – she can describe things she has never seen. And they're just like the reality' – which raises the question of how far what Rosy knows depends on what Paul sees – how far, more generally, 'reality' is the product of a particular vision.[7] Rosy averts her gaze from Paul's subversive activities, since anything that threatens the aristocracy threatens the other aspect of her vicarious existence that is lived through Lady Aurora. Rosy pumps her friend relentlessly on the home life of the peerage, with the result that she talks like 'a person in the habit of visiting the nobility at their country-seats'. She tries to make a reality of her vision of Paul and Lady Aurora staying together with her permanently, without success; but if Paul, perversely, is attentive to the Princess, there is still pleasure to be extracted from the Princess's attention to *her*, with its promise of material benefits.

That Rosy isn't sorry for herself might testify to the liberating powers of the imagination, if her 'gay, demented eyes' didn't take in the world the better to establish herself as its focal point. 'Your name, like mine, represents a flower' is her first reaction to meeting Hyacinth; her first reaction to his mentioning that his guardian is a dressmaker is, 'I never had a dress on in my life', and the request that swiftly follows for a pink and black dressing-gown is an attempt to reflect authentic boudoir society in her personal style, a grotesque mimicry of the social and sexual aspirations of those about her. 'If she wanted pink she should have pink; but to Pinnie there was something almost unholy in it, like decking out a corpse or dressing up the cat.' 'Image' matters all right; for getting it wrong only makes things worse, only emphasises the inhuman quality in Rosy (like the unromantic quality in Catherine Sloper). If the real, the ultimately significant thing is here, it lies somewhere between the reality laid bare in Pinnie's cruel simile and the poignancy of its effect.

2.

Hyacinth's introduction in a box at the theatre to Captain Sholto's friend is like some magical reversal of his being closeted in the upstairs room with Rosy. He finds himself abruptly in almost intimate rapport with a woman who is dazzlingly beautiful, a princess who proves, unlike Rosy, to represent the most modern political stance: 'She wishes to throw herself into the revolution, to guide, to enlighten it,' supplies her companion, Madame Grandoni. But if *liberté, égalité et fraternité* appear to have become an instant reality, Hyacinth is struck by the unreality of the situation: it seems to him like 'a play within the play'.

From this manifestly contrived point of departure begins his adventure with the Princess. Proceeding by way of her London apartments, it will reach its climax with his visit to Medley, the grand country house where Hyacinth is transformed into a companion fit for a princess and survives, despite warnings of danger, secure in her favour. This is the well-worn story-line of fairytale and like fairytale it will require of the reader some suspension of disbelief. Yet it is also the story of the impressionable but mistrustful Hyacinth who asks, as at Millgate and Rosy's bedside, why *me* and why *here*, and what sort of figure he cuts in consequence – questions that are superfluous to the requirements of romance, and persistently emphasise the disjunction between Hyacinth the nobleman and Hyacinth the author of his fate.

Although she hopes to have unearthed in Hyacinth a typical plebeian, the Princess is quick to uncover his French heredity and his intellectual interests; so that at their second meeting 'in an incredibly short time ... he found himself discussing the Bacchus and Ariadne and the Elgin Marbles' with her. It is she who draws the artist out of his soul into the light, she who offers him, in return for being taken to have a look at slums, an entrée into another sphere, one that has room even for the labours of a little artisan. When, on arrival at Medley, he sets out to 'take of it such possession as he might', it is as though Hyacinth were taking possession of the artistic heritage of the world.

He admires the pictures on the walls, the bindings in the library; in a hand 'even nobler than usual' he tosses off a note to Millicent, for the pleasure of writing under an heraldic letterhead. It is his first encounter with natural beauty, and he rambles in ecstasy through the park: 'His whole walk was peopled with recognitions.' Up till now we have been invited to share, and perhaps be amused by, the excitement of the *ingénu*; but gradually the reader becomes aware of an adjustment of the terms in which Hyacinth is presented, a certain pressure to recognise Hyacinth's aristocratic *Doppelgänger*, the rightful inheritor of a place like Medley, and of the Princess herself. Madame Grandoni informs him that he is 'one of those types that ladies like' and that he has, unlike herself, 'the appearance of nobility'. He is noble enough at any rate to pass for a gentleman in the eyes of Lady Marchant and her family, who ask him what pack he hunts with. Although we have been told that Hyacinth never so much as drops an 'h', this is stretching credulity a bit far; and the implausibility of his flawlessly aristocratic persona is only underlined by the appreciation of the Princess (who claims not to care for class-distinctions):

'You haven't a vulgar intonation, you haven't a common gesture, you never make a mistake, you do and say everything exactly in the right way. You come out of the poor cramped hole you've described to me, and yet you might have stayed in country-houses all your life. You're much better than if you had!' (298)

The Hyacinth who likes to think of himself as a born loser is suddenly in a can't-lose situation, good enough as an aristocrat, good enough as a plebeian. Pinnie, when she assured Hyacinth that 'a princess might look at you and be none the worse!' clearly had a fairytale in mind, and now it might be coming true.

Only evidently they won't live happily ever after. By the time Hyacinth leaves Medley, the Princess is positively festooned with warning signs – condemned out of her own mouth, condemned by her intimates, condemned by the tone of the narrative. Hyacinth has no sooner met her than we have the narrator's word for it that the Princess's faults 'were numerous' and that he is destined to discover this. Millicent has learnt from Sholto that 'she's a bad 'un' whose 'own husband has had to turn her out of the house'. Hyacinth, however, has already found the Princess to be 'too beautiful to question, to judge by common logic' such as Millicent's. The less conventional she seems, the more he admires her. 'I'm convinced we're living in a fool's paradise, that the ground's heaving under our feet,' she tells him, and he is thoroughly impressed:

> though he scarcely saw what she meant – her aspirations appearing as yet so vague – her tone, her voice, her wonderful face showed she had a generous soul. (165)

'Vague' is the operative word here. When Hyacinth first sets eyes on the Princess, 'a vague white mist' blots out the stage, and it will remain between his perceptions of the Princess's and the reader's, swathing an ironic subtext in unspecific epithets like 'beautiful, noble, wonderful'. The Princess is indeed unconventional, but as recorded in Hyacinth's consciousness she is never interestingly so. The second time they meet, she undertakes to tell him her life-story: how she has been 'humiliated, outraged, tortured' as the wife of Prince Casamassima . The reader might have expected here a slice of life served up verbatim, like Rosy's; but the details of the Casamassima family background 'remained vague' to Hyacinth. What he does observe is that the Princess's contempt for the old order is born of resentment for the way she has been treated. Here we do have a rare clue to the Princess's inner life, and one which helps to explain Hyacinth's interest in her, but it is promptly submerged: Hyacinth's induction 'didn't make her affect him any the less as a creature compounded of the finest elements; brilliant, delicate, complicated, but complicated with something divine'. This

virtually meaningless effusion, typical of his reaction to the presence of the Princess, may be compared with the portrait of the same
lady just supplied by her husband and Madame Grandoni. From
this conversation, as from another shortly afterwards, it emerges
that the Princess is profligate, capricious and utterly unpredictable
in her enthusiasms for men and for causes. Madame Grandoni
warns Hyacinth against 'being liked by Princesses!' and subsequently, on his arrival at Medley, urges him on no account to
prolong his visit.

Hyacinth, who has proved himself from childhood wary of
motive and intent, accepted the invitation to Medley in the first
place with the firm intention of 'knowing what he was in for'; and
even as he enjoys the Princess's company he is conscious that in
treating him as an old friend she is acting a part, though he cannot
think why. The reader now sees her play several parts: they include
that of 'barbarian' or scourge of the old order – who lives in luxuri-
ous surroundings, despite having hoped for a 'little honeysuckle
cottage', or a parsonage; that of social critic and of gracious lady –
who chooses to ignore, to his discomfiture, the real constraints on a
poor workingman's time; and that of seductress – who claims to be
'abject' while commanding him to stay, exploiting his lack of that
very social assurance which she will later claim him to possess in
large measure.

The incongruities are obvious, the irony is laid on heavily, the per-
formances teeter on the brink of parody. The Princess slips too easily
into the 'free, audacious and fraternising way' that suggests a keep-
fit instructress rather than a *femme fatale*, while Hyacinth's response
falls rather short of her advances (he suggests she might like Paul
Muniment better than him). He accepts nevertheless 'the cup of an
exquisite experience' being offered, taking a cautious look first to
see what's in it for him:

> it was purple with the wine of romance, of reality, of civilisation.... .
> He might go home ashamed, but he would have for evermore in
> his mouth the taste of nectar. (285–6)

So far, so good; but as Hyacinth remains in the thrall of the Princess
for several weeks, the reader may reasonably want to know more
specifically the ingredients of the potion that keeps him there. Later,
Hyacinth will reflect on his 'commerce' with the Princess, in which
'all without herself stooping she had only raised him higher and

higher and absolutely highest'. That he becomes her lover is naturally to be inferred from this sort of terminology, and also from the
narrative logic of his ascendancy, just as his fall is implicit when the
Princess turns to Paul. In fact, the nature of Hyacinth's or Paul's
relationship with her is never made explicit. Having, together with
Madame Grandoni and Captain Sholto, broadcast the news generally that the Princess takes up one young man after another, Prince
Casamassima assumes that Hyacinth and Paul are her lovers,
though Madame Grandoni, a self-appointed barometer of rising
sexual pressure in the vicinity of the Princess, will deny that there
was impropriety in Hyacinth's case, and Hyacinth will deny it to
Mr Vetch. The technicalities are unimportant: the point is that the
idea of the sexual relationship is there. Conflicting assertions and
denials only reinforce it.

And yet, although the silence that ensues after Hyacinth's first
evening with the Princess is characteristic of James's handling of
sex, here it is silence in a vacuum. There is no trace in the following
days at Medley of the atmosphere heavy with desire and electric
with emotion that we find in *The Wings of the Dove* or *The Golden
Bowl* – not the shadow of that dimple on the elbow that gave the
Princess's earlier incarnation, as Christina Light in *Roderick Hudson*,
fleshly reality. There are only ambiguous retrospective references to
the closeness of their 'commerce': 'his intimacy with the Princess
had caused any claims he might have had on Millicent to lapse';
'The desire to be with her again on the same terms as at Medley had
begun to ache in him...'; her 'tacit notification' in the company of
others that 'they must not appear too thick.'

A contemporary critic complained in this connection of James's
'suggestive decorum';[8] and the effect is indeed one of deliberate titillation. For the vocabulary of intimacy ostensibly refers to Hyacinth's
intellectual intercourse with the Princess. But this too is a relationship
whose substance is only to be inferred from retrospective references
of an unspecific kind – to pledges taken, ideas elaborated, to the
Princess's intellectual breadth and – when serious topics are set aside
– to her ability to make Hyacinth 'hang on her lips' with anecdotes of
foreign courts. It must all be taken as read. Those exchanges between
them to which the reader is actually party are with one exception
quite startlingly bland, which is not surprising, since as long as she
maintains her manner of treating Hyacinth as an equal and old friend
the Princess has abolished most of what elsewhere in the novel makes
for interest (one only has to listen to Prince Casamassima talking to

Madame Grandoni, or Hyacinth to Mr Vetch, or Millicent to Sholto, to see how much social and sexual tensions contribute to the climate of rattled nerves that prevails outside Medley).

The exception is their talk of the anarchist movement, with the revelation of Hyacinth's part in it. This is presented as a moment of great intimacy, where Hyacinth feels he has caught the Princess's attention as never before. Yet the scene somehow misses its effect: whatever might be the actual strength of Hoffendahl's conspiracy, it is dissipated in Hyacinth's almost mystic hyperbole: 'I've seen the holy of holies. ... there's an immense underworld peopled with a thousand forms of revolutionary passion and devotion' ; and when he talks of what he is actually pledged to do, his passion is converted into an air of well-bred deprecation that glosses the horror of the assassination – his 'little job' – and the pity of his sacrifice: 'Very likely it would be to shoot some one ... He should probably take little trouble to save his skin ... If one did that sort of thing there was an indelicacy in not being ready to pay for it.' The Princess, for her part, is moved by Hyacinth's impending fate, but feels she owes it to her revolutionary persona not to let him know it.

It's as if the 'mess of blood' in which it will all end were done up in a dainty parcel and deposited in her lap. One might find this coy handling even more offensive in respect of the political theme than in respect of the sexual one, were it not the natural consequence of Hyacinth's divided personality. Whether on account of his blue blood or his genteel upbringing, Hyacinth feels a constraint and a reticence towards too open a display of feeling; but he is also full of irrepressible 'swagger' – that is the actor, or, as his workmates assume, the Frenchman in him. He is the virtual embodiment of that 'suggestive decorum' which relishes the melodramatic and fantastic, and simultaneously distrusts it. Nowhere is this more clearly seen than in the ambivalence of his attitude to his experience at Medley, where, from the moment he sets foot in the house, he has been obsessed by his illegitimate parade of 'respectability', wondering continually whether the servants will see through him, imagining he is in a play and that the curtain may fall, even fantasising that the Princess might coldly unmask him before Lady Marchant as 'a wretched little bookbinder'. Hyacinth himself yearns for the 'strange, violent sensation' of some such decisive, melodramatic turn of events, and even though none of it happens, what is going on in his head has dramatic potential enough, since it directly confronts the question of his true nature and status, and hers.

The climax when it comes is thoroughly anticlimactic: 'He told her in short what he was.' This, for Hyacinth, is the last word in 'swagger', which also certifies the propriety, or decorum, of his position in the household. It is a gesture therefore that seems to guarantee the reality of the enchanted palace, and it is furthermore the supreme gage of his trust in the Princess. But it looks to us as though we have, after all, been fobbed off with Pinnie's version of Hyacinth's story, in which the ultimate truth is 'what he is', or what she and he believe him to be. The reader already knows all about that, and is more concerned to know what or who Hyacinth has become in the course of his association with the Princess, or at least what it proves her to be. Is he her lover? is he a hero? is she a witch? or, at least, is his a consciousness in which we can discern, through those 'vague white mists' in which Hyacinth drapes the Princess, some reflection of 'romance, reality and civilisation' vivid enough to convey the enchantment that she and her palace hold for him? As Hyacinth leaves Medley, it is difficult not to feel that what we have seen is merely a rehearsal of love and heroics, the superficial trappings of civilisation, and that Hyacinth's own probing, critical assessment of his story has become redundant in competition with the narrator's crude irony and the even less subtle dicta of the Princess's attendants, who tell us unambiguously what the Princess is, what Hyacinth is, and what will become of him: the Princess has no heart, and 'One of these days [he'll] see'; 'Certainly he'll have to be sacrificed' ... 'He's much too good for his fate!'

So resolutely does the narrator's point of view subvert Hyacinth's nebulous vision of the Princess that one wonders whether James couldn't have dispensed, in this connection, with so much help from her attendants, who belong to a more primitive tradition of story-telling. Their encounters with Hyacinth and with one another rely heavily on contrivance and coincidence, and their warnings and dire confabulations are repetitive and rob the story of the element of surprise and discovery. The position of Madame Grandoni and the Prince who, unlike Sholto, never mesh with the wider cast of characters, is conspicuously precarious in a novel which, even as he wrote it, James felt to be overpopulated (Ntbks 68), and can be attributed to their having made their first appearance in *Roderick Hudson*. Entering the sequel on Christina's coat-tails, they come already equipped with a certain perspective on her to which, once reinstalled, they can scarcely avoid referring. Hence the reports on past performance and the forecasts, the insistent, and insistently doom-laden presentation that lends *The Princess Casamassima* at times the tedious air of a documentary on some recurrent natural phenomenon, some act of God that is awe-inspiring, yet perfectly susceptible of explanation: Hurricane Christina, who returns every so often to blight youthful promise.

The Princess is the only major character that James carried over from an earlier novel. The problems inherent in such a procedure may not have struck him at the time, but that he was conscious of them later is suggested by the rather awkward apologia he made in the Preface to the New York Edition of *The Princess Casamassima*. The Princess, he claimed, 'had for so long in the vague limbo of those ghosts we have conjured but not exorcised, been looking for a situation, awaiting a niche and a function', and felt herself to be not 'completely recorded'(AN 73).

But if to be 'completely recorded' is her aim, what does that imply? The Christina Light of *Roderick Hudson* was a vain, capricious beauty, easily bored, attracted by novelty and the unconventional, who inspired passion in a young sculptor, betrayed and destroyed him. Yet she might not have betrayed him had she not been blackmailed into marrying Prince Casamassima. What is never clear is the sincerity of her intentions. 'I think she's an actress, but she believes in her part while she's playing it,' says Madame Grandoni (*Roderick Hudson*, p. 146), whose comments in her first incarnation are often sharply illuminating.

The later novel reveals Christina as essentially unchanged. She is still a sincerely vain and capricious flirt, attracted to Paul as she was to Rowland Mallet because he seems immune to her charm; and also sincerely attracted to Hyacinth and to the plebeian cause. If then she is to be completely recorded, we should expect in *The Princess Casamassima* to go further than this, to understand on some deeper level her character and motivation. Madame Grandoni and the Prince explain her only to a very limited extent. Christina is an angel, disappointed in the world as it is; she also hates the house of Casamassima and wants to injure it. She considers that 'in the darkest hour of her life she sold herself for a title and a fortune' – 'such a horrible piece of frivolity that she can't for the rest of her days be serious enough to make up for it'.

So much Madame Grandoni tells us, though she sounds now, with her rhetorical flourishes, like the agent of an actress who needs a more 'caring' image, and the Prince for one remains unconvinced of his wife's 'seriousness'. But what we learn from the two of them is no more than Hyacinth gathers from the Princess herself. Her commitment to the revolution never is explained further than in terms of her sincerity, and the grudge she bears against society. What is brilliant in James's conception of her is that this actually goes far enough, in summarising a type of terrorist mentality, as frightening as it is banal, that the Princess undoubtedly represents. If she *is* 'completely recorded', it is on this abstract level, and in a way that owes nothing to her encounter with Hyacinth. When they meet for the last time, the Princess makes as if to deny her very existence in Hyacinth's conceptual world:

'...Why am I so sacrosanct and so precious?'
    'Simply because there's no one in the world and has never been any one in the world like you.'
    'Oh thank you!' said the Princess impatiently. And she turned from him as with a beat of great white wings that raised her straight out of the bad air of the personal ... expressing an indifference to what it might interest him to think of her to-day, and even a contempt for it, which brought tears to his eyes. (521)

Hyacinth's extended stay with the Princess ends just in time for him to be with Pinnie when she dies. There is a sharp switch here from the inflated terms in which the Medley episode is handled to a more everyday currency. Grand projects left in the air give way to Lady Aurora's practical help, great ideas left unspecified to Mr Vetch's disclaimer of ever having had opinions except 'to frighten Pinnie', and Hyacinth's noble demeanour to his resumed habit of irritability. His subsequent trip to the Continent, financed by Pinnie's legacy, establishes a further distance between what already affects him as 'a far-off fable, the echo of a song', and the immediacy of his experience in Paris and Venice, which the reader through image and association is invited to share.

    At Medley, both the assassin marked to die and the bookbinder born noble seemed part of the unreal drift of the situation: characters who combine only to fade out in the shape of the half-hearted *chevalier servant* who offers to kill Sholto, if he troubles the Princess, because 'I shall have to kill some one, you know ...'. But in Paris Hyacinth's knowledge of time running out lends a vital urgency to his desire for experience: he must 'make a dash at the beautiful horrible world' represented by the city that witnessed the Terror. It is precisely his impending act of violence, and the violence done to his aristocratic father, that makes the site of the guillotine horribly fascinating to him. Yet in his capacity of Frenchman Hyacinth is impressed by the 'magnificent energy' of the Revolution, 'the spirit of creation', 'a sunrise out of a sea of blood' (perhaps also in his capacity of creative artist, for there is some seepage, in small purple patches, of James's own love of the lurid). The images on which Hyacinth's brain feeds will converge later in the insight that the monuments of civilisation are historically inseparable from suffering such as he has known and is to know; but meanwhile, in the here and now, past and present come together to minister to his deepest obsessions and needs.

If at Medley he found himself embodying a romance in which 'like some famous novel, he was thrilling', Paris is a reality in which Hyacinth feels he belongs as he never did even in London. His first *marquise* turns out to be only a confectioner's concoction – as might not be the case in 'some famous novel' – yet as he sits enjoying it in a boulevard café his appetite for life is as intensely felt by the reader as any thrilling romance; and the sense of 'the sweetness of not dying' that comes over him in the Place de la Concorde doesn't have the cloying taste of conscious heroism left by his earlier disquisition to the Princess on his elected martyrdom.

It is in Paris that Hyacinth really feels the cruelty of Paul's apparent indifference to his fate (at Medley, he hadn't seemed to notice the Princess's similar reaction): 'The tears rose to his eyes ... "How could he – how *could* he—?"' He who 'had dreamed of the religion of friendship' now knows that Paul is out of sympathy with him. Yet he has found companionship and a sense of identification in the spirit of his French grandfather who died on the barricades, a more congenial ghost than those of his parents. Hyacinth finds comfort too in thoughts of Millicent, who in the aftermath of Medley and Pinnie's death had proved surprisingly tactful and loyal: *she* cares what happens to him, she has promised to stand up for him 'if ever any one was to do you a turn—!' He had used to picture her in a red cap leading the Revolution, but now thinks of her as some 'Dacian or Iberian mistress' awaiting the return of a 'clever young barbarian' on 'the rough provincial shore'. Actually, as Hyacinth realises, she is likely to take advantage of his absence to see Sholto, but that relationship no longer distresses him. 'It was the general brightness of Paris perhaps that made him see sharp.' The brightness of Medley was the sort that dazzles; whereas Hyacinth's new clarity of vision, if it lets him see that he is losing Paul, also gives him insight into Millicent's 'large free temperament' in which 'many disparities were reconciled'. The disparities in his own temperament and situation come nearer to reconciliation in Paris than ever again.

We are informed that 'heaven knew he liked the Princess better'; also, that she is now Hyacinth's reference-point for culture and things foreign in general, and there is some winsome allusion to their recent 'intimacy'; but his harking back to Medley has, and will increasingly have, the quality of a blurred and faulty recording, whereas here in Paris it is Millicent who, as a 'loud-breathing feminine fact', is most audible in the text – partly because, like Paul, she is presented in direct flashback as well as through the medium of Hyacinth's reflections, partly also because of the specificity with which, sitting in the café, he tots up her pros and cons; her fake silver bracelets and vulgar speech habits versus her talking to him 'almost as if she had been his mother and he a convalescent child'. He at this point sees the Princess as a mother too – a mother goddess, who will rescue him from his fate – still his legendary creature, in other words, but his faith in the Princess is never so convincing as when he is considering her from the angle of his own story. It is appropriate that she should be reduced to a merely auxiliary function at the high point of that story here in Paris, where Hyacinth seems as right – right in himself, right in his relation to past and future, and in possession of his rightful inheritance – as in all these respects he seemed wrong at Medley.

Hyacinth's last link with that cardboard theatre of the passions is the long letter to the Princess that concludes the account of his travels; and it is here that the one false note in that account is struck. The Princess has asked him not to supply 'vague phrases' but 'the realities of his life'; he writes accordingly from Venice:

Through the chinks the hot light of the campo comes in. I smoke cigarettes and in the pauses of this composition recline on a faded magenta divan on the corner. Convenient to my hand in that attitude are the works of Leopardi and a second-hand dictionary. I'm very happy – happier than I have ever been in my life save at Medley ... (351)

This suggests, rather than reality, a lapse into some untypically dreary cul-de-sac of Jamesian travelogue, and the weakness of its connection with the matter in hand is sufficiently expressed in that limp last sentence. The letter isn't all written as flatly as this, or without any hint of self-mockery; and it has, of course, an important narrative function, which is to explain that, in the face of the accumulated beauty of the centuries, Hyacinth has 'lost sight of the sacred cause', and understands that the fabric of civilisation cannot be glibly exchanged for an improvement in the human condition. Nevertheless there does seem to be a slightly uneasy relation between the Hyacinth who is a master of his craft and the Hyacinth whose literary pretensions, earlier mentioned in passing, are now unequivocally asserted. Back in London, he finds renewed pleasure in his work in consequence of his recent aesthetic experiences; but he decides that binding books is 'much less fundamental' than composing them, and that he will write 'something', which will not be political:

> That was to be his transition – into literature ... It had occurred to Hyacinth more than once that it would be a fine thing to produce a rare death-song. (359)

Original or absurd, this new twist to his story goes nowhere, and his death will find only the most conventional artistic expression.

3.

It is James's story which makes at this point an important transition, a sudden shift registered by Hyacinth on his return from abroad as the shock of finding the Princess cosily ensconced in the intimate circle of Audley Court. In the faces of those about her he sees instantly that she has established a new domination, and reads at a glance the havoc that will ensue. The scene is highly dramatic, parodying the discovery of a nest of conspirators, and it introduces a narrative mode that alternates between an arch theatricality and an evident determination to bring matters into the open.[9] In what follows, hearts are worn on sleeves, authorial analysis is intensified, and the direction events will take unambiguously indicated. The atmosphere of conspiracy – of the hidden, the suppressed, the incalculable – that James claimed in his Preface to have tried for[10] is effectively dispersed.

Hyacinth himself sees, apparently for the first time, how much sheer pose there is in the Princess's slumming; and he challenges Paul hotly to make clear where he stands in relation to the Princess, to the people and to his friend: 'how will you like it when I'm strung up on the gallows?' *He*, Hyacinth, is the hero, *he* is in danger, and nobody cares for *him*. Rather oddly, given the lifeless bureaucratic patter that is Paul's response, Hyacinth ends up reassured that 'Paul was a grand person, that friendship was a purer feeling than love, and that there was an immense deal of affection between them.' The reader, on the other hand, is left under no illusion: 'He didn't even observe at that moment that it was preponderantly on his own side.'

It becomes obvious without the assistance of Madame Grandoni that Hyacinth's star is on the wane, that he will be supplanted, and, eventually, that he will die. Partly this is the cause, partly the effect, of Hyacinth's appearing, after the confrontation with Paul, to have lost his zest for the heroic role. He doesn't ask, as he once would have done, those questions that naturally occur to the reader, why he has been 'chucked' and why he must die: he feels the depth and pain of his predicament, without looking for the meaning of it. Only at the last moment, when the call to action comes, does he see himself in the frame of a historical logic which is also narratological: he is aghast at 'the idea of a *repetition*' (of his mother's crime). But by then his high-strung interpretive sensibility is all but reduced to a bundle of jangled nerves.

The narrator meanwhile, in a new extension of his authority, investigates and annotates the emotional consequences of the Princess's descent into Audley Court (her attraction to Paul, Rosy's anxiety on that score, Lady Aurora's distress, and so on); so that the psychological drama previously confined to Hyacinth's consciousness becomes a kind of soap opera of the domestic passions, perfectly adapted to Rosy's room and the little parlour of the cheap lodgings in Madeira Crescent to which the Princess has moved. Hyacinth is a percipient if intermittent observer of this drama; and his personal 'case', far from being lost in this shift of narrative focus, is illuminated in the light of other attitudes and other relationships.

Paul Muniment in taking up with the Princess proves not to be the 'successor to the little bookbinder' that Madame Grandoni anticipates: neither an exotic plebeian lover nor a votary of the aesthetic and intellectual values she stands for. It is a combination of curiosity and Rosy's nagging that brings him to the Princess, and once there he tells her that in order to please he wants 'to be as much as possible like Hyacinth'. He also seems, equally to her dismay, more impressed with her 'lovely home' than with the Princess herself; 'I like to see solid wealth,' he declares, and though she hastens to assure him she *'could* get money' for the cause, this Paul sounds as though he would happily forget about the cause and the Princess if he could move with Rosy into Madeira Crescent. 'Her life and mine are all one,' he tells the Princess on a subsequent visit, 'looking round the room again lovingly, almost covetously'. Rosy sanctions these visits on the basis that the Princess will help Paul to become prime minister. The reader can more easily see him as a party *apparatchik*, interested solely in feathering his own nest, or, under a different regime, as head of a company selling lifestyle interiors to the masses; for he seems to share his sister's enthusiasm for sofas, without her interest in their occupants. Hyacinth had already observed, in connection with her lust for everything 'tasteful', 'Rosy's transitions from pure enthusiasm to the imaginative calculation of benefits'. Perhaps Paul is merely his sister's brother.

If his is the soul of a bourgeois, the Princess lacks the soul of the artist, as is made plain on her encounter with Mr Vetch when he comes to beg her to help get Hyacinth off the conspiratorial hook. The old man pleads for his surrogate son with moving intensity; she resorts to a strenuous display of charm, to empty rhetoric, to phrases taken from Paul. As he did, she speaks of Hyacinth as 'a bloated little aristocrat'; she speaks of 'the people', inviting the retort: 'That's a silly term. Whom do you mean?' Mr Vetch, as he points out, is also one of the people, and the passion of the poor fiddler is cleverly set off by a comic vignette of the Princess using her own musical ability to improvise 'revolutionary battle-songs and paeans' on the piano.

But is *Hyacinth* simply looking for material comforts when, in conscious retreat from the street-horrors he now believes irremediable, he comes to Madeira Crescent on 'nasty winter nights'? Where are the hidden thrilling intimacies of Medley as he and the Princess sit together 'like very old friends' and he feels 'at times almost as if he were married' to her? Or is he still impressed against his better judgement, as Mr Vetch is, by the Princess's ability to act a part? He is fascinated by her housewifely ways, her modest economies, the details of her diet: her acting the *petite bourgeoise* presents itself to him as 'finished entertainment'.

The reader on the other hand, conscious of how often Hyacinth's restless roamings have ended in fuggy domestic interiors, may well

have an impression of *un*finished entertainment, may well wonder
if the theme of revolution hasn't been discreetly shelved here in
Madeira Crescent, the case of the workers parsimoniously boiled
down to a vicarious taste of lower-middle-class life ('On Sundays
they had muffins and sometimes for a change a smoked haddock or
even a fried sole'). Hyacinth himself is an uneasy mediator between
the matter of fact and the matter of fanaticism, or fantasy. There is a
sudden reference, as he sits by the Princess's fireside, to 'the ever-
lasting nightmare' of his relation to the cause: the phrase ought to
shatter the teacups, but doesn't, because the Princess has just belit-
tled Hyacinth's 'famous pledge to "act"' as 'like some silly humbug
in a novel'. He won't have to do it, she says, implying she knows
much more about Hoffendahl's plans than Hyacinth does. Hyacinth
is sceptical. He wonders if by claiming such involvement in Hoffendahl's activities she is merely giving herself 'cheap sensations',
and if secret, all-pervasive forces could lurk in such 'improbable
forms' as the Princess. He concludes that they could; but it's too late
for the reader not to have caught the hint that the conspiracy theme
is being handled in cheaply sensational terms, is being taken over
by the Princess as she is attempting to take over Paul and Lady
Aurora, and is, like everything else in the novel that she touches,
acquiring a dubious glamour. The 'hangman's rope' that in Madame
Grandoni's apocalyptic vision awaits the Princess really does
threaten Hyacinth, but we observe the Princess appropriate it and
translate it (elegantly, by way of French) into a means of appealing
to Paul: 'Do you consider that I'm in – really far ... And do you
think that *il y va* of my neck – I mean that it's in danger?'

   'Well, I'll look after you': Paul's reply covers for a multitude of
sins. How far and in what sense the Princess is 'in' it is never
explicit, but the subject of delicate obfuscation. Since this is exactly
the way the question of sex was handled, the reader finds it as
impossible as Hyacinth does to distinguish what she is doing for the
revolution from what she is doing with Paul. Certain 'acts' offensive
to her husband which Paul refers to cryptically might have taken
place in the anarchists' cell to which he supposedly conducts her, or,
alternatively, in Madeira Crescent where he returns with her late at
night. That *rentrée* under cover of dark, with her husband and
Hyacinth watching in the shadows, is a key scene, the fatal recognition that precipitates Hyacinth's downward spiral, and it works precisely because it brings into the sharpest focus the themes of
jealousy and exclusion already extensively investigated. Which is

why to see the Princess's sorties with Paul in Madame Grandoni's terms – that they go 'to that house to break up society' — must strike us as absurdly beside the point: we might as well be back in the theatre where Hyacinth first met the Princess, watching the Pearl of Paraguay's 'midnight meeting with the wicked hero in the grove of cocoanuts'.

To the same sort of cloak-and-dagger scenario belongs the Princess's declaration that she will save Hyacinth's life by assassinating the duke herself. Theoretically, hers is the sort of personality that – as distinct from Hyacinth's – could delude itself into murder; but the novel does not require it of her except for Hyacinth's sake, and he, killing himself, will pre-empt her. That she says to Paul, 'I love him very much' has little significance (it forms part of 'an exchange of amenities'). She is, after all, about to demonstrate, by her indifference to the books, masterpieces of craftsmanship, that he has bound especially for her, her comprehensive rejection of Hyacinth both as acolyte and artist.

What of her last-minute attempt to stop Hyacinth shooting himself? That final flurry and commotion undoubtedly has, in James's overall scheme of things, a sensationalist value of the kind she craves, but it also emphasises her redundancy in Hoffendahl's scheme. It shows how far she is from the controlling centre of the conspiracy: the call has gone out to Hyacinth without her knowledge, and it is left to Hoffendahl's man Schinkel, not to her, to snatch up Hyacinth's pistol after his death. The revenge of the plot is that the revolution comprehensively rejects *her*: she learns that it doesn't want her if the Prince cuts off her money.

Paul predicts that she will return to her husband. We don't have to believe that, but it would fit into the pattern of the book's closing chapters. Madame Grandoni returns to Italy; Lady Aurora, having lost Paul, re-enters society; and Poupin, that arch-enemy of the bourgeoisie, is to become foreman at the bookbinder's. Just as if Rosy had had the ordering of it, with her 'No, no; no equality while I'm about the place!', everyone takes up his or her ordained place in an ordered, hierarchical society; even Paul himself, for all the build-up of expectation that he would embody the revolutionary thrust, returns to Rosy's side.

Hyacinth too makes a move towards his former place or to the 'Plice' where he lived as a child, before he was aware of being different from everybody else. If there *has* been a fundamental upheaval, it has happened in Hyacinth's private universe, as a gradual liberation from the consciousness of his differentness that crippled him socially and emotionally. He now meets the Prince and Lady Aurora on an equal footing of sympathy and suffering, but unlike Lady Aurora, who thinks she wouldn't mind dying, Hyacinth thinks he would. He attempts to come to terms with his origins by trying 'more and more to construct some conceivable and human countenance for his father', to see through his own confusion of plebeian resentment and aristocratic disdain to the real man. In this new spirit of mature adjustment, the possibility is even admitted that Lord Frederick may not have been his father; not an idea Hyacinth entertains willingly, but he does now extend to Mr Vetch, once subject *in loco parentis* to the same resentment and disdain, a new understanding, reassuring him with a promise never to do the anarchists' work.

He has already returned to Millicent, recognising that the fate he always considered invidious has at least provided him with the opportunity to choose between 'the beauty of the original' as represented by the Princess and 'the beauty of the conventional'. As Millicent 'yields' discreetly behind a tree trunk to his encircling arm, Hyacinth seems to want to embrace a happy conventional ending.[11] Millicent is not at any rate seen to disadvantage where we are invited to compare her beautifully uninhibited condemnation of the Princess – 'Ah the vile brute!' – with the Princess's cold dismissal of Hyacinth behind his back as 'deplorably conventional', or her suspicious appraisal of him as 'less fresh than [she] first thought' with Milly's unqualified pleasure in finding the key to Hyacinth's personality. His secret, in her unimaginative handling, is promptly shorn of its mystique. '*She* wouldn't have been a nobleman's daughter for nothing!' Being an aristocrat is in Milly's book merely another incidental convenience to be taken robust advantage of, like the seat in the park which she hopes to avoid paying for. The fact remains that she gives due weight, as the Princess never does, to the part of Hyacinth that in his eyes chiefly constitutes his identity.

That is the best that Millicent can do for Hyacinth. She cannot prevent his life taking a tragic turn. Like it or not, Hyacinth isn't destined for the sort of future, in bondage to silver bracelets, of which we will catch a glimmer in *The Spoils of Poynton*, and which would have made a perhaps less conventional ending: he has yielded himself up to a different plot. Too quick to take up arms, he is trapped by the dramatic necessity which dictates that if firearms are part of the scene, a shot will have to be fired;[12] too captivated by his heritage, he is forced to repeat his mother's crime by committing murder, or his father's dishonour by breaking his word; too ready to resort to irony, he is submerged in a narrative of accumulating ironies: killing and being killed will really make him different from everybody else. Hyacinth finds himself alone in a cityscape now made irredeemably bleak. His story ends with the collapse of political energy, the failure of the religion of friendship, the contraction of the future to impossible choices. What price now *liberté, égalité et fraternité*?

The behaviour of the Princess, of Paul and Rosy and the Poupins, leaves him confused, without the capacity to 'see things sharp' that he had in Paris, without the sense of belonging anywhere. He turns finally to Milly: 'Mightn't she help him – mightn't she even extricate him?' The story that began with his regular revolutions at teatime to the respectability of Lomax Place concludes with his vision of 'a quick flight with her, for an undefined purpose, to an undefined spot'. He threads his way through 'the labyrinth' of the shop where she works and emerges from it to see, rather too sharply for his own good, the tableau that associates Millicent with his rival and from which Sholto's blank stare unmistakably excludes him. The panic, the silence, the familiar face that becomes a stranger's – all this has the feeling of nightmare, and the explanation of Hyacinth's suicide that it chillingly conveys is simply that he is scared to death, his fear of dying overwhelmed by the fear of being left alone like a child in the dark.

By redirecting our attention from the issues involved to Hyacinth's psychological disintegration, by presenting his final moments in terms of bafflement, searching, of a vision looming larger than life and, ultimately, of an absence, James makes a last bid to liberate Hyacinth from a more imprisoning narrative, the kind that deals in inflexible concepts like 'man whose life is over', 'man betrayed by his friends', 'man the dupe of the fair sex', 'man who dies for the cause' – concepts which Hyacinth is only too ready to apply to himself.[13] One might compare the closing pages of *The Ambassadors*, in which Strether manages to transcend those same concepts by accommodating pain in broader perspectives and a process of re-vision, and recognise that path as the one Hyacinth set out on when *he* was in Paris, the path where he has lost his way. He loses, specifically, that sense of proportion which Maisie Farange will find when she finally exchanges a story that is also impossibly ambitious for a child's portion of dignity and love. Yet we can see that, if his sacrifice of self wasn't for the greater good, it was perhaps some complex private reconciliation such as Fleda Vetch will appear to find. And we can see that he matters, as Milly Theale will at the moment of *her* final unwitnessed despair, not because he is noble but because he is suffering, because he had lived under the shadow of death and wanted a reprieve (which sets them both in a different literary dimension from the ill-fated youth who is Christina Light's first cast-off, Roderick Hudson). That we can best read how Hyacinth *might* have made an ending in these other, more success-fully realised endings is an irony he would appreciate; but it helps to redeem the banality of his 'doom', and confirms that he is party to that pursuit of understanding, that assault on life with all the resources of the imagination and intelligence, that attempt to har-monise it with a personal vision, which is James's recurrent theme.

This is the theme of Hyacinth's story, and it is one to which the Princess is not absolutely essential. It may seem perverse to say so, when she so resolutely goes through the motions of a restless quest for knowledge, but, like Mrs Monarch in 'The Real Thing', she can make nothing of the part assigned to her; and unlike Mrs Monarch she remains merely a programmed device. We are told that Hyacinth is to the last inspired by 'the great union of her beauty, her sincerity and her energy', that she has 'taken possession of his life', that 'No adventure was so prodigious as sticking as fast as possible to *her*'; but the extent to which he ultimately evades her influence and that of his other friends is the whole point of the book. What really influences him is his feeling for culture, milieu, history and, above all, his own history; which is another way of saying that it is in terms of these things that the reader forms an image of Hyacinth, not from categorical statements about what the Princess may or may not have done for or to him. Her influence only has observable effects in her initial encouragement of his cultural tastes which were in any case innate. And though she inspires him, as she inspired Roderick Hudson, to greater craftsmanship, Hyacinth's develop-ment as an artist is a mere thread of a theme that finally loses itself and peters out with his 'transition into literature'.

The Princess is, of course, the object of Hyacinth's devotion, play-ing Madame de Vionnet to Hyacinth's Strether, yet the least satisfac-tory parts of the novel are those where Hyacinth is singled out as her prince. She is never seen to be integrated into his experience of 'life' in the way that Madame de Vionnet is inseparable from Strether's imaginative embrace of Paris. Whereas it is hard to tell where her virtues end and Strether's imagination begins, there is so clear a dividing line between the Princess Casamassima as perceived by Hyacinth at Medley and as perceived by the narrator that it is impossible for the reader to see her as contributing to the glory communicated to Hyacinth by the place itself. On the contrary, once the Princess touches them, style, manners, the sense of the past, local colour – all the things that will bind Hyacinth to Paris – acquire a distinctly *ersatz* flavour.

It is true that she plays a key part in the betrayal, with Paul, of Hyacinth's religion of friendship; but again, not like Madame de Vionnet, whose chief concern at the end is that she shouldn't lose what the friend she betrays signifies; and not like Kate Croy in *The Wings of the Dove*, whose concern in the wake of a more deliberate betrayal is that she *can't* lose it. For Kate, even as she betrays Milly, as we shall see, re-creates her; while the Princess betrays Hyacinth almost by accident, hardly acknowledging that he is there: she gives the impression always of being on the lookout for a new supporting actor, even a new novel: her gaze stops briefly on Hyacinth only to appropriate for herself the version of his history ('scion of noble house sacrifices himself for revolution') that might have made a romantic hero of him. To her, Hyacinth is merely a bloated little aristocrat from whom she'll seize the pistol before he hurts himself.

Only, as we know, she doesn't. As she passes across Hyacinth's heaven, the Princess symbolises with her great white wings the aspirations of the revolution, but she draws up into her slipstream a vast load of cynicism that might otherwise devolve too heavily on the other aspiring revolutionaries. That is what the Princess really does for Hyacinth.

It would not be difficult to construct a version of his story, on the template for instance of *The Ambassadors*, that excluded the Princess altogether, yet allowed for Hyacinth's aristocratic tastes and anarchic sympathies. We could envisage the noble Lady Aurora, prettied up a bit, as Paul's insufficiently appreciated lover (compare Madame de Vionnet), who might become the focus of Hyacinth's desires and the means of his entrée into high life (inviting him perhaps to Inglefield, her family seat); but she would remain devoted to Paul (as Madame de Vionnet to Chad), who would in the end desert what Hyacinth believes in to set up 'a lovely home' (compare the return of Chad the rebel to the domestic decencies and the manufacture of mod. cons). One can further conceive just such a version of the story, only with Hyacinth relegated to the margin, which might be invented by Rosy, to whom the Princess isn't necessary either, except as a glamorous accessory.

The Princess Casamassima, if it isn't Christina's novel, isn't Rosy's either; and yet there is much of Rosy in its irrepressible vitality and assertive omniscience; and to a curious extent it reflects Rosy's limited vision of the world. What is its final negation of *liberté, égalité et fraternité* but the narrow view from her attic room, the restoration of the hierarchy in which she so fervently believes, the contraction of fraternal love to her brother's assurance that 'if *you* only keep going I don't care who fails'? It is remarkable, and disappointing, that in a novel where there is so much tension across social and sexual boundaries so little of it is released. Lady Aurora never gets closer to her plebeian Paul than Rosy's bedside, and Hyacinth, despite his growing attraction to the plebeian Millicent, never gets satisfactorily to grips with her; while both he and Paul pursue an intimacy with the Princess which seems always to hold out the thrill of some great tumble *de haut en bas* that never quite happens. That so promising an array of relationships should cumulatively come to nothing has something faintly unnatural about it, as if Rosy, that sexless, snobbish voyeur were arranging the whole scenario for her benefit. The very basis on which the novel purports to be constructed, that Hyacinth is Lord Frederick's son, is a confident assumption of a kind entirely characteristic of Rosy, which is no more necessarily true than Rosy's imagined perceptions of a world she has never seen.

This is not to suggest that Rosy's vision is coterminous with James's, least of all that he intended it to be. It does seem possible, though, that the dislike that Rosy inspires in many readers is the unconscious focus of their dislike of the book. Rosy after all does no one any harm; indeed, in her devotion to Paul and loyalty to Lady Aurora she represents something that at least remains intact amid the general desolation. Hyacinth may not be his father's son, but the bonds forged by love and protection between foster-parents and prostitute's bastard, between brother and sister, mother and son, are real.

At the end, Paul remains as tightly bound to Rosy as Hyacinth was at the beginning in his mother's 'terrible, irresistible embrace'. It is that affecting scene in the prison which is reflected on the last page of the book. In a vignette recalling Wallis's painting of the dead Chatterton,[14] Hyacinth lies as if asleep, one arm hanging downwards off the couch. There is a 'mess of blood' in his side, but the Princess prostrate over him covers it up. Almost a travesty of the *pietà*, the picture is as false as everything else she touches. Is Hyacinth, who always felt life had framed him to be the sacrifice, finally to be hunted down in this last weary resort of the picturesque? Only the ironic presence of Schinkel maintains that precarious balance between the cruel and the cute whereby the gaoler Mrs Bowerbank hoped to bring off her little scenario. The suspicion persists that the reader, like the dying prostitute, is expected in the face of fundamental truths to accept this substitute – to 'go off easier' for having, metaphorically speaking, seen Hyacinth's curls.

4

The Spoils of Poynton

1.

The lurking shadows of *The Princess Casamassima* and the nightmare
of Hyacinth's last days give way, in *The Spoils of Poynton*, to the
hideously patterned wallpaper in the guest bedroom at Waterbath
which keeps Mrs Gereth awake 'for hours'. There is absolutely no
glimpse in this account of difficulties between parents and children
of the disintegration of society as a whole. We are witness again to
self-sacrifice made ostensibly in the name of civilised values; but if
the 'mess of blood' in Hyacinth's side was, unlike the Princess, no
fake, here the notion of the 'real thing' seems to have returned us
safely to the realm of the connoisseur.

Poynton is ostensibly about taste, as *The Princess Casamassima* is
about politics. But the calculated appeal of both novels depends on
their projecting these abstract issues on to the domestic scene, where
the focus is on the interplay of character and tangible physical
realities. Mrs Gereth objects to the intimacy she observes between
her son Owen and Mona Brigstock, the daughter of the house, and
this has to do with her objections to Waterbath's 'intimate ugliness'–
an ugliness she considers 'the result of the abnormal nature of the
Brigstocks, from whose composition the principle of taste had been
extravagantly omitted'; and her discovery that one of the other
guests is a fellow-sufferer (moved to tears by their hosts' drawing-
room) marks the beginning of the 'tremendous fancy' that she will
take to Fleda Vetch.

That initial encounter is followed by a detailed discussion of
Waterbath, a fairly typical example, by the sound of it, with its
'strange excrescences and bunchy draperies', of rich Victorian
middle-class taste. Their demolition-job is as thoroughly agreeable
to the reader as it is to both women, and demonstrates that extravagance has its narrative uses as well as its aesthetic abuses:

The worst horror was the acres of varnish, something advertised and smelly, with which everything was smeared: it was Fleda Vetch's conviction that the application of it, by their own hands and hilariously shoving each other, was the amusement of the Brigstocks on rainy days. (4)

It is a lively and amusing passage, and as such it predisposes us to accept the narrator's suggestion that it's in Fleda's 'intenser consciousness' that 'we shall most profitably seek a reflexion of the little drama with which we are concerned.'

Already these stately cadences are lagging behind the drama that began with Mrs Gereth's recognition of Fleda. The approach of Owen Gereth and Mona Brigstock, laughing and 'romping' ominously, and the 'sensibly awkward' meeting of the two couples signals at once the plot's fundamental opposition of aesthetes and philistines. Mrs Gereth moves swiftly to fracture that opposition, detaching Owen from Mona so that he ends up with Fleda as the foursome proceeds to church. Fleda's consciousness registers this manoeuvre, and a great deal more, in a brief space. Mrs Gereth strikes her as 'masterful and clever, with a great bright spirit', Owen as 'absolutely beautiful and delightfully dense'; while she herself was 'prepared, if she should ever marry, to contribute all the cleverness', and 'her husband would be a force grateful for direction.' 'She was in her small way', Fleda, or perhaps the admiring narrator, further reflects, 'a spirit of the same family as Mrs Gereth.' Invited to stay with the latter, with the prospect of seeing her wonderful Jacobean house with its priceless treasures, Fleda envisages 'a future full of the things she particularly loved'. These things would appear already to include not only the spoils of Poynton but also Owen, and even to some degree the masterfulness of Mrs Gereth. Fleda, 'whose only treasure was her subtle mind', has hitherto maintained a precarious existence on the fringes of society. Now, she is clearly destined to take the centre of the stage, to link the present action with the future and to be the focus of romantic interest. Fleda in short – and the sequence of pages that brings us to this point is very short – is to become a heroine.

This blatant promotion, the prepackaging as it were of the story, the sharpness, slickness and dubious authority of the impressions urged upon us – all this has for the modern reader the flavour of a television commercial. The opening chapter of *The Spoils of Poynton* seems aimed at the consumer who expects to romp through its pages; indeed, it conveys the promise of a vital energy and sensual responsiveness that we shall see fulfilled in *What Maisie Knew*. And yet, programmed though we may be to respond to flashy appearances (like the bedroom wallpaper), *The Spoils of Poynton* demands of the reader a close, even painstaking scrutiny of the text. This is due to narratological complications of a kind not present in *The Princess Casamassima* or *The Portrait of a Lady*; but what *Poynton* does have in common with these earlier novels is a certain pressure exerted on the reader to admire the *quality* of the protagonist. We may exercise our independent judgement in wondering whether this isn't a retrograde step. If we, James's readers, are required to be connoisseurs, we must impartially examine both Fleda and *Poynton* as a whole.

In his Preface, James declares the subject of the novel to reside in 'somebody's excited and concentrated feeling about something' (AN 128); and it is one of a series of works, including *The Portrait of a Lady*, *The Princess Casamassima* and *The Ambassadors*, in which the protagonist's intensely personal vision is in conflict with a more worldly, cynical or humorous outlook that is sometimes represented by the omniscient narrator. Fleda is a typical Jamesian misfit, whose acute impressionability qualifies her to comment on her circumstances but who is too fine and sensitive to turn them to her own advantage. She is, furthermore, unlike Isabel Archer, afflicted with a strain of social insecurity which seems, as in the case of Hyacinth Robinson and Lambert Strether, to have magnified the sense of social responsibility; or, looking at it from a different point of view, to have produced that neurotic compulsion to meddle in other people's affairs which we observe in, for example, the telegraphist of 'In the Cage', in Laura Wing of 'A London Life' (1889), or the governess in 'The Turn of the Screw'.

In all these narratives, the point of view is critical: it makes all the difference for interpretation. But what is remarkable about *The Spoils of Poynton* is the extent to which critical views of it differ not necessarily from Fleda's but from one another, which suggests that the novel is puzzling and frustrating to a degree beyond, for example, 'In the Cage'. Its readers form factions as distinct and almost as vociferous as those of 'The Turn of the Screw'. What is wrong, or right, with *The Spoils of Poynton*, that it should excite such controversy?

The case is the more surprising if we consider the relative triviality of the issues involved. The power of beautiful furnishings to enslave hearts and minds hardly evokes the *frisson* that the ghosts at Bly do, and the death of a child must count for more than the destruction of a treasure-house, however wonderful.[1] Yet Fleda, who is only very indirectly responsible for that catastrophe, seems to inspire stronger and more personal feelings of sympathy or dislike than the governess in 'The Turn of the Screw'. Some critics, not necessarily taking their cue from James's Preface, in which she is so described, regard her as a 'free spirit', a follower in the 'Jamesian tradition of vital innocence' exemplified by Daisy Miller and the young Isabel Archer, only morally more admirable than either. Others, however, consider her at best a 'stumbling bungler', at worst culpably deceitful.[2] Yet the problem cannot be simply that of James's moral ambiguity. The moral line taken by Laura Wing in 'A London Life' is highly ambiguous, yet critics have shown little interest in her. Fleda Vetch on the other hand is undeniably both the focus of interest in *The Spoils of Poynton*, and of critical dissent about it.

One source of difficulty that presents itself mainly to the critic is that James's Preface to the novel and his notebook drafts reveal interesting discrepancies between his original intentions, subsequent satisfactions, and the story itself.[3] These texts are hardly the concern of the general reader, and the interpretation which follows – an attempt to elucidate the problem of *Poynton* – does not depend on them. Nevertheless, just as there are points in the Notebooks which indicate why something in the novel might go wrong, so there are points in the Preface where James does seem to be intimately in touch with the story that he actually wrote. As he searched for his narrative angle on the inarticulate spoils, 'Fleda Vetch', he claimed,

> marked her place in my foreground at one ingratiating stroke. (AN 127)

James is writing about Fleda here as if she were one of his privileged 'true agents'; and it is remarkable that he should use in such a context so derogatory a term, one which conveys to her detractors the essence of Fleda's dislikability. For it is because Fleda *is* ingratiating that she finds herself in a house, and a house of fiction, where she doesn't belong, with a function she is unable to fulfil. The problem of *Poynton*, as we shall see, is the problem of Fleda's place in relation to it.

2.

A year in Paris, 'arming herself for the battle of life by a course with an impressionist painter' has done nothing to prepare Fleda for the battle between mother and son into which she is now drawn. Poynton together with its contents has been, according to English custom, left not to the widow but to the son, whose appreciation of such things – according to his mother – is as defective as his taste in women. Mrs Gereth 'would have to give up Poynton, and give it up to a product of Waterbath – that was the wrong that rankled'.

Fleda is astonished by the speed – 'the great fierce bounds and elisions' – with which Mrs Gereth designates Mona the villain of the piece, whose 'hatred' the aesthetes have 'to reckon with'. 'She' ('Mona Brigstock, between these ladies, was now nothing but "she"') will prevent Owen from letting his mother take any one of the spoils from Poynton to the dower house, Ricks. 'She' will say,

> 'in that voice like the squeeze of a doll's stomach "It goes with the house – it goes with the house" ...' (11)

Mrs Gereth conveniently overlooks the consideration that it's by virtue of such refusal to compromise that Poynton is what it is. For the house itself only provided 'the matchless canvas for a picture': what has made it a 'complete work of art' is the contribution of the Gereths, and this, Fleda sees, can be attributed to 'the high pride of her friend's taste, a fine arrogance, a sense of style which ... never compromised nor stooped'. So that what Mrs Gereth is really objecting to is the addition to that harmonious whole of the haphazardly assembled 'maddening relics of Waterbath'. There can be no admixture of Mona Brigstock's taint, no living, as Mrs Gereth puts it, 'with such a creature's elbow half-way down her throat'.

Yet the link between the two styles is Mrs Gereth herself, who combines the arrogance of the one with the crudity of the other. As if chunks of the Poynton which Fleda perceives as 'written in great syllables of colour and form' had dropped into her workaday vocabulary, Mrs Gereth makes an extraordinarily vivid impression almost every time she opens her mouth. The capacity to impress is what we expect of great art, but Waterbath has it too: all three of them – Waterbath, Poynton and Mrs Gereth – impress Fleda sufficiently on occasion to make her cry, or feel sick.

Fleda also perceives, as she wanders through the great house, that 'Poynton was the record of a life', without ever understanding how smoothly for Mrs Gereth aesthetic ideals translate into the terms of physical existence. Soon, though, Fleda is to be made directly and even physically aware of the depth, the intimacy – going far beyond mere admiring contemplation – of Mrs Gereth's attachment to her possessions: 'Blindfold, in the dark, with the brush of a finger, I could tell one from another. They're living things to me, 'she explains to Fleda and a bemused Owen – things that are not however for Mrs Gereth, as they will prove for Fleda, a substitute for personal relationships, but which provide a permanent focal point for her human affections and disaffecuons. The 'things' represented her marriage, the partnership with a husband who shared her collector's passion:

> '... They were our religion, they were our life, they were *us*! And now they're only *me* – except that they're also *you*, thank God, a little, you dear!' she continued, suddenly inflicting on Fleda a kiss intended by every sign to knock her into position. (20)

The position of guardian of the treasure, inseparable in Mrs Gereth's eyes from that of cherished daughter-in-law, is a magnificent offer – though it is never clear that Fleda relishes the second as much as the first. What is clear is that she will strenuously resist being written into Mrs Gereth's drama as the antithesis of the so summarily written-off Mona – an attitude which later earns her the rebuke of being 'a stiff little beggar'. Using Fleda in her schemes doesn't preclude Mrs Gereth's being fond of her, and she will be perpetually astonished that, after the initial outpouring of imaginative sympathy, Fleda gives so little of herself in return. James, when he came to write the Preface, seems to have felt for Fleda a similar proprietorial affection, and not least because of her narrative function, or place in his scheme of things. Fleda's position in the novel, as he with hindsight saw it, was that of a 'free spirit' engaged with 'fools' who were the 'fixed constituents' of the action (AN 129); and in the opening chapters of the book she is conspicuously on display, not only as the detached intelligence through whom James got his angle on the story, but as intelligently detached – embodying, that is, a point of view that has depth and perspective, and which shows up the other protagonists as hopelessly blinkered. Fleda attempts to find a compromise solution to the looming crisis, or at least to reduce it to sensible proportions: the lovers, she supposes, 'wouldn't after all smash things nor burn them up'. She appears rational, conciliatory and sensitive, where the others are fanatical, obstinate or merely obtuse. As the philistines – Owen, Mona and Mrs Brigstock – prepare to descend on Poynton, the free spirit is capable of 'an amused diplomatic pity' for them, and reflects on Mrs Gereth's

> almost maniacal disposition to thrust in everywhere the question of 'things', to read all behaviour in the light of some fancied relation to them. (16)

Fleda concludes that although, like Mrs Gereth's, her taste was her life, 'her life was somehow the larger for it.'

So insistent is the suggestion that Mrs Gereth's outlook is narrowly limited, her passion perhaps even a sterile one, that it prompts one to reflect that it was actually Fleda's life which was defined at the outset in relation to the question of the 'things'. As when Hyacinth Robinson first came to the house of the Princess, it was on her journey to Poynton that Fleda's future seemed to expand, holding among other expectations the promise of a romantic interest. But the effect of Owen's arrival with Mona – a bad sign for herself – is to drive her further into the aesthetic embrace of the treasures. Fingering brasses, holding velvets 'in a loving palm', Fleda reflects wistfully that

> Mrs Gereth's remaining would have offered her an apology for a future, stretching away in safe years on the other side of a gulf ... (14)

It *is* an apology for a future – the 'gulf' being, presumably, that into which any other kind has disappeared – and yet it is striking that Fleda should conceive of her future in such terms, of Poynton as a retreat from the world outside – almost, as a final resting-place. Here, after all, is a girl with her youth before her, and fresh from Paris, the city synonymous in James with 'life' as well as art. But Fleda finds in Poynton 'all France and Italy with their ages composed to rest'. It is as if her own life had stopped there and she herself were serenely absorbed into her own vision of art eternal and inviolate. The picture is a beautiful one, but it is also slightly chilling, like seeing the 'long and bland' vistas of Poynton converge in the 'dead wall' in which Isabel Archer saw her future as Gilbert Osmond's museum-piece.

The reader turns from it with relief to the advent of the Brigstocks, whose visit like their home is described with a sharp specificity, nailing their preposterousness at every step of the guided tour. Mrs Brigstock brings with her 'a "lady's magazine"', a 'horrible thing with patterns of antimacassars'; she raps Mrs Gereth's porcelain with her big knuckles; Mona's big feet are encased in mannish patent-leather shoes which appear to interest her more than Poynton does. Although Fleda divines that 'her ignorance was obscurely active', when pressed to respond to the aesthetic Mona exhibits a 'belligerent blankness', an impermeable surface that enables her effortlessly to deflect on to softer targets like her mother the malice of the narrator. Of her uncouth silences it is rather mildly observed that

> She was a person whom pressure at a given point infallibly caused to expand in the wrong place (17)

– rather like the Poynton which she envisages improved by the addition of a winter garden 'thrown out'. Fleda is shocked by the idea of such a 'shiny excrescence on the noble face of Poynton'; it reminds her of the conservatory at Waterbath, replete with 'untidy plants' and a stuffed cockatoo, in which she had caught a bad cold. For all she can mimic the extravagant mode, Fleda hates to be trapped in it. Hence her horror when Mrs Gereth's profession of fond attachment to her 'things' swells into an encomium of Fleda herself as the girl who appreciates them, and whom she proceeds to present to Owen, with rather tasteless rhetorical trimmings, as a better class of wife. Mrs Gereth is never afraid to go too far. Even more outrageous is her parting address to the recalcitrant Mona, in which her rudeness rises in a thrilling crescendo, figured by her tossing after Mrs Brigstock 'the female magazine with the what-do-you-call-'em? – the grease-catchers. There!'

The despised publication is caught by Mona, who

> from the force of habit ... had popped out, with a little spring, a long arm and intercepted the missile as easily as she would have caused a tennis-ball to rebound from a racket. 'Good catch!' Owen had cried ... (23–4)

It is the gage of battle that Mrs Gereth hurls, and it links her with the hitherto impassive Mona in a moment of vital interaction. Between

such formidable opponents, Fleda is left helpless, in the position of
prig in the middle.

3.

Mrs Gereth is, and will remain,

> puzzled to conceive why a good-natured girl shouldn't have con-
> tributed more to the personal rout of the Brigstocks – shouldn't
> have been grateful even for the handsome published puff of Fleda
> Vetch. (94)

But Fleda is furiously offended by the 'puff' – the unintended insult
to her dignity, which has come dangerously close to exposing her
secret attraction to Owen. Her humiliation is not quite as extreme or
as public as Fleda makes out, since only Owen witnesses it and he,
when he returns to Poynton to announce his engagement, is clearly
unaware of complicated subtexts, having, as Fleda has already
observed, 'no more sense for a motive than a deaf man for a tune'.
His is the sort of mind which, unlike Fleda's, thinks of one big thing
at a time: latterly it has been Mona, now it is Poynton. 'Naturally I
want my own house you know,' he tells Fleda, and he wants it complete with the 'furniture' – a word which, 'on his lips, had somehow
to Fleda the sound of washing-stands and copious bedding'.
Aware only of Fleda's sympathetic disposition, Owen gratefully
assigns to her the job of seeing Mrs Gereth 'safely and singly off the
premises'. In this manner, Fleda becomes intimately implicated in
the affair of the tables and chairs, her moral worth, as it were, to be
defined in terms of how many pieces exactly Mrs Gereth won't get
away with; she is also put in the invidious position of betraying
either her and Poynton, or Owen's trust. Her loyalty to her friend
and to the aesthetic ideal on the one hand, her tenderness for Owen
and respect for the law on the other, mesh together in Fleda's over-
worked consciousness into a tangle of emotion and rationalisation, a
knot which gathers into itself all the threads of the narrative, a
nexus of interest, but one which continually threatens to strangle
action and development.
Fleda finds two ways of escape from her difficulties. One lies in
fantasy. At Poynton, instead of pushing Owen's cause, she dreams
of what 'might have been that could never have been'. The other lies

in flight. She goes up to London to help her sister Maggie prepare for marriage to a poor curate – and there, by chance, she runs into Owen, who in his gratitude attempts to buy her a present.

From dreaming amid Poynton 's works of art to being offered in a big Oxford Street shop a string of comically specific items is a drop into bathos from which our heroine never really recovers. Owen's incongruous selection – 'a travelling-rug, a massive clock, a table for breakfast in bed, and above all ... a set of somebody's "works"' – demonstrates that to him one object is as good as another. But to Fleda, objects have associations, significance. She thinks Owen, whom she sees as 'immensely in earnest', would like to buy her the 'splendid stuffs' that lie 'tumbled about': an idea that sounds faintly improper, and would in those days definitely offend notions of 'form', especially in the sort of mind that can convert 'furniture' into 'copious bedding'. So that we are surprised to find Fleda attributing Owen's not buying dress-material for her to his 'delicacy' – his wanting not to draw attention to her poverty. It is Fleda who is immensely in earnest, and her reading of signs provokes amusement and scepticism: the high seriousness of the idea that splendid stuff has immanent meaning survives the encounter with Owen with its value slightly marked down.

That Fleda sets great store by 'form' is evident in her suddenly perceiving everywhere the absence of it. She refuses as improper his offer of lunch, envisaging 'a romp in a restaurant', but consents to a walk in Hyde Park where, thinking about gentlemen in novels who break out on the eve of their marriage, she is both thrilled and frightened to find herself so openly playing the part of rival to Mona. She is acutely conscious of what Mona might think, but

> she had by this time to think for Owen as well as for herself ... He wanted to stay with her – he wanted not to leave her: he had dropped into complete silence, but that was what his silence said. (44)

She finds Owen's behaviour 'extravagant and even inconsequent'; but the reader may well see it as natural self-assertion, popping up here in reaction to the pressure put on him elsewhere – expanding in the 'wrong' place, as Mona did in response to Mrs Gereth's overbearing manner at Poynton. And the more Fleda, without any supporting evidence, pushes the idea that she stands in some sort of relation to *Mona*, the more the reader is inclined to assume that she does not. It is a natural reaction to the sort of narrative weighting which – like the pressure on Owen and Mona – produces expansion in the wrong place, forming excrescences on the story that may strike the reader as peculiar. One such excrescence is the story in which Fleda nearly becomes Owen's wife and mistress of Poynton, and over it hangs a huge question-mark.

Is Fleda as unreliable a narrator of her own experience as she is an unreliable *chargé d'affaires*? Is she simply indulging in a 'subjective adventure', to use Robert C. McLean's notorious phrase?[4] 'Notorious', because the implication of McLean's article is that the 'subjective adventure' is coterminous with Fleda's romantic illusions, and because it has perhaps led to the tendency to see the novel in reductionist terms of Owen's good faith versus Fleda's bad faith, or vice versa. There *is* a 'subjective adventure' going on in *The Spoils of Poynton*, but not one which has exclusively to do with Owen.

James's text seems deliberately to imply that Fleda's romance is illusory, or very much open to question, at least as far as the episode when Owen, on a diplomatic mission to Ricks, is understood by Fleda to be communicating that he finds her 'different' from the other woman who is 'so ugly and vulgar, in the light of this squabble'. He doesn't actually *say* this, for Fleda catches his meaning '[c]learer than he could have spoken it'.[5] So when Owen, in his vague, conciliatory way, says that he 'could put up with' Ricks, Fleda promptly hears him say, in 'unsounded words', that he wants to live there, and live there with *her*, since he couldn't possibly mean that Mona would put up with Ricks. These are both quite unwarranted assumptions: Owen has told her that it's Poynton he wants, and on another occasion that 'Mona had taken a tremendous fancy' to Ricks. Fleda thinks she is bringing logic to bear on Owen's disjointed utterance, and yet up pops this soap-bubble of her own fantasy. What is demonstrated here is her instinctive recourse to notions of logic, order and propriety to hold in check the disruptive power of impulse and imagination – which becomes the more obstreperous for being suppressed.

Fleda firmly believes that Owen's fiancée has an inalienable right to him, in the eyes of the law and of society. (Her own precarious social standing means that she appreciates, as the Gereths, enjoying different circumstances, don't, the horror of social disgrace and the protection of the law.) But, just as her concern with 'form' gave Fleda the idea, in Oxford Street, that Owen had lost his, so her obsession with being 'right' towards Mona dangles alluringly before her the image of a Mona who isn't 'right' at all, but vulgarly pushy and sexually permissive.

The conviction that Owen *must* prefer her to someone like that is the basis of Fleda's hopes and hence of the ethical inconsistency in her believing that he ought to stick to Mona, while praying that he won't. This will worry only readers who believe that James has lost in Fleda some putative moral line; what James keeps, of course, at this point is the obvious explosive potential, as in any sealed system with a weak spot, of Fleda's suppressed romance, which she cherishes like

> some dangerous, lovely, living thing that she had caught and could keep – keep vivid and helpless in the cage of her own passion and look at and talk to all day long. (74)

Even without the metaphor, Fleda's position here anticipates that of the *déclassée* telegraphist in 'In the Cage' and her consoling fantasies about Captain Everard. Fleda thinks she is beloved, but the reader is given every encouragement to think that, like the telegraphist, she is a deluded spinster who takes refuge in dreams from material and emotional deprivation.[6]

Nowhere is this more clearly indicated than in her first visit with Mrs Gereth to Ricks. We shall see that fondest of all Fleda's fantasies is her evocation of the maiden-aunt who had made her home there and who, Fleda maintains, 'had deeply suffered', leaving a house which is 'faded and melancholy, whereas there had been a danger it would be contradictious and positive, cheerful and loud' – in the style of Waterbath, the reader mentally notes, or of Mona and Owen romping together, or indeed of Mrs Gereth when provoked. To Fleda it is evident that

> the maiden-aunt had been a dear; she should have adored the maiden-aunt. The poor lady had passed shyly, yet with some bruises, through life; had been sensitive and ignorant and exquisite: that too was a sort of origin, a sort of atmosphere for relics and rarities, though different from the sorts most prized at Poynton. (36)

And the 'relics', the humble bits and pieces, of the maiden-aunt, 'made her even wonder if it didn't work more for happiness not to have tasted, as she herself had done, of knowledge'.

'Knowledge' in James is a highly charged concept: not having it usually implies, as in *What Maisie Knew* and *The Ambassadors*, being shut out from 'life', or, on a more superficial level, from sexual relationships. But Fleda's reference to 'knowledge' here, when her friendship with Owen has scarcely begun, seems to signify her acquaintance with the very best in furniture and porcelain: once again she defines herself, subconsciously, in relation to 'things'. Consciously, she celebrates the spirit of the maiden-aunt, clearly finding her 'small prim parlour' – 'practically a shallow box' – a more homely and appropriate retreat from the world than Poynton. The implied identification is a perilous one for Fleda: maiden-aunts have seldom been regarded as heroic figures, and being 'sensitive, ignorant and exquisite' is but a short step from seeming too good for or too comically inept at the business of life and human relationships.[7] Fleda will be astonished and pained when told reluctantly by Owen that Mona 'wanted to know what right you had to meddle. She said you weren't honest'; but the reader can easily see the source of Mona's resentment, not in the idea that Fleda is any kind of rival, but in another version of her story that is dropped into the narrative like the sort of ugly, incongruous little item Mona would be bound to pick up: that among her circle of acquaintances Fleda's 'tendency had begun to define itself as parasitical' and that

> people *were* saying that she fastened like a leech on other people – people who had houses where something was to be picked up ... (40)

It is her sister who tells Fleda what 'people' are unkindly saying – which suggests a touch of malice in their relationship, a hint perhaps that Maggie resents the sister who regards her as 'doomed' to the curate but who nonetheless has her eye on the couple's 'small spare room' and won't hesitate to use it as a bolt-hole. When Mrs Gereth visits her there, Fleda observes 'how characteristically she looked at Maggie's possessions before looking at Maggie's sister'; but it is *Fleda's* view of the soiled tablecloth and 'smelly' shops that has already defined Maggie's circumstances, and Fleda in relation to them – as sensitive, superior and alien.

Laura Wing, Fleda's counterpart in 'A London Life' sees herself very similarly, if not similarly placed; but Fleda never evinces for any person that uncomplicated attachment Laura feels for her cuddly small nephews and which, almost as much as financial dependence, ties her to the hearth of her disappointing sister Selina. So that, even more than in Laura's case, working against the stereotype of the neurotic spinster is the very real pathos that Fleda inspires because she doesn't belong *anywhere*. The only home to which she has a right is with her father, who with his collection of penwipers, ash-trays and brandy-flasks is an embarrassment to her, and who encourages Fleda to live off other people. As Mrs Gereth's companion, whether at Poynton or at Ricks, she is at least glad to have 'a use not universally acknowledged'. Fleda tends to see herself, as she sees her sister, in terms of her usefulness; and for all her sensibility, we never have any palpable sense of how deep her affection for Maggie or for Mrs Gereth might actually be, though we have her word for it that 'she should have adored' the no-longer palpable maiden-aunt. We see vividly enough the picture in Fleda's head of the maiden-aunt, and also the picture she has there of herself as Owen's beloved, but it is quite difficult to see *Fleda*, as Mrs Gereth, Maggie and Owen variously complain. And not only in the sense of knowing *what* she is. Sometimes we lose track even of *where* she is; for she jumps on and off trains so fast that she becomes a mere blur of anxiety divorced from any physical identity or external *point de repère*. It is this desperate search for a place to be 'right' which is Fleda's true subjective adventure.

The greater then is her shock when, summoned again to Ricks to join Mrs Gereth, now in residence there, Fleda finds that it no longer represents an asylum for self-effacing spinsters – that

> the maiden aunt had been exterminated – no trace of her to tell her tale. (52)

4.

While Fleda 'sees' and 'hears' those things which compose a somewhat suspect account, Mrs Gereth, unseen and unheard, has left her indelible mark on the novel in the tracks of the 'mighty' removal vans that have brought the spoils from Poynton to Ricks.

During the last days at Poynton, Fleda had cast her friend in assorted heroic poses – back to the wall, going down with the ship, and so on; but far from steering straight into martyrdom, Mrs Gereth changes tack continually, leading into whatever wind will produce the biggest squall. What was initially her distaste for the 'product of Waterbath' becomes resentment at the injustice of English law, and, finally, the claim that the 'great wrong Owen had done her' was 'his failure from the first to understand what it was to have a mother at all, to appreciate the beauty and sanctity of the character. ... One's mother ... was a subject for poetry, for idolatry.'

The extravagance of her attitudes is markedly at odds with the quiet harmony of Poynton, where no single item has the bad taste stridently to claim the limelight. Mrs Gereth has no fear of publicity. She is, she assures Fleda, ready to be dragged out of the house by constables. Having a stronger grasp of reality than Fleda, she in fact accepts that the young couple must eventually displace her; and her reaction isn't to cast about like Fleda for some notionally absolute solution, but to head straight in the direction dictated by her capacity for improvisation, her preference for the temporarily expedient, maximally impressive move. Generously interpreting Owen's permission to remove a few of her favourite things, she takes, if not literally every object, enough wonderfully to reproduce at Ricks the effect of Poynton.[8]

Fleda's recognition of this effect and of the crime that produced it, one of the novel's great moments, and virtually the only one brought about by Fleda herself, is a masterly blend of comedy and high drama. She is overwhelmed by the beauty of the transfigured Ricks, in which what appeals to her most is 'a certain gorgeous audacity'. Mrs Gereth stands before her as the embodiment not of 'good taste' but of the creative spirit which made the aesthetic whole out of the materials at her disposal, the creative spirit without which they would add up to so much less – as would Mrs Gereth. 'Wherever she was she was herself the great piece in the gallery.' It isn't Mrs Gereth's nerve that is suddenly brought home to Fleda, as she sees her in her triumph, so much as this bond between creator and created – the vital infusion of life that makes art.

For Fleda, it isn't a case of unmixed joy, for the safe house of Ricks is now contaminated by Owen's illegally removed furniture. Instinctively, she feels guilt by association; but what really shocks her is the spirit of anarchy, even of violence, that walks abroad in Mrs Gereth's blithe *démarches*, bringing humiliation upon her young friend, wiping out the maiden-aunt, and worst of all – as Fleda will perceive from the uneasy comfort of her stolen Louis-Seize bed – striking at what she holds most in reverence:

In the watches of the night she saw Poynton dishonoured; she had cherished it as a happy whole, she reasoned, and the parts of it now around her seemed to suffer like chopped limbs. (53)

Mrs Gereth's attitude to the 'things' is quite different. '"Upon my word", she laughed, "they really look better here!"' This need not be taken at face-value (the narrator having hinted that the effect is in fact rather cramped); Mrs Gereth is engaged in appreciating not the transported spoils, but the transporting of them: 'Her elation ... was not so much from what she had done as from the way she had done it' – on a basis, as she explains in detail, of clever timing, military rigour and unstinted expense, but also by deploying her personal reserves of courage, charm and energy. She outfaced those servants likely to give the game away, she sweet-talked the packers into staggering expenditures of overtime ('I made love to them ... they found me wonderful'); she 'lifted tons with [her] own arms.'

And now, 'I'm tired, very very tired.' This prosaic comment brings into focus rather effectively the world in which Mrs Gereth operates, a world in which loads get hauled, where cups get dropped and old ladies worn out with the physical strain of it all; and reminds us how different is the world that Fleda has created, the cloistered spiritual world of the maiden-aunt, whose bruises were not, we imagine, caused by bumping into packing-cases. Fleda had, indeed, vividly imagined Mrs Gereth's departure from Poynton amid 'a tussle, dishevelment, pushes, scratches, shrieks', but held it incredulously at a distance, like certain other visions of physical rough and tumble – the 'romp in a restaurant' with Owen that never took place, or the Brigstocks' hilarious shoving as they varnished the woodwork of Waterbath. It is for her to be spectator and interpreter: she tries to make sense of the drama in symbolic, if not moral terms; Mrs Gereth on the other hand, whose concern is to prolong the drama ('What indeed was her spoliation of Poynton but the first engagement of a campaign?'), makes it *felt*, through her visceral relish for the fight with Owen:

'... Oh he may burn me alive!' she cried with a happy face. 'Did he abuse me?' she then demanded. (77)

It is at this point that Mrs Gereth sees in Fleda's betrayal of her *tendresse* for Owen a new path to victory. She will return the spoils 'for' Fleda if Fleda will 'get Owen away' from Mona – if necessary, as Mrs Gereth makes all but explicit, by offering the sexual favours that Mona is assumed to have offered him. Fleda finds herself in a dilemma that characteristically presents itself as the problem of whether to go or stay. She dislikes being bullied by her hostess, but dislikes even more the idea of departing in open pursuit of Owen; so she stays on, amid what she censoriously calls the 'ill-gotten gains', and as Mrs Gereth scans the paper every day for the news of Owen's marriage which fails to materialise, the alternative, 'advertised and offered' bride squirms in

> a kind of bath of boldness ... as if a fierce light poured in upon her from windows opened wide ... (94)

The metaphor suggests the bright impunity of Poynton, and Fleda's position demands that she exhibit it; but she resists with the battered superiority of unreconstructed Ricks, dusting down once more her inveterate complaint against her friend:

> She had no imagination about anybody's life save on the side she bumped against. ... Mrs Gereth had really no perception of anybody's nature – had only one question about persons: were they clever or stupid? To be clever meant to know the 'marks'. (94)

Not for the first time when the way forward seems obscure, Fleda has retreated to the moral high ground, where the gulf between her and her friend is clearly visible as the difference between idealism and cynicism. But on another level – the level of plot, which imposes the question, what happens next? – it can be viewed, more interestingly, as the difference between Fleda's conservatism (keeping the peace, keeping secrets, keeping the lid on) and Mrs Gereth's paramount concern with moving things on. As Fleda is perfectly well aware, Mrs Gereth, knowing the 'mark' of Fleda to be her refinement and sensitivity, and knowing also that it is her weak spot, bumps against it to a very deliberate end. For days Fleda is bombarded with tasteless hints that she should embark on a sexual adventure with Owen, till she can take it no more and leaves Ricks, which is exactly what Mrs Gereth wants. Her parting injunction at the station, 'Only let yourself go, darling – only let yourself go!', handing unequivocally to Fleda the stirring part that she herself can no longer play, seems strangely to invoke the rumbunctious spirit of Waterbath, and promises to lead the narrative out of the delicate, convoluted ironies of the previous chapters into excitement and revelation.

But in those chapters our heroine's progress is disappointing. From being 'advertised and offered' (a phrase that unhappily recalls the 'advertised and smelly' product smeared on everything at Waterbath), she has come to figure 'in the queer conversations of Ricks as a distinguished, almost as a dangerous, beauty'. We know as well as Fleda that these commercial blow-ups are parodies, and yet Fleda's own romantic self-image can't be taken seriously either, since there is as yet no evidence that Owen reciprocates her sentiments. 'To know she had become to him an object of desire gave her wings that she felt herself flutter in the air': but the trouble with Fleda's hesitant flight is that it takes her out of a story that is increasingly seen to work in terms of the concrete and specific, of striking poses and unambiguous gesture, of coup and counter-coup, into a narratological limbo, where she 'resembled – or thought she did – a lonely fly crawling over a dusty chart'.

5.

So much for the 'dangerous beauty', who, returning to London, makes no attempt to contact Owen but spends her days wandering aimlessly in 'the great unconscious town'. There is some reference to friends whom she has lost touch with since cleaving to Mrs Gereth, whose failure now to materialise indicates to Fleda, as it does to the reader, that she has no usefulness and no grip on anyone's attention outside the Ricks–Poynton axis. A similar half-hearted attempt to connect with another dimension of her existence consists in the brief interlude in which Fleda considers withdrawing to Maggie's and, 'concealed in this retreat', taking up painting again. (She had given it up after her visit to Waterbath, where 'the sight of the family splotches had put her immensely on her guard.')

The sudden drop into life before Waterbath makes a jarring transition to her meeting with Owen in front of the picture-framer's window. Fleda, one has the impression, only just makes it: she nearly fell out of the story altogether. It takes Owen to bring her up again – 'his pull was tremendous', and it consists in his looking exceptionally handsome. Made acutely conscious of his sex-appeal, of her neglected role as mediator and of her father's tasteless parlour when she takes him home for tea, Fleda once more acknowledges the reader's mundane concerns. There is even a promise of farce as she nervously deals out the 'vulgar' cups and saucers and plates and Owen clumsily tries to help her: 'this made indeed for disorder.' A sort of knockabout comedy does ensue, but it involves the clash of minds, not of crockery.

Owen has come to discover from Fleda whether he must resort to the law or whether his mother will in fact return 'every blessed "stolen" thing'. The double quotation marks suggest the 'stolen' is Mona's contribution, connecting with an earlier moment at Ricks when Owen had dismissed the Brigstocks' talk of 'stealing' as 'none of their business' – causing Fleda to note with satisfaction, 'no one so slow could ever have had such quick transitions.' But what Owen is demonstrating, and will continue to demonstrate, is the reverse of her own analytical intelligence. He dislikes rows, and likes romps; he wants his marriage, and above all, as everything in the novel demonstrates, he wants his house; and these concepts appear to hang together in Owen's world-view not logically, but by a sort of spontaneous attraction. So he can say to Fleda of Mona: 'Oh she's all right. Mother must come round', and when it transpires that Mona isn't and mother won't, he is at a loss.

As they talk over the teacups, and Owen's thoughts dart from one definite step to another that might or might not be taken – his marriage, or bringing in the solicitors – Fleda, confronting her ethical dilemma, is preoccupied with his position in relation to Mona and herself. Will Mona release him from their engagement? And does he want her to? She has nothing more to tell Owen than that his mother is hanging on 'to tire Mona out'; but she draws out the conversation, directing it by means of leading questions to what she wants to know: can Mona, if she cares so much for the things, really care for *him*?

Then, with the ground prepared, she poses the crucial question: does Owen still love Mona? Her persistence is rewarded. Owen, who has until now 'stared' and looked 'befogged', unsuccessfully deflecting Fleda's enquiries and taking the initiative only in what directly concerns Poynton or his tea, all at once responds to Fleda's question with a lively expression of his liking for her and growing distaste for Mona.

Clearly this is a pivotal point in the novel, and it is worth observing that a close study of the text reveals Fleda as leading Owen up to it. For his declaration, which will be followed in a later episode by a proposal of marriage, has been regarded by some critics as a sudden deliberate move on Owen's part to trick Mrs Gereth into returning the things, intending them for Fleda as Owen's wife. According to Robert McLean, Owen, suspecting Fleda of withholding information,

> determines to follow the lead of his adversaries in practicing deception. He decides that only a profession of love will get him the spoils. (McLean, p. 217)

This 'conspiracy' theory (for it requires that Owen involve the Brigstocks in his scheme) radically alters the picture. The view of Fleda it posits – implicit in the whole idea of the subjective adventure – as somewhat less than the sum of her self-expectations is, I think, intrinsically valid; what is much harder to accept is the promotion of Owen to such a responsible position *vis-à-vis* the plot of the novel. Making those 'quick transitions' that Fleda had observed isn't at all the same thing as the quick thinking coupled to action Owen would be exhibiting if his profession of love wasn't spontaneous. The conspiracy theory, moreover, demands that Owen should have a capacity for abstract reasoning and calculation that is not only nowhere apparent in the text but implicitly denied: 'there were lots of things, especially in people's minds, that a fellow didn't understand. Poor Owen went through life with a frank dread of people's minds'; and as we have seen, the concept of ulterior motive is completely beyond him.

It might be argued that the latter estimate of 'poor Owen's' capacities is merely Fleda's, and quite mistaken. If this were so, and appearances in Owen's case so deceptive, we must presuppose a level of plot which is not reflected in the narrative and is much lower than that on which James is accustomed to excite interest. If Fleda falls into a deliberate trap, then her subjective adventure becomes no more than an objective misadventure. The point of 'In the Cage' or *The Ambassadors* is not that the telegraphist and Strether are deliberately misled, but that, confusing appreciation with understanding, they totally mistake the nature of those they are dealing with. That is why they are interesting rather than merely pathetic. So it is with Fleda. The strongest objection to the conspiracy theory is that it is an interpretation which devalues James's lightness of touch, and replaces it with crude irony. If we take the tea-party in West Kensington at face-value, as displaying the protagonists' very different qualities of mind, it is a comic set-piece of such brilliance that any further interpretation of it seems redundant: to uncover what Owen is really up to by peering, as it were, under the tablecloth is to act rather in the manner of Mrs Brigstock, who now bursts into the room and sees in the sprawling tea-things and the biscuit Fleda has dropped 'a vivid picture of intimacy'.

Owen's declaration of love is not in itself so very improbable, if seen in the light of those 'quick transitions' we know him capable of. What *is* a little odd, though, is the manner of his making it. He begins on an authentic note, as he replies to a delicately phrased enquiry from Fleda that his affection for Mona 'seemed to go all to pot as this horrid struggle came on'. And the content of Owen's further remarks is plausible enough; but what we hear sounds increasingly like a recording made in Fleda's consciousness. Mona, he declares, 'made just the same smash' of their prospects and happiness 'as if she had kicked over that tea-table'. It is his way, and Mona's, to smash into things, but it is Fleda who expects them to do it; and hearing that Mona abuses her as 'a pretty girl' is also what she expects, and a reflection of the satisfaction and guilt – both exaggerated – she felt in Hyde Park. And what Fleda felt so strongly Owen didn't have then – 'a right to speak out' – is what he now declares that Mona 'has given [him] at last by her confounded behaviour'. Why 'at last'? Has he been waiting all along for Mona to put a foot wrong? *Fleda* certainly has.

'You ask me if I don't love her', Owen continues, 'and I suppose it's natural enough you should ...'; what *was* natural, however, for any third party to ask, in view of Mona's attachment to the spoils, was whether *she* really loved Owen. The question Fleda put later and with much greater caution – whether *he* loved Mona – was not natural, and to say gratuitously that it was sounds suspiciously like Fleda talking, not Owen.

It might therefore naturally be assumed that Owen's declaration is merely a further episode in the 'subjective adventure', were it not firmly authenticated by the narrative voice, which this time makes it clear that he is actually speaking; and, proceeding rapidly in his new lyrical vein, he is assuring Fleda that 'there's only one person on the whole earth' he 'really' loves when he is 'pulled up short' by (so Fleda assumes) the sound of approaching footsteps.

Yet the fact that he *is* interrupted suggests that the scene is still being scripted by Fleda; for every time her romance has seemed about to take off, Fleda herself has interrupted it, 'dashing' away, with the result that it never progresses beyond a certain point. Now, just as

Owen clutches her arm and asks her to guess the 'one person' he loves (and he has made it clear the answer isn't 'Mona'), she cuts him off; she sees the door about to open and breaks in with, 'Your mother!'

The juxtaposition of phrases cannot be accidental, though I don't think we need see it as the sign of a hidden story (Owen's Oedipal passion for his mother?).[9] I take this rather as James's little joke, and a joke furthermore against Fleda. For it is odd that, hearing footsteps on the stairs, she should assume 'the visitor would simply be Mrs Gereth.' Since the whole point of Mrs Gereth's dispatching Fleda to London was to facilitate her being alone with Owen, and since a maid is there to tell any visitor they *are* alone, Mrs Gereth is 'simply' the last person Fleda might have expected to burst in on them. Fleda, it seems, is fed this unthinkable thought in order that she should come up with 'Your mother!' at a place where it gives rise to a teasing ambiguity, just as the start–stop rhythm of her own story is becoming a little monotonous. It is as if, instead of getting *that* story firmly under way, Fleda were caught blowing a narrative bubble that bursts before our eyes.

Mrs Brigstock has come to beg Fleda to use her influence with Mrs Gereth and, taken aback to find Owen there, is doubly at a disadvantage. Fleda recognises, and feels sorry for, the limitations of a mind that 'strayed and bleated like an unbranded sheep'. She also recognises the opportunity to 'let herself go', which to Fleda means using social skills rather than sexual ones, or demonstrating to Owen that she can handle the situation with 'simplicity and tact'. But she lets herself go too far, answering for Owen 'as if she had been his wife', and even suggesting to the respectable Mrs Brigstock that she might regard Fleda as 'one of those bad women in a play':

> The remark was disastrous: Mrs Brigstock, on whom the grace of it was lost, evidently thought it singularly free. (121)

It is disastrous because Mrs Brigstock takes it as evidence of Fleda's being indeed a 'dangerous beauty', and departs forthwith to Ricks, where her telling his mother that Owen is ensnared will prompt Mrs Gereth to return the spoils to Poynton too soon. And disastrous because Fleda's remark leaves her not in the position of a free spirit who kicks over the conventions for love, nor even of the conventional hostess who thinks only in terms of *savoir-faire*, but of someone who – like Dr Sloper in *Washington Square* – can only be 'clever' at the expense of others.

That this is not quite the heroine's part is figured by Fleda's finding, after a characteristically prompt retreat, a new refuge with
Maggie and her husband. In 'the mean little house in the stupid
little town', the curate's fork drawing diagrams of drains on the
tablecloth grimly incises a lapse from the ideals of Poynton, leaving
Fleda adrift, in her sensibility and snobbery, somewhere between
the squalid and the sublime. 'Sublime' is what she hopes Owen is
being: not putting himself in the wrong. But she is 'sure' he will
write and when he does, makes a specious excuse for allowing him
to see her at Maggie's.

All the evidence of the text now suggests that Owen's feelings,
and his proposal of marriage, are genuine – in the sense that he
means what he says at the moment when he says it. 'I don't think I
can have *really* loved her, you know,' he tells Fleda serenely; she
remembers how recently he told her he '*really* loved' someone else,
and she laughs – which surprises him (if he didn't mean it, he might
have expected her to laugh). Now, making to Fleda the physical
advances he has made to Mona, the change in his situation seems to
him self-evident: 'Everything *is* different when I know you!' he tells
her. Basically his attitude is the same as when he told her he 'could
do' with Ricks: he simply has a ready appreciation of whatever is
thrust under his nose.

This then looks like the moment of truth, long anticipated: Fleda
reacts to Owen's proposal as calmly as if she had written the script
herself. But all at once she loses her nerve, panic-stricken when she
finds the narrative frames moving too fast, obliterating the unrealis-
tic picture of herself installed at Poynton with no sacrifice to virtue or
propriety. She tells Owen, 'you've been right and good, and it's the
only comfort, and you must go', to return only when Mona's written
word has stamped him legally a free man. The pain of her ethical
dilemma is nicely counterbalanced by Owen's finding her 'painfully
perverse'. His grasp is of the tangible and straightforward: his hand
on Fleda's wrist stops her backing away, and he utters what sounds
like a line from some intellectually unintimidating play: 'Do you
mean to tell me that I must marry a woman I hate?' At this, her
deliberately dry and sentenntious manner breaks down:

'... She must love you – how can she help it? *I* wouldn't give you
up!' said Fleda. ... The great thing is to keep faith. Where's a man
if he doesn't? If he doesn't he may be so cruel. So cruel, so cruel,
so cruel!' (135)

And she makes yet another dash for the stairs. It is the sort of scene Dr Sloper wanted to bring about but couldn't, because his daughter resisted his attempts to make drama out of her private sorrow. Preoccupied like the Doctor with her own romance, Fleda takes a similarly teleological view of events and now gives that view a similarly melodramatic colouring. For all that she expects to end up with Owen, his proposal alarms her: 'It was all too horribly soon', and she hates hanging on in the hope that Mona will drop out: 'it's like waiting for dead men's shoes!' Her father thought Catherine Sloper was waiting for *his* shoes, but from the moment she kept quiet about that, Catherine had the story in her power. Fleda, again like the Doctor, loses her grip on it. For, as she is about to discover, Mona is very much alive and kicking; and has, so to speak, put the patent-leather boot in.

6.

After Owen's departure Fleda waits to hear from him that he is free, sensing in the stillness Mona's 'magnificent dead weight'. The news of his release never comes. Instead there comes from Mrs Gereth a summons to London, where Fleda finds herself already incorporated all too literally into her friend's new story-line, which assumes she will have done 'what a healthy young woman must like'; she is told that Owen is 'sick with love' of her, and they are to be hustled off to the Continent in Mrs Gereth's charge: 'when once I get you abroad together — !'

At the cost of her seeming at such moments ineffably crude, it is Mrs Gereth's function in the novel to advertise certain realities of life, and in particular those belligerent and sexual impulses which in Fleda are repressed, in Owen unfocused and in Mona concealed and held in reserve. Yet she never loses her ability to make something impressive out of these raw materials. She describes to Fleda how Mrs Brigstock came to Ricks with the information that Owen was at Fleda's feet, begging her to intercede and stop Mona being 'killed'. 'If a cow should try to calculate, that's the kind of happy thought she'd have,' comments Mrs Gereth, and reveals to Fleda her own exquisite scheming with such satisfaction ('I had effaced myself like a saint') as to evoke Poynton itself, with Mrs Brigstock like some blundering beast trapped in its impersonal beauty.

'Of course I was delighted that Mona should be killed ...'. The interview between the two matrons seems in point of fact to have

been rather a decorous affair, but Mrs Gereth's account of it, drawing on the more extravagant reaches of her idiolect, has the kind of
narrative impact that is lacking in the sagging melodrama of the
previous chapter, for all its pressures of wrists and lips and dashes
upstairs. The difference is that between the art which imitates life
and the art which produces it.

Mrs Gereth has returned the spoils to Poynton. Why didn't she
wire Fleda before making her move? It doesn't seem to matter that
her action – one of the 'great fierce bounds and elisions' Fleda had
from the first observed in her handling of narrative – is inherently
implausible: 'Mrs Gereth stood there in all the glory of a great
stroke.' Dazzlingly, it obliterates a difficult old woman who has
repacked some crates with things that didn't belong to her, substituting for those sober facts a grand theatrical climax, the moment of
reversal and recognition. Compared to this, Fleda's attempt now
lamely to pick up her own story seems like her retrieval of the biscuit that caught Mrs Brigstock's eye on the floor in West Kensington
– the biscuit that was the spurious clue to a romance that wasn't the
real story.

Fleda has a spoilsport tendency always to be reading ahead of the
reader; and now persistently, almost methodically, she anticipates the
point where her hopes will be dashed. She wires Owen audaciously
at Waterbath but says as she sends the telegram that she is 'prepared
for the worst'; she implies that she 'did things' when she last saw him
that might make us tremble, but tells Mrs Gereth that Owen's love
hasn't made her happy: 'It's anguish – it was from the first; from the
first there was a bitterness and a dread …'. It is as if Fleda were
doomed to represent the spirit of anticlimax: even Mrs Gereth
appears at last to accept it. At any rate she doesn't argue when told
she has been quite mistaken about Fleda and Owen: 'You've only had
it from my own mouth that I care for *him*!' says Fleda. Which isn't of
course true: she had told Mrs Gereth that 'He's enough in love with
me for anything!'

Inconsistency is a fact of life, but here Fleda seems to make a
deliberate attempt to muddy the narrative stream. What is going on
here? Is Owen her puppet, the invention of her fantasy, or is she his?
Does he '*really* love' her or doesn't he? These are all questions left
glaringly unresolved, to puzzle readers and critics alike. Even
Owen's last communication, in which he asks Fleda to take from
Poynton 'a remembrance' ends in a tease: 'You won't refuse if you'll
simply think a little what it must be that makes me ask.' Fleda

thinks, but she is 'baffled'. Together she and Owen make a muddle in the novel as they did with the tea-table in West Kensington, when Fleda 'was aware she produced more confusion than symmetry', and for the same reason: because she tries to impose order on the random, vulgar element in life, now epitomised in Owen's having, apparently, drifted off into the Waterbath orbit.

The circumstances now call on Mrs Gereth's greater competence in straightening things out and assembling a coherent picture. 'If he's at Waterbath he doesn't care for you. If he cares for you he's not at Waterbath,' she observes bluntly. It is exactly the sort of simple distinction between Waterbath and salvation Fleda had happily endorsed when they first met, but now it earns her passionate rebuff:

> '... The tangle of life is much more intricate than you've ever, I think, felt it to be. You slash into it,' cried Fleda finely, 'with a great pair of shears; you nip at it as if you were one of the Fates! ...' (155)

This rather strikingly recalls that passage in the Preface to *The Spoils of Poynton* where James describes how he grasped the 'germ' of his novel in the story told him of a woman at odds with her son over some valuable furniture. When he had 'ten words' James silently cut his informant off: he had 'the perfectly workable little thing'; the rest of the anecdote was dismissed as 'clumsy Life again at her stupid work' (AN 121). Fleda opposes to Mrs Gereth's trenchant judgements and bold strokes her own habit of conscientious deliberation; but 'slashing into life' is the writer's privilege, and she is the more creative artist when she follows Mrs Gereth's lead. It was they who between them – and with very little to work with – invented Mona the monster. And if we compare Mona the monster with another Mona whom Fleda conjures up in ostensibly altruistic debate with Owen – Mona withdrawing from her engagement from 'a very high motive', Mona as exemplifying self-sacrifice, a Mona who is in fact an unconvincing replica of Fleda herself – we see again the difference between art that has vitality and a lifeless copy of it.

This is not to deny that James's novel leaves room for rational explanations of Mona's behaviour, or that it is Fleda's function to supply them. When she no longer has anything to gain by disingenuous approaches to Owen, she presents Mona altogether plausibly, as 'a person who's upset by failure and who blooms and expands with success'. Thoroughly unpleasant to Owen while the spoils were at Ricks, when 'the pressure was removed she came up again. ... her natural charm reasserted itself.' And yet, even as she takes the myth out of Mona, Fleda implicitly recognises her affinity with some impersonal force of nature, the latent energy that erupted in response to Mrs Gereth's challenge at Poynton, and which operates the dynamics of the novel far more effectively than Fleda's cautiously regulated stop–go mechanism. The 'massive maiden at Waterbath' has let herself go, and Owen can no more resist her 'natural charm' than a barrel going over Niagara: 'Before he could turn round he was married.' [10]

So Fleda loses Owen; and what is odd is how little she appears to mind, the extent to which her desire for him is sublimated in the vision of Poynton made whole again. This disconcerting equanimity is based on something more profound than simple satisfaction in Owen's having done right by Mona, a prospect which hadn't after all stopped Fleda from trying humiliatingly to get him back. Hers is the resignation of the religious, and as such it is very different from Mrs Gereth's. She who 'bumped' and 'prodded' more sensitive creatures ruthlessly has real cause to resent Fleda now. But with nothing to gain by aggression, Mrs Gereth has no more use for it. In one of those easy transitions from a kind of emblematic impregnability to physical susceptibility that Fleda (the 'object of desire' who never yielded to it) is incapable of, the proud chatelaine has become an exhausted old woman who leans on her friend for support; and it is she, not Fleda, who makes palpable in gesture and word the pleasing tenderness of their reconciliation, telling Fleda: 'I'm tired of *them*: I'm not tired of you.' By 'them' she means here the spoils; but she isn't so tired of them as to blot them from memory: she will come to speak of them as if they were errant children through whom she still clings to life, and a focus of the affection between herself and Fleda: 'We can always, as time goes on, talk of them together.' One has, as ever, the impression that to Mrs Gereth the spoils, when not for collection or redistribution are, more generally, for making an ado about – just as to James the despoiled Poynton meant not cataloguing the *objets*, but finding the human 'story in it'. Indeed, it isn't clear that by 'talking of them' Mrs Gereth doesn't refer to her real errant children, Owen and Mona, from whose renewed association she promptly pulls a new thread of drama: that Owen 'has ended by hating her and he hates her now more than ever ...'; that he won't live with his wife.

Fleda isn't reluctant – as one might expect – to discuss the mystery of Owen and Mona, and indeed takes 'satisfaction' in talking of them 'serenely and lucidly'; but she refuses ever again to talk about the spoils. 'The reconstituted splendour of Poynton ... the beauty that ... had safely crept to its home' is sacred to her – not a subject for conversation, but the object of self-effacing adoration, and source of the 'strange peace that had descended like a dream'. So Fleda muses at Maggie's, in that state of arrested animation which is her natural element and which she had found at Poynton before the irruption of the Brigstocks.

She is interrupted now by an invitation. If her husband was there to share Poynton, Mrs Gereth wants her friend there to 'bear' Ricks:

> 'It looks just like Waterbath; but, after all, we bore *that* together ... you'll at any rate be a bit of furniture. For that, a little, you know, I've always taken you – quite one of my best finds. So come if possible ...' (169)

Of course, when Fleda gets there, Ricks looks nothing like Waterbath. For Mrs Gereth has once more made it beautiful, this time with the effects of the maiden-aunt.

Fleda's admiration is extreme, but less extreme than the discrepancy evident to the reader between cause and effect. What she sees, after all, is no more than a few rooms nicely done up; but it makes a peculiar impact on her:

> The girl's heart gave a leap ... Mrs Gereth was all unwitting; she didn't in the least know what she had done. Therefore as Fleda could tell her, Fleda suddenly became the one who knew most. That counted for the moment as a splendid position; it almost made all the difference. Yet what contradicted it was the vivid presence of the artist's idea. (171)

Characteristically, Fleda introduces a confusing 'contradiction': her position, all too evidently, isn't as splendid, as vividly visible, as that of the artist. Yet *she* is the person called upon again to bear witness to the creative spirit – burning now with a purer flame. For what makes the *real* difference is that, this time, the exhibition of Mrs Gereth's talents hasn't made the place wrong for Fleda. On the contrary, Fleda sees more clearly than ever before that her place is where James saw it when he wrote in his Preface:

The thing is to lodge somewhere at the heart of one's complexity an irrepressible *appreciation* ... (AN 129)

At last Fleda feels herself safely lodged: her hold on the story is secured.

People said, it will be recalled, that she 'fastened like a leech on other people – people who had houses where something was to be picked up'. What Fleda now picks up at Ricks is

a voice so gentle, so human, so feminine ... the impression some-how of something dreamed and missed, something reduced, relinquished, resigned: the poetry, as it were, of something sensi-bly *gone* (172)

– and the story, according to her fantasy, of 'a great accepted pain'. Despite denying that this is *her* story ('I'm happy,' she tells Mrs Gereth, who is unimpressed), she feels at home with the shade of the maiden-aunt as she has never felt quite at ease anywhere: 'Poynton was too splendidly happy'; but 'there'll be a ghost or two' there now – ghosts which '*she* [Mona] won't see.'

Fleda's vision seems to imply superiority, putting her one up for example on Catherine Sloper, who doesn't recognise the artist in people or 'see' as those James endows with an 'intenser conscious-ness' see. But ghosts, like fantasies, be they or be they not 'real', are no use to the reader unless he or she actually sees or feels some-thing memorable at the point where apparition and imaginative construct intersect: the terrible recognition of 'The Jolly Corner', or the sombre unease of 'The Turn of the Screw'. At the beginning, Fleda was a vivid reflector of the comedy of taste; and at the end, even in the dimmer guise of one of Poynton's ghosts, we can see in her the attrition wrought by being too tasteful; but what is the ghost of Ricks? – merely the shadow without substance of Fleda's unfocused yearning for 'what might have been that never could have been' and of what she now perversely denies actually *was*. If Catherine Sloper, who also remains an old maid occupied with her needlework, comes out of it all rather better, that is because, hav-ing admitted to a broken heart, she simply turns her back on us, without our doubting that there *is* a real story where she has left her substantial imprint; whereas Fleda lingers on hugging in her lap a bundle of such limp satisfactions that the reader is inclined to share Mrs Gereth's irritation with her. The tapestries Fleda is making to hang on the walls of Ricks certainly suggest the way in which her story has battened, leech-like, on to that of Poynton.[11]

Some months after Owen's marriage, Fleda receives his letter from abroad, in which he asks her to go down to Poynton and take as a remembrance 'something of real value'. It is for Fleda not only an unambiguous sign of there having been something between them, but the chance to define her position in the story in the specific, emblematic terms in which the story works. Uncertain as she is of Owen's motivation, Fleda is certain of that, and of its value to her: whatever item she picks up in Owen's house, 'it should be one of the finest because it was in the finest he saw his symbol.'

Fleda's 'passion' for Owen is not extinguished: 'what had happened had made no difference' to it. Yet she finds a 'secret rapture' in having instead of Owen an object belonging to him. Tentatively – having little sense of relative values – he has suggested the Maltese cross, a rare little ivory crucifix; and were James as simplistically well-intentioned as Owen, he might have left Fleda with that potent symbol of self-sacrifice. But for her, it is emphasised, the choice is not self-evident:

> At bottom she inclined to the Maltese cross – with the added reason that he had named it. But she would look again and judge afresh; she would on the spot so handle and ponder that there shouldn't be the shade of a mistake. (180)

Fleda puts off the trip to Poynton: able to visualise the 'whole place', she spends weeks 'in a luxury of comparison and debate', happy to set aside her vast, vague ethical and emotional burdens for the pursuit of the specific thing that will give her most satisfaction. It is amusing – endearing, even – to visualise her so, fingering in her imagination tapestries, up-ending vases; and it brings her sharply into relief as the person who defines herself, and is ultimately defined, by the 'marks'. You can be catastrophically wrong in your choice of lover, but about your choice of souvenir there mustn't be *the shade of a mistake*. Given one last opportunity to experience that 'excited and concentrated feeling about something' which, James implied, justifies her central role, this is what Fleda makes of it.

The Poynton in which she does her mental rounds excludes Owen and also Mrs Gereth:

> for once at least, her possession was as complete as that of either of the others whom it had filled only with bitterness. (180)

Proof against the passage of time and the ravages of love and hatred, this is the Poynton in which Fleda first found herself – a place of refuge, a retreat from the 'tangle of life'. Her story had seemed arrested there before it began, and now it returns to that still point. Fleda has it all wrapped up, safely concluded, as she sets out on her journey: 'She pictured her return that evening with her trophy under her cloak': she holds Poynton complete and inviolate, as Poynton holds her.

7.

'Poynton's *gone*?'
... 'What can you call it, miss, if it ain't really saved?' (184)

The conflagration, often regarded as a judgement on the vanity of human desires and mere 'things', is less portentously interpreted as a ironic comment on Fleda's illusory constructions, the futility of salvage operations when there are no pieces to pick up.[12] But the manner of Poynton's going is also the positively reassuring mark of a proper narrative, substituting for Fleda's obliterated haven the safe confines of fiction. It is a flamboyant theatrical coup worthy of Mrs Gereth, exhibiting that apparently reckless energy which allies her to Mona Brigstock, and by virtue of which they have between them exercised control over the story. Now the very atmosphere, the gale and the 'wild rain' and unstoppable fire, is letting itself go – in accordance with that operative principle that Fleda distrusted and failed to take account of. Had she not stated at the beginning that the lovers wouldn't burn things up? But now they *have* – not, of course, by literally setting light to Poynton, but by having left, in their careless way, inadequate caretakers. Similarly inadequate fire-fighters, who in the station-master's words 'don't come up to a *reel* emergency', have done the rest.

Here, then, is a supreme instance of 'clumsy Life again at her stupid work', getting in the way of the story. But the story that is spoilt is Fleda's, not James's. 'Life', as he explained in his Preface, is 'all confusion and inclusion': that is, almost by definition, Waterbath, filled as it is with romping and 'the sweepings of bazaars'; and art, which is 'all discrimination and selection', is by the same token Poynton. But the writer must slash into the one in order to deploy it with what James called 'the sublime economy' of the other (AN 120).

And Mrs Gereth, who as we know can make a work of art out of the most unpromising materials, has done her improving on nature to remarkable effect: for she seems all along positively to have encouraged the spirit of Waterbath, which remains rampant in the pages of *Poynton*, overwhelming by the arbitrary move, the extravagant gesture, the element of vulgar surprise Fleda's pursuit of form and harmony, romping exuberantly away from her draft of the story, and perhaps from James's too: there are times indeed when Fleda's romance looks uncannily like Mona's projected winter garden, that excrescence on the face of Poynton the idea of which Fleda so deplored. It wouldn't have gone with the house: whereas Fleda's was to be, quintessentially, the story of how *she* went with the house, of her union with the aesthetic ideal. That is the story which has gone for good, like the furniture, with the house.

But will the winter garden survive, as an offshoot of vitality, a bubble barely able to contain the tangle of life, the breeding-ground of moral and psychological insight? Or is it an unfortunate extension of Fleda's Poynton, a barren retreat, a place not of life-in-art but of death-in-art, where even Mrs Gereth in the shape of a stuffed cockatoo has been finally silenced? It is certain only that after the fire the logic of the narrative must return Fleda to Ricks, the ultimate destination of her subjective adventure, where she will revel with the ghost of the maiden-aunt in 'the poetry of something sensibly *gone*' – a story, that is, of love and loss, but one which, when we come to compare it with *What Maisie Knew*, will seem strangely bloodless and attenuated, standing in much the same relation to the canvas of James's *Poynton* as the shadowy impressions of her infancy bore to Maisie's later experience of life. And if the '*reel* emergency' – the matter of life and death – is to make the connection between art and life, between Poynton's design for living and the livelier designs of Waterbath, then Fleda doesn't 'come up to it'. Unlike Mrs Gereth tossing their magazine after the Brigstocks, Fleda cannot launch a story; unlike Mona who caught it, she is never part of their game: she is all false starts, ineffectual feints, and lunges in directions that disappoint the reader. If, as James's Preface implies, Fleda was by 'understanding' to speak for the inarticulate spoils (AN 127–8), her voice is drowned by that of Waterbath, which speaks for *The Spoils of Poynton* as a television commercial might undertake to put across some highbrow message: simplifying, vulgarising certainly, but making that vital link between life and art. And Fleda meanwhile, a casualty of Waterbath indiscriminacy, is lumped together with the 'things', defined in relation to them, characterised ultimately by Mrs Gereth as 'a bit of furniture'.

The problem of *Poynton*, I have suggested, has to do with Fleda's position in relation to it; and that this position hasn't been quite what she at least intended is recognised by James in his Preface, where Fleda is qualified as a 'free spirit ... "successful" only through having remained free' (AN 129–30). For if Fleda *does* remain 'free', it is at the cost of remaining on the margin of the real story, able to admire the creative process but unable adequately to emulate it. 'You make things "compose" in spite of yourself,' she told Mrs Gereth, who 'didn't in the least know what she had done'. It is possible that James too was charmed by Fleda's sympathy for the artist and remained in ignorance of some of his best effects, as exemplified in Poynton seen not from Fleda's point of view but from Waterbath's, which places her idea of the real thing – her moral and aesthetic absolutism – in a more genial and accommodating perspective. Owen took Fleda, Mona took the magazine: the spirit of Waterbath, which we as readers might emulate, simply takes things, for profit or pleasure, as they come. At any rate, 'the handsome published puff of Fleda Vetch' which is James's Preface should not mislead us into seeing in Fleda a value extravagantly beyond that which Mrs Gereth puts on her: for the Preface itself, we must remember, was written in the service of a commercial endeavour.

5

What Maisie Knew

1.

What Maisie Farange knows is that she doesn't know her lessons. Shuttled between her divorced parents, Ida and Beale, her education is a haphazard affair, and proper schooling always has for her the attraction of the unattainable. As the prospect of it becomes increasingly remote, Maisie feels 'as if she were flattening her nose against the hard window-pane of the sweet-shop of knowledge'.

Her mother regards it as the governess's function to keep Maisie out of her life, and her father comes to regard it as Maisie's function to keep the governess in his. Pretty Miss Overmore follows her charge to Beale's bachelor establishment, where she will proclaim herself 'in a false position', because her real purpose in coming there is not to be with Maisie. The child observes that adults make a fuss about who is living under whose roof, or paying whom visits – her affectionate friend Miss Overmore doesn't, for example, care to receive Ida's emissary and second choice of governess, Mrs Wix. But Maisie herself no longer minds about her own abrupt switches of residence, because there is now someone in each house to pay attention to her. She concludes that: 'Parents had come to seem vague, but governesses were evidently to be trusted.'

Not to be trusted, though, as soon becomes plain, to teach Maisie geography, history or French. Mrs Wix's grasp of academic 'subjects' proves as weak as her emotional grip on Maisie is tight, while Miss Overmore goes off with Maisie's father to inspect a 'splendid school in Brighton' and returns married to him, with less time for lessons than ever. The new 'Mrs Beale' and her charge are 'left to gaze in united but helpless blankness at all Maisie was not learning'.

The low tone of her upbringing is evident, but James also conveys, more poignantly, the lowering atmosphere of Maisie's days, spent hanging about in the 'dead schoolroom', hanging over banisters to catch the sound of a doorbell or a rustle of silk, with – hanging over everything – the sense that her primary duty is to learn. It's not that Maisie is academically inclined, but that her needing to be taught is the basis of all the security she has known. She would really like to be taught by a man, because that would put her in the position of little girls 'of exalted status' who go to expensive schools. Conversely, she supposes that anyone who actually gives her lessons wouldn't be in Miss Overmore's false position. That's why it's natural, on hearing that her mother has 'picked up' a gentleman, for Maisie to wonder whether, when she next stays with Ida, this gentleman might not become her tutor.

Miss Overmore finds her question 'sweet'. Maisie's ingenuous remarks have long been a source of amusement to her adult entourage, and she is resigned to 'infallibly producing' an echo of laughter. The experience has taught her that

Everything had something behind it: life was like a long, long corridor with rows of closed doors. She had learned that at these doors it was wise not to knock – this seemed to produce from within such sounds of derision. (32–3)

Maisie appears not to know about sexual activity and its associated taboos (sexual attraction is something she can see all around her); and the idea that sex in this restricted sense is the 'something' behind everything which she is ignorant of is not only underpinned by the plot, which is constructed on a network of illicit couplings, but signalled by the brightest flashes of the narrator's wit: his coda, for instance, to the fact observed by Mrs Wix that Ida's necklines are cut remarkably low:

She was always in a fearful hurry, and the lower the bosom was cut the more it was to be gathered that she was wanted elsewhere. (70)

When Ida, wanted elsewhere, doesn't return to her relatively new husband, Maisie asks him if her mother is doing what she wants. 'Up to the hilt!' replies Sir Claude. The unconscious innuendo (for Sir Claude is never crude) demonstrates James's use of an easy irony to frame someone, place him or her at a distance from and at the mercy of the narrator. And if the device is reminiscent of *Washington Square*, Maisie like Catherine Sloper is at one further remove within the picture, not only because she doesn't understand irony, but because she feels uneasy with language in a way the other characters in both novels, eloquent or merely noisy in their different ways, are not. For Maisie and for Catherine, the question of opening one's mouth at all, except to stuff it with a cream bun, is problematic.

One thing Maisie has learnt is that frankness can be a mistake, that what you say can be twisted to reflect badly on you – like something her father once said to her about her mother which made her nurse, Moddle, very angry with him. Bearing insults from one camp to the other makes the child as vulnerable as if she were crossing a minefield, where Ida in particular, always menacing and unpredictable, is likely to erupt. It is for this reason that Maisie, especially in her mother's company, takes refuge in being 'stupid' – in not repeating, pretending not to understand, what she has seen and heard. A 'new feeling, the feeling of danger' is met by 'the idea of an inner self, or, in other words, of concealment'. Those adults who are more tolerant of Maisie's solecisms also exploit her 'stupidity'. 'It isn't as if you didn't already know everything, is it, love?' says Mrs Wix, and she is not referring to 'subjects'. Maisie is right instinctively to distrust language: for Mrs Wix's 'everything' stands precisely for the one thing that Maisie knows nothing about.

It's from such behaviour on the part of her mentors that she forms the idea of a knowledge that is fascinatingly central to everyone's experience except her own, and which despite their evasions they seem on the whole to want, even to expect her to possess. To find out what it is Maisie is obliged to keep asking questions (although in her anxiety not to cause offence she is often relieved not to get a straight answer); so that the growth of her inner self to be inferred from her silences is accompanied by more blatantly advertised epistemological investigations. In *Washington Square*, what Catherine ought to have known was set grimly in front of her like an unpalatable dish which, equally grimly, she turned her back on, with the result that, while we know what she felt, we never really do discover what, if anything, she learnt; but Maisie's story seems to offer a guarantee right from the title-page that we will find out what Maisie knew; and throughout it the words 'know' and 'knowledge' resound like drumbeats accompanying the child's march towards revelation, and rising, on the beach at Boulogne, in a splendid crescendo:

She judged that if her whole history, for Mrs Wix, had been the successive stages of her knowledge, so the very climax of the concatenation would, in the same view, be the stage at which the knowledge should overflow. As she was condemned to know more and more, how could it logically stop before she should know Most? It came to her in fact as they sat there on the sands that she was distinctly on the road to know Everything. She had not had governesses for nothing: what in the world had she ever done but learn and learn and learn? She looked at the pink sky with the placid foreboding that she should soon have learnt All. (208–9)

This passage is a conspicuous milestone on what might be called Maisie's low road to knowledge, where 'knowledge' has dubious overtones, and is attained with spurious certainty ('learning All' mimics Mrs Wix's 'knowing everything'). 'I ... despair', the narrator puts in, as she sits on the beach, 'of courting her noiseless mental footsteps...'; and it is these steps that trace on a parallel track – not always noiselessly, but certainly unencumbered with Mrs Wix's baggy rhetoric – Maisie's high road to knowledge. This is the private path of her inner development as she learns what she *really* needs to know – how to survive unharmed in a dangerous environment. What is her position in the world? Who are her 'real' parents, who cares for her, who pays for her? (Little girls at smart schools would know.) She has to learn to understand conversations in which the same word is used to mean different things and different words to mean the same thing, and to distinguish permissible from impermissible behaviour, while trying to make out if there is some fundamental basis of right and wrong on which everything rests.

It is by this high road to knowledge that Maisie will come to a deeper understanding of her situation. And her progress is analogous to that of the reader who, feeling along the way for reference-points in the plot, say, or in language, is trying to map out the framework of the story. But what if the frame suddenly shifts, or falls away altogether? Then the reader may feel as Maisie feels when made in the company of the maid to loiter on the corner of the street, conscious of irregularity but also of 'diversions': don't street-corners, like closed doors, hold out the promise of surprises? Behind Mrs Wix's notion of it there's a wider conception of knowledge, and the things behind the doors in the corridor, what Maisie doesn't know, are a figure of *all* that she is missing. The reader who wants to catch some sense of that will not assume that all doors are bedroom doors and all noises from within bedroom noises. That would be a crudely reductive reading, positively inviting 'sounds of derision'. One such reading is what we may call the social worker's casebook version of *What Maisie Knew*, according to which Maisie is the helpless victim of a milieu where she is exposed to trivial values and perhaps even physically at risk. From a small child held 'on knees violently jolted', her calves pinched 'till she shrieked', to 'a long-legged stick of a tomboy' taking chocolates and cake from a kind gentleman, to a smartly dressed little girl waiting for the same gentleman on a bench 'where you see the gold Virgin' is, some readers may suppose, but a short step.

To read Maisie's story in such terms, however, is to ignore entire dimensions of the narrative, which clearly reveal things as having a different slant – tilted as in 'some wild game of "going round"'. That is how Maisie sees herself clinging to Miss Overmore – being 'saved' by her, as her father puts it. 'Being saved', one of the key concepts in the story, tilts quite giddily, depending on whose point of view we take, and, slanted from Maisie's, the emphasis on the physical merely reflects the fact that for a child, life is most vividly apprehended in physical terms. Maisie notes how people look, how hard they hug her, what they give her to eat. Ida's proficiency at billiards may suggest that her daughter also gets slammed about and indeed her embrace feels to Maisie like smashing into 'a jeweller's shop-front', but there are other angles from which to view Ida's attributes – her mother's glamour and physical prowess are part of the very powerful impression Ida makes on the child. Having the body of a little girl makes Maisie potentially vulnerable, but the narrative slant towards the physical in the first part of the story tilts her into a dimension beyond the immediate concerns of her elders, and where she herself doesn't worry too much about what's happening behind the scenes, as long as she's kept in a jolly whirl. One can feel – one doesn't have to 'know' – why a restless, leggy child might find bounding about with Miss Overmore a welcome change from the schoolroom where Mrs Wix, who 'had not the spirit of adventure', 'took refuge on the firm ground of fiction, through which indeed there curled the blue river of truth.'

Mrs Wix 'knew swarms of stories':

> mostly those of the novels she had read ... They were all about love and beauty and countesses and wickedness. Her conversa-

tion was practically an endless narrative, a great garden of
romance, with sudden vistas into her own life and gushing foun-
tains of homeliness. (28–9)

That Mrs Wix's is a distorted vision is as plain as the 'straighteners',
or corrective glasses, on her nose: those vistas into her life, for
instance, afford Maisie no glimpse of Mr Wix ('dead for ages')
though they converge repeatedly on the figure of a small daughter,
Clara Matilda, who came to a premature end under the wheels of a
hansom in the Harrow Road. The searing effect of this tragedy, of
Mrs Wix's having been, 'with passion and anguish, a mother', is
what forges the initial bond between Maisie and her new governess:
'something in her voice at the end of an hour touched the little girl
in a spot that had never even yet been reached'; and she naturally
falls into a dutiful and affectionate filial role in return for Mrs Wix's
devotion, knowing to trust this 'greasy grey' old woman in the
instinctive way children cuddle a security blanket of the kind that
superior governesses like Miss Overmore think too shabby for their
nursery. Despite her alarming appearance, Mrs Wix makes Maisie
feel safe.
   It is, conversely, because of his beautiful appearance that Mrs Wix
puts her trust in Sir Claude. On the sole evidence of his photograph
Mrs Wix knows – without having ever met him and against all the
odds – that Ida's new husband is 'a perfect gentleman'. Perfect
gentlemen protect the 'distressed beauties' of Mrs Wix's mythology.
The reader knows why Sir Claude, bearer of gifts, brings not one but
two umbrellas to Mrs Wix in her garden. One is to protect himself
against the innuendo that rains down on him there. Suspecting Ida
of being about to 'bolt' – which would result in Mrs Wix's being separated from Maisie, Sir Claude and her livelihood – the old
governess puts to Sir Claude the idea that 'they should seek refuge'
in a *ménage à trois*: 'Any roof – over our heads – will do for us; but of
course for you it will have to be something really nice.' Sir Claude
takes cover in a glance at Maisie, in which she reads 'that the accom-
modation prescribed must loom to him pretty large.' But Mrs Wix,
thoroughly embattled, leaping the hurdles thrust in her way
('"bolting with *you*?" Sir Claude ejaculated'), ends triumphantly in
a mighty charge:

'...Take hold of *us* – take hold of *her*. Make her your duty – make
her your life: she'll repay you a thousandfold !' (84)

Mrs Wix's real refuge is her idea that Sir Claude and Maisie will save one another from bad influences (she wants him to stand for Parliament), and by so doing ground Mrs Wix firmly in a respectable position. But the river of truth that runs through this fiction makes a fairly obvious detour round the salient issue of Sir Claude's financial – not to say sexual – requirements. (Just what coin does she expect Maisie to repay him in?)

Maisie and Sir Claude, then, are substitutes for the dead daughter and husband, features in a wider landscape in which fiction is a surrogate for the life Mrs Wix never had. This makes her, at least from the social worker's point of view, somewhat of a compromise candidate for the job of rescuing Maisie, an unsatisfactory replacement for the 'good lady' who came forward to help do so on the second page of the book, but was instantly wiped off it. Mrs Wix is good for Maisie because she gives her security, but also bad for her because she confuses fact with fiction and her own interests with Maisie's. It is however so frequently the case in real life that a woman fulfils the maternal function in one respect and neglects it in another that one wonders why critics should trouble to debate, as they have, whether Mrs Wix is a good or a bad person.

Yet if argument, dissatisfied, focuses on her it is because there is a real difficulty here, and there always will be for critics who try to channel the truth through a fictional construct such as Mrs Wix. It is odd that this governess who gives Maisie the impression of having 'sidled and ducked' through life, who has even been heard to drop an 'h', should acquire 'a new tone' when she lands in France and starts telling Sir Claude in no uncertain terms how to deal with Maisie's maid and 'the scandal of [his] connexion' with Mrs Beale. Odder still when this oracle of rectitude is observed to give Sir Claude 'a great giggling insinuating naughty slap'. Oddest of all, perhaps, is finding the duffer who couldn't follow the instructions for children's board games understanding and entering with apparent ease into the sophisticated verbal and psychological games that are played at Boulogne. In short, the pieces of Mrs Wix don't come together into an entirely plausible whole.[1] She is like a pantomime dame, at once vulgar and splendid, and the two qualities can't be separated out: when one comes to the fore, it is still framed in the perspective of the other, as if seen by an adult over the shoulder of a small child who sits fascinated by the spectacle.

To say that its structure depends on the superimposition and interrelation of such different perspectives is not to reduce *What*

Maisie Knew merely to a conglomeration of theatrical effects and different viewpoints, though these are important features of James's technique. It is, rather, to point out that we are faced here with a multidimensional system of visual, narrative and linguistic frames which at certain points resists the reader's attempts to impose on it his or her own imaginative or logical constructs (just as certain facts of life will resist Maisie's attempts to do the same). As we have seen, to define Mrs Wix as 'good' doesn't quite fit the case; definition is perhaps more a matter of seeing how two frames relate. For example, in certain aspects Mrs Wix seems to replicate Ida, to be a manikin contained in that larger presence. But although Maisie, angled a certain way, can also be seen as a projection of Ida, she certainly isn't Mrs Wix in microcosm: they seldom operate within the same frame at all. Sometimes, the real picture seems to lie beyond the frame: the narrator indeed identifies the exact point where Maisie is bonded to Mrs Wix – the sense of safety – in Mrs Wix's 'tone, which in spite of caricature remained indescribable and inimitable' – that is, virtually outside the novelist's capacity or inclination to depict it. But then, at other times, the frames slide together, so that hot and bothered Mrs Wix becomes the focus of all the novel's warm concern for Maisie. And so on. The shifting frames can disclose where the spatial interacts with the temporal or the scenario with the narrative, or where what we see becomes what we 'know'.

For Maisie when she was little, the 'actual was the absolute, the present alone was vivid'; but as she grows older, her consciousness takes on extra dimensions where the framing process can take place. She is old enough, when Mrs Wix puts to Sir Claude her startling idea that the three of them might run away together, to feel 'with trepidation' that her fate is in the balance, but still young enough to be distracted by the phenomenon of Mrs Wix's 'coming out', or taking the boards:

> So the sharpened sense of spectatorship was the child's main support, the long habit, from the first, of seeing herself in discussion and finding in the fury of it – she had had a glimpse of the game of football – a sort of compensation for the doom of a peculiar passivity. It gave her often an odd air of being present at her history in as separate a manner as if she could only get at experience by flattening her nose against a pane of glass. (85)

Perhaps because it will find an echo later in the metaphor of 'the sweet-shop of knowledge', which in turn triggers an association with the theme of Maisie's exclusion from sexual knowledge, this passage may seem to provide a basis for interpreting her role in the novel as merely that of an exploited innocent, or untarnished mirror of her milieu. This view is all right as far as it goes – which is as far as Miss Overmore goes in finding Maisie's ingenuousness 'sweet': it does bring out an important aspect of the novel, which is that Maisie is *sexually* innocent. But it risks overlooking an equally important aspect, which is that Maisie is not a passive victim of her environment. (This aspect is in fact eventually picked up by Miss Overmore, and by Ida: they are the adults least overwhelmed by Maisie's sweetness, and are punished for it by its reflecting badly on them.) The figure of the pane of glass which so vividly conveys Maisie's sense of helplessness does not suggest that 'the doom of a peculiar passivity' is something to be accepted willingly. On the contrary, we may infer that Maisie is at this point feeling peculiarly frustrated. On the occasion of Sir Claude coming to tea when 'the ideas [for their joint salvation] were produced', it 'was extraordinary how the child's presence drew out their full strength'. If Maisie is a spectator of events, she is also a participator in them, with all the strength of a child's imagination. *What Maisie Knew* is the story of her struggle to escape from the helplessness of knowing and to transform her experience into what Maisie *wants*.[2]

2.

The danger feared by the good lady who intervened unsuccessfully to save Maisie was specifically that, used by her parents as a channel of verbal abuse, Maisie would be contaminated. '"Poor little monkey!" she at last exclaimed; and the words were an epitaph for the tomb of Maisie's childhood.' But the narrator promptly over-rides her concern, stating categorically at the outset that those in charge of Maisie's 'little unspotted soul' 'would be able to make nothing ill' of it. It's a reassurance that the story isn't going to be sordid. On the other hand, it is unlikely to be interesting if Maisie is merely a stainless container for the corrupting thing contained. And of course she isn't. The whole point is the interaction between Maisie and the baser elements that surround her. And when James comments in the Preface, 'I lose myself, truly, in appreciation of my theme in noting what she does by her "freshness" for appearances in themselves vulgar and empty enough', he doesn't mean that

Maisie is a refining influence in the way that Fleda Vetch aspired to be, but that Maisie has introduced interest, colour and excitement where intrinsically there was none, transforming appearances (as James further elaborates) into 'the stuff of poetry and tragedy and art' (AN 147). It's not a question of their making nothing ill of Maisie – of her remaining intact and unravaged like Fleda's ideal of Poynton, but of Maisie making something of them, as Mrs Gereth reconstructed Ricks with the materials to hand. And it's a process in which James, indiscriminately exploiting the lurid fascination of monkeys and mimicking, tombstones and tragedy (they are all, for Maisie, part of the same circus), is deeply implicated.[3]

Maisie peers into her experience of life as if it were not a sump of turpitude but a jewel box, which she picks over with a child's desire to emulate the grown-ups, and a child's susceptibility to the flashier pieces. Catherine Sloper, it will be remembered, with the same general instincts ended up looking like a sofa; but Maisie's paternal home offers no such model of solidity. Nor does her mother's, though when Maisie is first about to move there her nurse Moddle draws up a list of

> ever so many pleasures that she would enjoy at the other house. These promises ranged from 'a mother's fond love' to 'a nice poached egg to your tea', and took by the way the prospect of sitting up ever so late to see the lady in question dressed, in silks and velvets and diamonds and pearls, to go out ... (18)

Whereas Catherine Sloper's own, secret story (her greediness, Morris's love, her love of finery – a package of incongruous elements very much like those on Moddle's list) sits awkwardly on the margin of the narrator's elegant satire, from a certain point the story of Maisie seems to shape itself to the child's requirements, as if she had the privilege of selecting its component parts, and from a better catalogue than Moddle's. It all starts with the advent of Sir Claude, a self-confessed family man ('there *are* no family-women' he assures Mrs Beale). Ida's 'fond love' and poached egg are rapidly discarded in favour of Sir Claude's and his chocolate creams, and Maisie herself is the person who gets to go out with him, and a lovely new greatcoat to wear. Like her mother, who 'carried clothes, carried them as a train carries passengers', Maisie finds herself to be a dynamic force, somebody who gets things moving. If a little girl like her can draw a man like Sir Claude into her slipstream, she can carry the reader with her too, can become a heroine, as she will perceive her mother to be in other people's stories. Ida never lets herself get stuck in a position where she might appear marginal: when the points switch, she simply changes direction (a habit which nearly lands her in South Africa). It's small wonder then that Maisie believes she too can carry the story where she wants it to go. In this respect she is very different from Catherine, who can only stop the story by lying down in front of it.

The points switch for Maisie when Mrs Beale meets Maisie's new stepfather and finds in the child a pretext for getting to know him. 'What seems to have happened', she tells Sir Claude, 'is that she has brought you and me together.' It impresses Maisie as 'the happy truth'. Faced with the unfamiliar spectacle of these grown-ups who appear not only to like her but also each other, she too spots the possibility of a relation between them 'in connexion with herself'. Running from Sir Claude's embrace to Mrs Beale's, Maisie 'felt entrancingly the extension of the field of happiness'; and she *sees herself* as the bonding force in it.

Maisie's world is transformed because she brought her stepparents together; but what transforms her perception of that world is her assumption that she has a central and permanent place in their lives. 'How shall I ever leave you?' she demands of Sir Claude on relatively short acquaintance (adopting, we observe, the manner of one accustomed to doing the leaving, like her mother). Determined that they shall never be parted, and afraid that when she moves back to her father's they will be, she repeats Mrs Wix's wishful thinking as if it were gospel truth:

> 'He makes me his duty – he makes me his life,' Maisie set forth to her stepmother.
> 'Why that's what *I* want to do!' Mrs Beale, so anticipated, turned pink with astonishment.
> 'Well you can do it together. Then he'll *have* to come!' (100)

Mrs Beale is rightly astonished by this exhibition of an egotism as rampant as her own and even less discreet, while even Sir Claude seems fairly uneasy to find himself the object of converging strategies. 'All the same', he breathes, 'if you hadn't had the fatal gift of beauty——!'; and Maisie instantly assumes he refers to her, though it's in fact not clear that he didn't mean Mrs Beale. The child's fatal gift – if that's what it is – is to reflect the brighter side of things.

Mrs Beale, for example, acquires much-needed lustre from the shine Maisie has taken to her. For Maisie has no intention of excluding her:

> 'You're both very lovely; you can't get out of it!' – Maisie felt the need of carrying her point. 'And it's beautiful to see you side by side.' (102)

By openly approving their association Maisie plays into her step-parents' hands, yet they are playing into hers by suggesting a domestic arrangement more appealing to the child than Mrs Wix's alternative. First, Sir Claude and Mrs Beale mirror the most present-able aspect of her real parents (Ida and Beale are 'awfully good-looking'); second, since their ostensible common interest lies in Maisie's education, they are bound to assign to it an importance which Mrs Wix, with her weakness in 'subjects', cannot. It is Maisie who raises the question of her lessons, but Mrs Beale's enthusiasm for learning is revived in order to please Sir Claude, who seems genuinely concerned for Maisie's education. Classes with 'awfully smart children' (Maisie's ideal of respectability) never materialise, but courses of lectures at a public institution offer a cheaper alternative. And although Mrs Beale's self-interest is blatant (Sir Claude is to join them at the lectures), her educational initiative heralds a new dawn for Maisie, darkened only by her wondering whether she 'shouldn't be a low sneak in learning to be so happy without Mrs Wix'. The effect on her spirits when the 'dream of lectures' becomes a reality is described in one of the most exhilarating passages in the book. What's important is that doors should open; it doesn't really matter if what's behind them isn't so very exciting:

> The institution – there was a splendid one in a part of the town but little known to the child – became ... a thrilling place, and the walk to it from the station through Glower Street (a pronunciation for which Mrs Beale once laughed at her little friend) a pathway literally strewn with 'subjects'. Maisie imagined herself to pluck them as she went, though they thickened in the great grey rooms where the fountain of knowledge, in the form usually of a high voice that she took at first to be angry, plashed in the stillness of rows of faces thrust out like empty jugs. 'It *must* do us good – it's all so hideous,' Mrs Beale had immediately declared; manifesting a purity of resolution that made these occasions quite the most

harmonious of all the many on which the pair had pulled together. Maisie had certainly never, in such an association, felt so uplifted, and never above all been so carried off her feet, as at the moments of Mrs Beale's breathlessly re-entering the house and fairly shrieking upstairs to know if they should still be in time for a lecture. Her stepdaughter, all ready from the earliest hours, almost leaped over the banister to respond, and they dashed out together in quest of learning as hard as they often dashed back to release Mrs Beale for other preoccupations. (126)

Mrs Beale's principal preoccupation, to Maisie's disappointment, has failed to join them. It seems that Sir Claude doesn't find the same virtue as Mrs Beale, teeth gritted, finds in cut-price education, because he hasn't arranged for Maisie's piano-lessons either, on the grounds that 'the real thing, as he said, was shockingly dear, and that anything else was a waste of money.'

Mrs Beale has a different explanation for his absence at the lectures ('He says he doesn't want you mixed up'), from which Maisie gets her first inkling of something between her step-parents she doesn't know about. Nor does she want to know, as she assures Mrs Beale: 'Whatever it means I don't in the least mind *being* mixed.' This Maisie who doesn't want to know – as opposed to the Maisie who is assumed to 'know everything' – is the Maisie whom Mrs Wix will come to despair of as being thoroughly shifty, someone who will never stand still when Mrs Wix wants to pin a 'moral sense' on her. It's this shiftiness that lets the child mix herself up intricately in the schemes of her elders; and the more she 'knows' – that is, recognises awkward issues like money and sex and steers away from them, the more they value her in their scheme, in which the child's willing presence is like a guarantee of probity. It is, of course, a spurious probity (hence Sir Claude's scruples), and Maisie derives from it a spurious sense of her own importance. This is the real corruption of Maisie, and Mrs Wix contributes to it as much as anyone. Maisie thinks that a word from her will bring Sir Claude into line; she begins to assume she has the power to direct events, not realising – because she has no *real* knowledge of them – that forces like money and sex also have power and exert their pull on the story too. Indeed Maisie is just beginning to feel she is pulling things her way when two incidents disrupt the peaceful process of her education, jolting it into a different, less settled perspective.

Walking in Hyde Park with Sir Claude, Maisie meets her mother, supposedly playing billiards in Brussels, with her current lover, the Captain; and subsequently, out with Mrs Beale, she bumps into her father, supposedly at Cowes, with a woman who vanishes but whom Maisie meets later in an apartment to which her father, virtually abducting her, has brought her in a cab. Apart from this obvious symmetry, the two encounters resemble one another in that each strikes the reader as both arbitrary and contrived, as having that quality, described by James in another context, of being 'as queer as fiction, as farce' (*The Ambassadors*, p. 389). The first is introduced by Sir Claude's comparing, in improbably literary vein, Hyde Park to Shakespeare's Forest of Arden, himself to the banished duke, while Maisie is 'the artless wench', and 'Rosalind' is the distant female figure with swain who turns out to be Sir Claude's wife.

The second episode begins with Maisie's abrupt deposition in the apartment of 'the Countess', a miracle of luxury with palm trees and electric light, in which Maisie feels as though 'the Arabian Nights had quite closed round her.' The first episode turns to melodrama, the second is more like a scene from pantomime: the effect is to make a compelling spectacle of circumstances which would impress us as appalling yet essentially banal had Mrs Wix, for example, described them, but which appear quite different apprehended through a child's fascination with the rhetorical and flamboyant. Despite a persistent emphasis on the false and theatrical (and Maisie is faking it as much as anyone), James is doing something subtler here than, for example, Tolstoy does when he manipulates the point of view of his *ingénue* Natasha Rostova to show what he saw as the essential vacuity of the theatre.[4] James expands what he called in *Washington Square* the 'circle of our observations and sensations', where Tolstoy seeks to restrict it. The device of the play-within-the-play indulges Maisie's taste for the mystery and glamour of artificial forms, though it also lays her open, as she faces the footlights, to concomitant risks of panic and confusion. She experiences in the first little scene an intense private drama and enacts in the second a more public one; yet so expertly tailored is the production to the size of the heroine that we never lose touch with a child's sense of proportion. And while we can follow on the bottom (narrative) line the development of Maisie's maturing vision, the technique of the scenario encourages us to develop more flexible and intuitive ways of perception, a sensitivity to sight and sound, to echoes and reflections – which is how Maisie has learnt to learn.

Her father asks her if she won't come to America with him, hoping she will refuse, so that he can then repudiate her with a clear conscience. The Captain, in a desperate attempt to improvise conversation, asks her if she won't come back to Ida. Maisie fully understands that neither parent really wants her. Yet the Captain proves pleasant and reassuring; and Maisie, rather charmed, is anxious to respond with adult civility when suddenly he pierces her guard with a most unexpected tribute to Ida's virtues that concludes:

> 'My dear Maisie, your mother's an angel!'
> It was an almost unbelievable balm – it soothed so her impression of danger and pain. She sank back in her chair, she covered her face with her hands. 'Oh mother, mother, mother!' she sobbed. (117)

Like Mrs Wix – whom Maisie finds he strangely resembles – the Captain has tweaked Maisie's filial chord. She sees in his picture of an Ida who 'has had everything to suffer' a revelation of real sorrow; and, as Mrs Wix might, Maisie rapidly improvises a script that will take care of the distressed beauty and of her own heartfelt emotion: 'Say you love her, Mr Captain, say it, say it!' But the *jeune premier* fails to play his part convincingly:

> Mr Captain's blue eyes fixed themselves very hard: 'Of *course* I love her, damn it, you know!' (118)

and Maisie's moment of truth passes as if it were indeed only a fiction. Trotting cheerfully enough back to Sir Claude, she naturally doesn't tell him she had briefly contemplated living with the Captain and her mother; less naturally, she doesn't tell him anything at all, and positively enjoys his consequent irritation. Anger can be a bond, as the example of her parents has obviously taught her. So the episode which began with Sir Claude asking for Maisie, by way of the housemaid, 'the same as if you was a duchess' ends with her sense of her importance to him undiminished, and how disingenuous the 'artless wench' has become will be demonstrated in the apartment of the Countess. Maisie sees through Beale's clumsy overtures and histrionic poses: when she cries, 'Dear papa, I'll go with you anywhere', she is simply taking her cue from his hypocrisy and from the extravagant opulence of the room. She knows that pretending not to know (in this case, that her father really wants to be shot of her) can annoy her parents, and is therefore the policy best calculated to restore her to her step-parents. The narrator comments in this episode on 'the small strange pathos on the child's part of an innocence so saturated with knowledge and so directed to diplomacy'. The pathos is that all her guile only just makes Maisie a match for the brutal candour with which Beale plays on her fear of abandonment. His suggestion that one day Mrs Beale and Sir Claude won't need Maisie any more provokes a *cri de cœur* ('They *won't* chuck me!') which recalls her parting command to the Captain not to love Ida 'only for just a little'.

The arrival of 'the Countess' destroys Maisie's composure irretrievably. It's not just the intrinsic shock of the woman's dreadful appearance ('she might have been a clever frizzled poodle in a frill, or a dreadful human monkey in a spangled petticoat') but that this 'short fat wheedling whiskered person' with her friendly overtures fits nowhere into Maisie's mental construct of the world. Like an actress mastering a challenging piece who finds her lines suddenly translated into an unknown language, Maisie finds there to be 'something in the Countess that falsified everything'. She beats an undignified retreat home to her stepmother, obliged to accept money for the cab from her father's new mistress: Sir Claude's 'duchess' is a little girl again, struggling not to seem socially inept, while the Countess, behaving as a real countess might, assumes in the matter of who'll supply the cab-fare a crushing authority:

> 'Stepmothers *don't* pay! ... No stepmother ever paid in her life!' (149)

and there looms for an instant, behind this bedizened figure of corruption, the vaster, murkier issue of what an education can be if bought, like Maisie's, on the cheap – and who stands to gain by it.

3.

Returning to Mrs Beale's, Maisie is once more abducted – this time by Sir Claude, to Folkestone, to 'the sea which represented in breezy blueness and with a summer charm a crossing of more spaces than the Channel'. The space that is crossed unmistakably denotes the transition from the first part of the story to the second, which is properly Maisie's. It marks the end of the arbitrary displacements which brought Maisie face to face with one spectacle after another. From now on, it is her mental footsteps that determine the path she will take and the course of the story, from Maisie mystified to the mystery of Maisie.

At first, she only saw what was in front of her nose. Now Maisie sees in her experience a pattern, with the result that she can infer from the configuration of the bits that are there the shape of those that aren't. She realises that Sir Claude sometimes has to make himself scarce because he is Mrs Beale's lover and that there is 'a kind of natural divergence between lovers and little girls'.[5] All the same, it is Maisie who has bolted with him, is going abroad with him, is alone with him and the housemaid, not the most punctilious of chaperones. Here's a new version of her story, its masterplot perhaps – for it strikes Maisie as magically, even divinely inspired: she believes it 'a miracle' wrought by Mrs Wix, who miraculously stays away, and when Ida, the bad fairy, comes after them it's only to announce that she's leaving the country, leaving her child, leaving Sir Claude. 'I'm free – I'm free!' he exults as he kisses Maisie good-night. Next day he and she cross the Channel, bringing her to new, thrilling sights, sounds and tastes, to the 'great ecstasy of a larger impression of life', and to a hotel suite with a 'little white and gold salon which Maisie thought the loveliest place she had ever seen except perhaps the apartment of the Countess'.

It's all too good to be true, so that, from the first, Maisie tries by strenuous rationalisation to give the fairytale a solid basis, and the narrator effortlessly undermines her rationalisations by the irony of his commentary: 'Oh decidedly I shall never get you to believe the number of things that she saw and the number of secrets that she discovered!' Sir Claude always enjoyed expeditions of any kind with Maisie; but Maisie, sounding like one of the errant adults, considers this entirely plausible explanation of his initiative as a pretext for 'best carrying off' 'what was between them'. She lets herself believe that Mrs Beale is in love with Sir Claude rather than the other way around – a delicate adjustment to the plot which is given a heftier wrench by Mrs Wix, whose prompt arrival in Boulogne puts an end to Maisie's carefree happiness.

Determined to rescue Sir Claude from the 'fiend' Mrs Beale, Mrs Wix drives him, under the bombardment of her warnings and reproaches, back across the Channel to London, in order to break finally with his mistress. Waiting anxiously for his second coming, she and Maisie imagine Sir Claude 'completing' the 'sacrifice of Mrs Beale'; and yet Maisie finds she can't arrange her own feelings to fit this new development. The morality of the schoolroom tells her that plotting against her former companion is behaving like a 'low sneak', and added to this is the complication of Maisie's aesthetic sense, telling her that it isn't right to exclude 'the flower of the Overmores' from the beauty and romance she finds in Boulogne. 'Why shouldn't we be four?' she demands of Mrs Wix, latching on to what might be called her 'straight' plot, because it shows her grasp of reality – that lovers aren't properly paired with little girls, and that her step parents' illicit relationship brings benefits all round. Faced with Mrs Wix's objections, in which the word 'immorality' looms large, Maisie tries to rearrange the morality of the affair to accommodate it in her plot. Her father having dropped her for 'the Countess – and for her whiskers!' strikes Maisie as so wrong that it must be right to be caught up by Mrs Beale: 'She's beautiful and I love her! I love her and she's beautiful!' The sentiment has a dignified ring, but there's no more moral fervour in it than in that of a child at the pantomime, invited to boo the ogre, and Mrs Wix is canny enough to realise that she herself has had a close shave ('even if I haven't whiskers – have I? – I dare say there are other ways in which the Countess is a Venus to me!'): thwarted in her own plot, Maisie might opt for Mrs Beale's, and sacrifice Mrs Wix.

But the latter finds support unexpectedly in Mrs Beale, who, deserted in turn by *her* spouse and declaring herself 'free' too, precedes Sir Claude's return to Boulogne and by 'making love' to Mrs Wix seems to Maisie rather too easily to have secured her allegiance. Maisie is disconcerted by this development, which ought to have facilitated her straight plot: it begins to look ominously as though the two governesses were playing a different game from Maisie, in which she herself, the key piece, doesn't seem to have a place on the board. So the moment comes that Mrs Wix has dreaded, but it isn't Mrs Beale that Maisie has chucked her for: the child wants

'Him alone or nobody.'
'Not even *me*?' cried Mrs Wix.
Maisie looked at her a moment, then began to undress. 'Oh you're nobody!' (229)

It's the sort of behaviour that, when she was little, Sir Claude had warned Maisie against: 'we take care what we say. ... I think we must on the whole be rather nicer here than at your father's.' The gentlemanly Sir Claude is a product of civilisation, and he includes in the unpleasantness from which he wishes to preserve Maisie the disruptive effects of primitive emotion. For him, the good life is the quiet life – even if the decorum is only superficial. Mrs Wix, on the other hand, has only the most rudimentary notion of decorum – she seldom takes care what she says – and her sense of right and wrong and her passions come from a single, deep wellspring. To her, saving Maisie means saving her from Mrs Beale, and to this end, as they sit on their bench in Boulogne, like some old pelican she feeds Maisie with her own bleeding heart:

> 'Has it never occurred to you to be jealous of her?'
>   It never had in the least; yet the words were scarcely in the air before Maisie had jumped at them. She held them well, she looked at them hard ... 'Well, yes, since you ask me.' She debated, then continued: 'Lots of times!' (213)

Mrs Wix, who thinks she 'probably' made a fatal mistake in not being a Catholic, probably sees in the figure of the gilded Virgin on the church that presides over these confabulations a herald of that heavenly kingdom in which they'll all three 'live together without a cloud' with Maisie as the immaculate partner of Sir Claude. In the obverse scenario, Mrs Beale reigns as Queen of the Night, with Sir Claude a 'poor sunk slave' in sexual bondage. 'She won't mind in the least his hating her,' Mrs Wix embroiders enthusiastically. '... She'll only hate *us*.'

> 'Us?' the child faintly echoed.
> 'She'll hate *you*.'
> 'Me?' Why, I brought them together!' Maisie resentfully cried. (233)

There's something comic but also clumsily damaging in Mrs Wix's attempt to suppress with her account of events, in which all is 'hatred' and 'adoration', the more complex and interesting drafts that Maisie produces as she tries to combine the good and the beautiful into a workable design for living. Fleda Vetch similarly searched for a place to be right that would be harmonious

and stylish and safe, but failing to find it chose instead to promote
'the tangle of life'. Nothing is more evident in *What Maisie Knew*,
on the other hand, of the clarity of intention and effect, and the
sense of balance, epitomised by that 'complete work of art' which
is Poynton. Nothing is clearer to the reader than the significance
of those factors – psychological, social, financial (things that
Fleda's story-telling blurs) – which suggest that Maisie is the flaw
in her own 'straight' plot, the one piece that can never fit. Yet we
also see that, unlike Fleda's, Maisie's dreams are anchored to an
affection we have no reason to doubt, and that, if Fleda's are hot-
house fantasies, the story Maisie will construct is the natural,
unforced flowering of the phrases casually sown in the path of her
development:

> 'there *are* no family-women' … 'make her your life' … 'I'm free –
> I'm free!' … 'one got [what one wanted] – Mrs Beale always said
> *she* at all events always got it, or proposed to get it – by "making
> love" …' (53,84,173,222)

What Maisie wants is Sir Claude, and he wants Maisie, as a refuge
from the emotional scenes which 'every woman he looks at' makes.
The child knows better than to behave like that:

> 'Oh your friend here, dear Sir Claude, doesn't plead and shriek!'
>   He looked at her a moment. 'Never. Never. That's one, only
> one, but charming so far as it goes, of about a hundred things we
> love her for.' (183)

What's in it for Maisie, on her part, and for the reader, isn't merely a
question of sampling 'a hundred places for the best one to have tea'.
The mutual sympathy between the young man and the little girl
gives the novel something it would otherwise utterly lack: without
the air of enchantment, a little hazy at the edges, that is perfectly
conveyed in Sir Claude's encomium, about a hundred things we
might love Maisie for – her bright curiosity, her sophisticated airs,
her hearty appetite – would merely be charming so far as they go.
  Maisie and Sir Claude have a great deal in common,[6] including a
habit of duplicity developed under pressure, and an innate gentle-
ness. His 'characteristic kindness' becomes the basis of Maisie's
security, and all the more reason, when he does say something
unequivocal, to take him on trust:

'... I give you my word ... that I'll never, never, forsake you. Do you hear that, old fellow, and do you take it in? I'll stick to you through everything.'

Maisie did take it in ... she buried her head on his shoulder and cried without sound and without pain. (85)

Sir Claude's pledge defines for the child the line her story should take as effectively as if he'd clapped blinkers on her; and adult readers might well mistrust it as a *Leitfaden* threatening to lead into the insipidity of Mrs Wix's romances or into the crude ironies that Beale, for example, deals in (he will chuck her! – poor little monkey – and there's an end to it). If this is not the case – if we *do* feel that Sir Claude's relationship to Maisie is the lifeline of the novel, it is because Sir Claude is Maisie's line to life, her means of access to an existence that isn't circumscribed by other people's plots. He broadens her horizons, literally and figuratively; he lets her spirit expand in an atmosphere free of recrimination and retribution. That's why, when Ida materialises before the happy couple in Folkestone the reader shares Maisie's sense of shock:

the light of foreign travel was darkened at a stroke; she had a horrible sense that they were caught ... (157)

But we are shocked also because, reflected in the shape of her mother, who had herself been 'caught' in Hyde Park, Maisie's position is suddenly defined in different terms, terms that may even suggest there to be something positively unhealthy in her trip to the seaside. From the minute Maisie joins Sir Claude in his carriage outside her stepmother's house, she *is* caught, framed in a fictional perspective which gives their departure together the air of an elopement, emphasised by the further flight to France. There, the pressure rises steeply – not just the emotional pressure on Maisie when Mrs Wix and Mrs Beale turn up in hot pursuit, but the pressure on the novel itself to resolve the protagonists' conflicting plots. Can James *handle* it – the reader may wonder uneasily – other than through the shrieking safety-valve of Mrs Wix? Will it devolve into mere bathos or pathos, or into something more lurid, as Sir Claude becomes increasingly *louche* and self-conscious and so does the narrator, with his reference to 'the more than filial gaze of his intelligent little charge', which gives Sir Claude ' – poor plastic and dependent male – his issue'. Sir Claude's instinctive refuge from his

difficulties at this point is to make a sort of blind grab at Maisie.[7]
Her subsequent grab at him is part of a more conscious strategy of
escape:

> 'I'll go to him – I'll find him.' ... And with decision she quitted
> the room. (235)

4.

Maisie's seizure of the initiative, her departure in search of Sir
Claude, introduces twenty pages that constitute the climax, and the
vindication, of her masterplot: the most intense and dramatic
account of the experience of love in James's fiction. The shift of tone
in them is marked; so too is a shift in James's method whereby the
narrator is no longer perceptible as a distinct entity, Maisie no
longer the mirror he angles to catch a distorted picture of passing
events. Instead, what 'happens' is the construction of Maisie's
thoughts, the reflection of Maisie's vision.

What she sees 'in a flash' when Sir Claude returns to France in
Mrs Beale's wake is that 'he was different – more so than he knew or
designed.' His superficial qualities – the 'light fresh clothes' that
'gave him a certain radiance', 'his beautiful smiling eyes', 'his easy
brilliant French' – are observed by Maisie as opposed to absorbed
into the fabric of her mind, which is being rapidly overlaid with
different sorts of perceptions, differently expressed: 'he had rather
markedly not caused her to be called to him' – implying he's with
Mrs Beale – and when he denies it, Maisie has 'the faintest purest
coldest conviction that he wasn't telling the truth'. Later, 'she had
never seen him so nervous.'

Though these observations have a stiff adult poise (very different from the manner in which Mrs Wix might have expressed
them), what is going on is something more complex than a simple
framing process that makes Sir Claude, seen in a maturer perspective, suddenly appear a bit of a cad. That would be to take a narrowly reductive view, whereas what is emphasised here is
Maisie's expanding consciousness; not the easy if disagreeable
satisfaction of placing the villain, but Maisie's uneasy apprehension of things that cannot always be placed, or named – an apprehension now sharply focused when the child finds herself
confronted, not for the first time, by an apparently baffling

equation between fear and love. What gives Maisie 'a settled terror' isn't the bald fact of Sir Claude's being Mrs Beale's lover: the
'gulf' that she feels between herself and him isn't an abyss of
immorality, it is whatever has swallowed up the former terms of
their friendship, a profundity of emotion that can't be expressed
because language itself has changed its frame of reference. Sir
Claude tries to reassure her concerning Mrs Beale: 'We do nothing
in life but quarrel'; 'I want to see *you*'; 'I want to see you alone' –
words which are true but which don't reflect the particular truth
that Maisie wants to see. Being together at 'a nice little intimate
table as they had so often been in London', being offered the solid
consolation of rolls and coffee, can't prevent her from recognising
behind these 'restored familiarities' a fundamental change in their
relationship; only Sir Claude's unremitting sympathy, his insistence that it was 'really and truly' Maisie he wanted to see can –
momentarily – do that:

> She felt an instant as she used to feel when, in the back garden
> at her mother's, she took from him the highest push of a swing –
> high, high, high – that he had put there for her pleasure and that
> had finally broken down under the weight and extravagant
> patronage of the cook. 'Well, that's beautiful. But to see me, you
> mean, and go away again?' (243)

If Sir Claude's assurances can no longer offer the kind of certainty
Maisie and the reader want, metaphor sometimes 'really and truly'
can. Here, marking the high point of Maisie's emotional experience,
it marks it as real and true, as a love story conceived by the imagination of disaster that is always conscious of the drop beneath the
swing and the imminence of collapse.[8] For without that imagination, as the romance of Catherine Sloper makes plain, love stories, if
they survive at all, lead a repressed existence.

It's the imagination of disaster which, in another time of life
and another novel, brings us to the end of the journey taken by
that middle-aged innocent Lambert Strether, whose lunch in a
riverside restaurant in Paris is recorded with a similar appreciation of local colour as the breakfast in a quayside café where
Maisie remains sensible to the charm of unfamiliarity despite the
unfamiliarity of Sir Claude's charm and the disturbing impression
that 'she had never before seen him in the state in which he had
been given back.' It takes a long time for Strether to get to this

point *vis-à-vis* the object of *his* unfocused desires, because he
started too late to learn the language of evasion. Maisie, familiar
with that language from infancy, knows instinctively how to use it
in the game of capture and possession that is being played in
Boulogne. She holds out on Sir Claude when he tries to find out
from her which way Mrs Wix will jump, just as he hesitates to tell
her his plan, saying,

> '...You mustn't make *me* risk everything.' (244)

Maisie is 'struck with the force of this': it's her acknowledgement,
rather as a Brownie salute mimics adult reverences and rituals, that
in James's fiction the refusal to name is invested with all the power
of the things *not* named – fear, love, horror, death. Here it means that
Sir Claude's remark conveys not the languor of a reluctant ladies'
man but the intensity of a lover; and for the brief moment that he
lays his hand on Maisie's across the table, he and she are the fore-
runners of Kate Croy and Merton Densher, of Charlotte Stant and
Prince Amerigo, held together in a moment of peculiar intimacy
under the sign of the unnamed, at the very point where their paths
will take that natural divergence which Maisie had observed
between lovers and little girls.
   Observed in his naturally divergent state, Sir Claude doesn't
look or sound too good. With 'a mottled face and embarrassed but
supplicatory eyes', he must ask Maisie to make up 'a quite unconventional little household' with him and Mrs Beale. It is Maisie
who assumes the air of a realistic and responsible adult, as she
presses the claims of education ('Then who'll teach me?'); of
philanthropy – what will Mrs Wix live on? of the affections –
doesn't he understand how Mrs Wix *loves* him? (She is sufficiently
realistic nonetheless to see that 'if Mrs Wix clung, it was all the
more reason for shaking Mrs Wix off.')
   Yet at the critical moment, when Maisie's choice will settle her
fate and the direction of the novel, she feels 'the coldness of her
terror':

> it seemed to her that suddenly she knew, as she knew it about
> Sir Claude, what she was afraid of. She was afraid of herself. ...
> There was but one thing Maisie wished to do, and after an
> instant she expressed it. 'Have we got to go back to the hotel?'
> (250)

Maisie has learnt to say what she wants in terms of what she doesn't want. Making statements puts you in a spot, pins you down: Sir Claude doesn't suggest that 'they might for instance start off for Paris', though he looks to Maisie as if he would like to. Instead, he suggests a walk.

So they set off, dawdling, window-shopping, doing 'all the old things as if to try to get back all the old safety' – the safety, that is, of those days when life had the glamour, but also the simplicity, of a fairytale, when it was just a question of finding the right words and everything would fall into place, everyone be happy ever after. '[D]on't you remember? I brought you together!' cries Maisie nostalgically, but they aren't anxious to return to Mrs Beale at the hotel. Maisie walks the streets of Boulogne as if compelled against her will to read a novel for adults, retreating from the knowledge and the self-knowledge that lies at the end of that road: 'If they were afraid of themselves it was themselves they would find at the inn.'

Instead of the rush to review the options, even to close the case, heralded by the conversation in the café, what we have now is a slow-motion sequence from a silent film, as Maisie clutches Sir Claude's hand in a 'mute resistance to time'. Reflected in shop-windows and Maisie's consciousness, he is looking better now: his eyes 'seemed to propose to come straight off with him to Paris'. We don't hear his suggestion that they should go over to the station to meet the Paris papers, we see Maisie's 'mental picture of the stepfather and the pupil established in a little place in the South'; and his saying where the train standing near the bookstall is going – 'To Paris. Fancy!' – isn't a communication, it's a signal: 'She could fancy well enough.'

Bursting into speech again, Maisie asks Sir Claude to take her to Paris. It's a natural enough request from one with Maisie's sense of style, one who felt from the moment of her arrival in France that 'her vocation was to see the world', and who has been told that 'there *are* no family-women', that Sir Claude is 'free' and must 'make Maisie his life'. But Sir Claude hesitates – an equally natural reaction, as the reader can appreciate. What would a young bachelor *do* in Paris with a little girl, without money, without a maid or either of her governesses? It's probably the thought of the noise those two ladies would make when they caught up with him that makes him blench. But Maisie doesn't see it like that:

> conscious of being more frightened than she had ever been in her life … she seemed to see her own whiteness as in a glass. Then she

knew that what she saw was Sir Claude's whiteness: he was as frightened as herself. (254)

The one-sided intensity of this confrontation – quite *un*natural in the circumstances – has a parallel earlier in the story, when Maisie, meeting her mother for the last time in the hotel garden at Folkestone, invokes the name of the Captain, who, she fondly believes, is going to take care of Ida as Sir Claude is going to take care of her. When Ida is dismissive of the Captain – 'the biggest cad in London!' – it provokes Maisie to a singular display of emotion:

'Well, he was kind about you then; he *was*, and it made me like him. He said things – they were beautiful, they were, they were!' She was almost capable of the violence of forcing this home, for even in the midst of her surge of passion – of which in fact it was a part – there rose in her a fear, a pain, a vision ominous, precocious, of what it might mean for her mother's fate to have forfeited such a loyalty as that. There was literally an instant when Maisie fully saw – saw madness and desolation, saw ruin and darkness and death. (169)

Ida could but take a dim view of Maisie's excitement, for what the daughter saw didn't reflect any real experience of the mother's (Ida at first could hardly recall who the Captain was). What Maisie 'fully saw' in her mother's fate, and 'knew' that she saw in Sir Claude's white face is her own fear, and passion, and fear of her passion; and it is the completeness, the certainty, of her vision that links the two episodes. For Maisie, seeing is believing; and if for the reader believing is seeing – if one doesn't dismiss what she sees as childish fantasy, it's perhaps because in James's fiction what's real often flashes out from just a sudden shift in perspective, or violent twist such as Maisie gives the narrative here, forcing it to reflect her own premonition of love and the loss of it. The fact that it *is* a premonition – a 'vision ominous' – indeed suggests that there is a 'real' end to her story, and Maisie already knows what it is.

The moment exemplifies how we are offered a choice: to draw on our extraneous knowledge of life and other novels to reconstruct *What Maisie Knew* retrospectively from the point where she will lose Sir Claude (we knew it all along); or not to seek reality beyond the distorted yet intensified images of Maisie's imagination (this is all we know, and it's all we need to know). Most readers will take up both options simultaneously, which isn't surprising, since to know the same old thing will happen and yet want to extract the last idiosyncratic thrill from seeing it happen is almost to define the voyeuristic pleasure excited by works of fiction. *The Ambassadors* – James's own favourite among his novels – is a case in point.

Its hero, author of a notoriously naïve 'straight' plot, is fated to stumble across a story-line he wasn't following but the reader was. Whether Lambert Strether, the editor of a magazine, is covertly running his own masterplot is a matter of debate, but his position at the intersection of two narratives, one commonplace, the other a thing charged by his imagination to the point of explosion, is certainly Maisie's as she stands on the station platform. The train that took Strether out of Paris led him 'as if by appointment' to an inexorable deadline, to the revelation that satisfies the reader's expectations and brings down the whole edifice of illusion that Strether has constructed in the 'vast bright Babylon', the enchanted playground of his innocence where the good and the beautiful were one and the same. Paris – 'Well, isn't that the *real* thing,' Maisie had asked Sir Claude, 'the thing that when one *does* come abroad——?' Maisie can't but see the train that will take her in to Paris as a direct line back to the never-never land she once shared with Sir Claude, where there was never any question of finding oneself, or facing a decision, or reaching the last page of the story. But Sir Claude knows that the idyll has gone as far as it can go; and his dilemma is also James's: from here, the story can only become boringly repetitive (Maisie discovering Paris as she did Boulogne), or more impossibly lurid than what Strether saw on his day-trip to the country. (Put Maisie and Sir Claude in a boat together, and all you'd get would be some inane splashing about.) The scene is set, then, for a final conflagration, as Strether's imagination of disaster might conceive it, or, taking a more prosaic view, for a tidy finish to the novel. And Maisie wants out. Wasn't it her mother who said 'I must go to that new place'? – her mother who is always sweeping past, rushing away, leaving few tracks in the novel except for the example of her dynamism and a rhetorical leave-taking of Maisie that raises getting out of difficulties to an art form. Maisie is her mother's daughter, after all. In a sequence as odd and intense as a dream, Maisie suddenly finds she has the power of utterance, she understands and speaks French, she asks the porter to get them tickets:

'*Prenny, prenny. Oh prenny!*' (254)

But the last magic doesn't work. The porter wants her money, Sir Claude wants her decision; and as the train moves away, perhaps the reader hears the 'faint receding whistle' of that other train that Strether didn't catch, the train that was his metaphor for the life he hadn't led, the life which takes us out of other people's stories on a journey which, like Maisie's eager question – ' isn't that the *real* thing ...?' – doesn't have an ending. Her mother had once said: 'there are plenty of trains', but there was only one train for Strether, and there is only one for Maisie and she has missed it:

> She had had a real fright but had fallen back to earth. The odd thing was that in her fall her fear too had been dashed down and broken. It was gone. (255)

The swing has collapsed that made such heart-stopping flights. Maisie remains merely a disappointed little girl standing on the platform with an armful of reading matter, the pink and yellow novels which Sir Claude had told her were the 'natural divisions' of literature in this foreign country 'for the young and for the old'.

5.

On a page suddenly washed clear of excitement and passion, Maisie now reduces the problem to simple terms: she will abandon Mrs Wix if Sir Claude will abandon Mrs Beale. This solution has the elegance Maisie is looking for, but its inadequacy is promptly demonstrated when they do return to the hotel by the child's reaction to the evidence of Mrs Wix's impending departure. In the Maisie who says of Mrs Wix 'I'll let her go', and then at the mere sight of her battered old box insists, 'I must see her – I must see her', we see, precisely, reflected 'out of the confusion of life' (as James puts it in his Preface) the two sides of 'that bright hard medal, of so strange an alloy, one face of which is somebody's right and ease and the other somebody's pain and wrong' (AN 143). And we can also see that Maisie perceives how her altogether decent, respectable feeling for Mrs Wix gives her leverage with Sir Claude, enabling her to make a bargain with him remarkably tough for one so generally amenable: if he will now go and make a final break with Mrs Beale, she herself will go up into the town and wait till Mrs Wix takes the boat without her. 'I won't even bid her good-bye … I'll sit on that bench where you see the gold Virgin.'[9]

It is as if Maisie herself were dangled before us like James's 'bright, hard medal' – and who is to say of the alloy of which she is composed which is the baser element, her love for Sir Claude or for Mrs Wix? Some – Beale's friends, for instance, those by whom she was 'handled, pulled hither and thither and kissed' and pinched till she shrieked – may regard Maisie's proposition as that of a brazen hussy; others may see in it a sort of saving grace, a fastidious turning away from the squalid row the reader is confidently expecting on their return to the inn. Maisie is in for a dénouement as enjoyably full of shoving and shrieking as her father's drawing-room; and her distaste for it is a mark of the gap that has opened between her story and those of the grown-ups.

Mrs Wix makes it happen, Mrs Wix who on the point of departure offers Maisie 'another chance' to come away with her on the boat. Maisie asks Sir Claude if he will come too, 'as if she had not already seen that she should have to give him up. It was the last flare of her dream.' Her attitude to what follows is that of a weary participant in meaningless adult games. Across and above her, Mrs Beale and Mrs Wix enact a hectic charade, the one representing injured middle-class motherhood, the other divine authority, and producing between them merely a poor impersonation of Ida, who seemed effortlessly to combine these roles but didn't stay to be examined in either. To Maisie now, glamorous Mrs Beale appears compromised and vulgar, while magisterial Mrs Wix is simply baffling:

> '… Have you lost it again?'
>
> Maisie surveyed – for the idea of a describable loss – the immensity of space. Then she replied lamely enough: 'I feel as if I had lost everything.' (260)

Undismayed by this rejoinder, Mrs Wix pushes the issue of Maisie's lost moral sense, as if by reiterated pressure on that particular point the novel, like a fruit-machine, might suddenly yield up its treasures. In her dogged pursuit of Maisie's soul she clearly prefigures that other unnamed governess, at Bly, who also has cause to wonder what her little charge knows, and whose anxiety is perfectly expressed in Mrs Wix's accusation to Maisie: 'You were *with* them – in their connexion!' Had Maisie's story been told by Mrs Wix, it might well have become an anodyne version of 'The Turn of the

Screw', a tale of the struggle between good and evil, with trappings of Gothic horror. But what is most shocking and disturbing in that tale as it is told by Miles and Flora's governess is not the existence of the malevolent spirits as such, but the idea of the actual, scandalous physical connection between Miss Jessel and Peter Quint, and the idea of the children's innocent flesh in contact with that pollution; and by far the most horrific scene in the book is the last, when the governess clutches Miles 'with passion' and is left holding a dead body – not the least of the horror being the discrepancy between her graceful description and the reader's impression of something limp and inert.

In rather the same way James expresses the essence of Maisie's vulnerability in all the grasping and clutching to bosoms that takes place in the gilt salon, and its pathos in her physical reaction:

> as if she were sinking with a slip from a foothold, her arms made a short jerk. What this jerk represented was the spasm within her of something still deeper than a moral sense. She looked at her examiner; she looked at the visitors; she felt the rising of the tears she had kept down at the station. They had nothing – no distinctly nothing – to do with her moral sense. (261)

What's shocking and disturbing here is not the fate of the latter entity, 'nipped in the bud' as Mrs Wix puts it, 'killed when it had begun to live', but the image of resilient, warmhearted impetuous Maisie stultified and repressed. The effect is similar to that of the death of Miles. This is not the place to pursue the parallels between two women adept at telling stories and who use children to compensate for emotional or sexual deprivation; but it is just perhaps worth noting that if 'The Turn of the Screw' was to make evident a connection between being possessed by another and death, there is a less evident but curious connection (curious because unintentional echoes are very rare in James) between the facts that Mrs Wix 'touched the little girl in a spot that had never even yet been reached' and – a few lines further on – that Mrs Wix 'had had a little girl quite of her own, and the little girl had been killed on the spot'.

The governesses' tale is one of love and death, but the knight's tale[10] ends on a very different note, that deliberately puts Maisie out of reach of primitive emotions and grabbing hands. 'I've not killed anything.' Sir Claude refutes Mrs Wix's accusations:

'on the contrary, I think I've produced life. I don't know what to call it – I haven't even known how decently to deal with it, to approach it; but, whatever it is, it's the most beautiful thing I've ever met – it's exquisite, it's sacred.' (261)

As if indicating to a reader more sophisticated than himself the true significance of things, Sir Claude holds up for our admiration Maisie the ineffable who always, if unknowingly, finds the pulse of the story, and who has finally exhibited something 'exquisite' (virtue? charity? fortitude?) in refusing to give up Mrs Wix.

This is of course not how it really was, as Maisie is quick to point out. She *had* agreed to give up Mrs Wix, but only to force Sir Claude to give up Mrs Beale: it wasn't, as Sir Claude is now implying, evidence of a superior morality, it was simply the necessary term in a hard bargain. But Sir Claude, always the perfect gentleman, and 'recovering himself rapidly on the basis of this fine appreciation' of Maisie, behaves during this final scene with the greatest possible consideration to everybody. Even when he tells Mrs Beale, 'She hates you – she hates you', it's as if he only wanted to say what we had all along hoped Maisie would say herself, in order to relieve the child of an uncomfortable burden. Nevertheless, it's a feeble effort on his part to reduce to three blunt words all the complexity of Maisie's response to Mrs Beale: rather like Maisie offering 'I'd *kill* her!' as a sop to Mrs Wix's view of what that response should be. On both occasions, it's a case of finding a quick exit from a tricky corner; for Sir Claude, according to the narrator,

> was out of it now, or wanted to be; he knew the worst and had accepted it: what now concerned him was to prevent, to dissipate vulgarities. (264)

'The worst' might mean the separation from Maisie, or it might mean Mrs Beale's shortcomings, or both; but if the worst for him is what's best for the child, Sir Claude is promoting it. 'She hates you' removes Maisie from any risk of contamination by her stepmother, who seems to be emerging as the villain of the piece, while Sir Claude emerges as protector of the innocent child *and* of the fallen woman, heroically sacrificing his interest in the former, heroically sacrificed to the interests of the latter. But 'the worst' for him isn't all that bad: he's free at least of importunate requests to take the Paris train – free, too, to leave Mrs Beale at any point, since without the pretext of making a family for Maisie she will lose her most solid claim on him.

No wonder Sir Claude wants out, for at this point he comes out of the story wonderfully well. 'We *can't* work her in,' he declares ('quite exuberantly') of Maisie. 'It's perfectly true – she's unique. We're not good enough – oh no!' Sir Claude's tale can have no other hero than Maisie (and it's one of the things we love *him* for); yet his cricket-watching, bun-munching 'Maisie-boy' ends up in a 'beautiful' and 'sacred' story which is not altogether our heroine's. It tells nothing of Maisie fascinated by the foreign and the exotic, by the Captain and the Countess and the Countess's gilded monkey-cage; it doesn't speak of Maisie pale with passion for Sir Claude, or of the 'madness and desolation ... ruin and darkness and death' that she saw in her mother's future. These are things Sir Claude wouldn't need, or want, to read about; and his final solution, that Maisie shan't live with nasty Mrs Beale, that the good old nurse shall look after her, that her parents will provide the cash, is as simple and salubrious as a bedtime story. Perhaps it isn't good enough for Maisie, or perhaps she's too bad for it. At any rate, it excludes her – 'We *can't* work her in' – from what wasn't a 'we' till *she* brought them together.

'You're free – you're free,' says Sir Claude theatrically, upon which Mrs Beale shoves the child into the centre of the room – 'the cynosure of every eye and not knowing which way to turn'. Maisie recognises that the stage is set for the high point of her personal drama: 'here at last was the moment she had most to reckon with', the moment of confrontation with Mrs Beale; and the reader too is encouraged to recognise it, as the moment where on a deeper level the novel's central theme will be resolved:

> Somehow, now that it was there, the great moment was not so bad. What helped the child was that she knew what she wanted. All her learning and learning had made her at last learn that ... (263)

The child who doesn't know what the grown-ups know now becomes in herself the object of intriguing speculation, holding our attention more closely than she could as a participant in a mere melodrama. For we aren't told, in so many words, exactly what Maisie wants; we can only try to infer it from what she does. She puts Mrs Beale a question: 'Will you give *him* up? Will you?' Why does she ask that, having already accepted that she can't have Sir Claude herself? Her question doesn't quite convey the same anxiety as her question to the Captain, who she feared *would* give Ida up. Does she want Mrs Beale to promise she won't leave Sir Claude, as Maisie is leaving him? Or has she found where she stands with regard to the moral sense? The only certainty is that when she reiterates the question Maisie provokes a big row in which Mrs Wix is able to give the moral issues a thorough airing, and Mrs Beale, reduced to yelling abuse, comes off so badly that one can't help observing how effectively 'all her learning and learning' (the example perhaps of her pretty governess 'making love' to her father and Sir Claude) has taught Maisie to exert pressure on a person's weakest spot. '*Do* you hate me, dearest?' asks Mrs Beale, who is reduced almost to tears (she cares, evidently, what Sir Claude thinks of her). Maisie looks at her 'with new eyes'; and puts her question a third time: 'Will you give him up?'

It is possible, then, that Maisie wants Mrs Beale to stick with Sir Claude (since she too after all loves him), though most readers will assume that Maisie wants her permanently removed from Sir Claude's environment (because she's bad, or because she's Maisie's rival). Sir Claude, on the other hand, states his position quite unambiguously. It is to Mrs Beale now that he makes the pledge he once made to Maisie. He hasn't forsaken her, and

'... I don't mind giving you my word that I never never will. There!' he dauntlessly exclaimed.

'He can't!' Mrs Wix tragically commented. (267)

It isn't tragedy, of course; not even for Mrs Beale, who remains 'erect and alive', though not popular with anybody. It's a burlesque performance which barely attempts to conceal that this is a triumph of the commonsense view: *we knew* Maisie couldn't keep Sir Claude; *we knew* he'd choose the woman rather than the little girl ('stepmothers don't pay'). It's as if – together with Maisie and unable to *see* – we had been listening to those intriguing noises behind the closed door in the corridor, which now turn out to be merely the echo of a long-running serial for adults, repeated all down the line. It's actually Mrs Wix who points out in the tone of an experienced viewer-voyeur that Sir Claude hasn't, in spite of everything, given Mrs Beale up. She had already explained to Maisie that the wonderful white-and-gold salon 'isn't ours now'.

Maisie's fairytale is over. With no longer any place for her in Boulogne, or part for her in the plot, she knows when to go; and the clean break she now makes with Sir Claude is performed with a dignity not easily distinguishable from virtue. Yet there's no trace in Maisie of the self-conscious altruism that Lambert Strether evinces in similar circumstances, of his bleak satisfaction 'not, out of the whole affair, to have got anything for myself'. For whereas Strether leaves still giving us to understand that his position always was that of a spectator, Maisie, when the chips are down, reveals the size of her stake:

'I love Sir Claude. I love *him*.' (265)

She knows that much then – but everybody else knows it too: she need hardly state it, and only says the words because the situation seems to demand them. And the way Sir Claude twists them neatly against Mrs Beale ('She hates you') is one more indication that speech is dangerous, that Maisie had better say nothing, to prevent what she says becoming part of someone else's story, like the 'beautiful things' Maisie heard the Captain say about her mother, which might be the beautiful things she heard Sir Claude say to her, and heard him say, finally, to Mrs Beale. The best story for Maisie was the story of the time before Sir Claude needed to say beautiful things to her, when he and Maisie could jump on a bus to the park and do things that didn't ask to be talked about. And perhaps what Maisie really wants is not so much to preserve Sir Claude from the contamination of Mrs Beale as to preserve her love story from the contamination of the predictable. To be the vessel of purity, not scoured like Strether by ascetic resolve, but holding intact within itself the precious fiction – to be that, to have that and be able to get away with it before it comes to pieces, is surely the freedom that Sir Claude clumsily offers Maisie. He seems to understand the urgency of her 'Shan't we lose the boat?' Mrs Wix appears to be in no such hurry. The fuss and the scandal were *her* story, after all. Indeed, to square the Mrs Wix who virtually beckoned Maisie into the story with the Mrs Wix who escorts her officiously out of it is one of many adjustments the reader is forced rapidly to make to bring the past and the future into some sort of coherent picture as Mrs Wix and her companion are hustled away across the gangplank. What will become of Maisie now?

There is a view that it's as well that Maisie should enter adolescence under Mrs Wix's 'respectable tutelage'[11] – a view that appears to find in some conception of Mrs Wix's character the 'sense of support' that Maisie found in her, 'like a breast-high banister in a place of "drops", that would never give way'. But what we know of Mrs Wix's tutelage, which hasn't been a conspicuous success either morally or academically, doesn't seem to promise any more for Maisie – as other critics have observed – than an existence of genteel poverty, limited physically, intellectually and emotionally. Even fishing about rather desperately like Maisie's nurse for the elements of a hypothetical future, we can't get much further than Moddle's 'poached egg' (probably), 'a mother's fond love' (certainly): dead Clara Matilda's shoes in place of Ida's 'silks and velvets and diamonds and pearls'.

'It *must* do us good – it's all so hideous' Mrs Beale might have said of this prospect, as she said it of the lectures they attended during the brief period consecrated to educating Maisie. But the child had responded differently – had 'almost leaped over the banisters' to escape to the great world beyond the schoolroom; and how will she escape now, if Mrs Wix is a banister that will never give way? Safe on board with Mrs Wix, what is Maisie being saved *for*? To see her 'surrounded by the quiet sea' is to see her cut off from a great range and depth of experience: 'the immensity of space' in which, back at the hotel, when Mrs Wix had tried to nail her, Maisie had searched 'for a describable loss'. Exactly what Maisie has lost is as indefinable as what Sir Claude claimed she had found in associating with him ('I've produced life – I don't know what to call it'); it may be even that she will find consolation in some region indescribable in James's novel, beyond the reach of the vicarious imagination. But she won't look for it in Mrs Wix's endlessly recycled tales of 'love and beauty and countesses and wickedness', because they won't seem the real thing any more.

Mrs Wix doesn't look back to the frontage of the hotel while it is still visible across the water: she doesn't have to, because she knows it all already. Maisie, who has to see in order to know, does look back, but her non-committal answer to Mrs Wix's enquiry – 'He wasn't there' – leaves her companion obliged on her behalf to fit the empty balcony of the salon into the appropriate background: 'He went to *her*.' All doors, for Mrs Wix, are bedroom doors. But Maisie forecloses on this line of speculation, which can only return exhausted (like Sir Claude) to the same old scene. Maisie is safe when she is stupid; and her final words, 'Oh I know!', leave Mrs Wix all at sea, still with 'room for wonder at what Maisie knew', suspecting that her frame doesn't contain the full picture and that Maisie is edging out of it; cheated of the last gasp at Maisie's 'knowledge'.

As for us, who likewise will never know precisely what Maisie knew, or wanted to know, or knew she wanted, we do know that all this talk of Maisie knowing this and knowing that doesn't add up in itself to any real knowledge – we suspect, indeed, that it is merely a literary device. And put like that, it may sound a bit of a cheat; but we have only to turn to the novel itself to see we aren't being short-changed. It's perhaps just a question of letting literature produce life in its own indescribable but instantly recognisable way – as Sir Claude claimed to have produced it with Maisie. We are cheated only if we assume a literal connection between the truth and the word. Though Sir Claude's sin, according to Mrs Wix, was 'Branded by the Bible!', nobody sees it as a blot on his countenance; he looked from the first, and somehow he looks at the last, 'the perfect gentleman'.

What fictions teach us needn't involve 'learning and learning', but the price can be high. Maisie paid it for the knowledge of what 'the perfect gentleman' might signify in her own story; but without Sir Claude, she wouldn't have had her own story. And, as he said of the piano-lessons that the child never had because he couldn't afford them, the real thing is shockingly dear, and anything else is a waste of money.

6

The Wings of the Dove

A young American woman is wandering through London's National Gallery, hoping by a quick plunge into the mainstream of European culture to catch a few 'great moments'. But she feels 'too weak for the Turners and Titians', which strike her as 'truly for the larger, not for the smaller life', and pauses instead to watch the earnest, bespectacled women intent before their easels. And Milly Theale, heiress to a fortune, the darling of London society, reflects: 'She should have been a lady-copyist – it met so the case.'

Like Isabel Archer in the gallery at Gardencourt and Hyacinth Robinson in Paris, Milly is peculiarly conscious of the discrepancy between her 'case', or personal situation, and the 'larger life' implicit in art's scope, its permanence, its coherent and essentially truthful vision. Milly has come alone to the gallery this particular morning to avoid a visit from her doctor, who in her absence will have to break bad news to her companion, Susan Stringham. For Milly's real 'case' is one of fatal illness; and it demands that she stop deceiving herself and assimilate the picture of the future on its own terms. Her vulnerability, and her sense of being unequal to the task, is touchingly conveyed as she feels a 'compassionate admiration' for the 'misguided efforts' of the lady-copyists. The silent gallery strikes her as a 'refuge': she feels as if she were at the bottom of the sea. 'The case', she tells herself,

> was the case of escape, of living under water, of being at once impersonal and firm. There it was before one – one had only to stick and stick. (205)

When Milly leaves the safety of the gallery, it won't be to ask what the doctor said, but to confront in Susan's dumb, desperate gaze the certainty of her impending death.

The Wings of the Dove is about taking refuge and breaking for freedom, about putting a bold face on disturbing realities, about love, betrayal, and the weak going to the wall. These and other themes that James liked to 'work' accrete to the initial image which struck his imagination, described in his notebook drafts as that of 'some young creature ... on the threshold of a life that has seemed boundless, condemned ... by the voice of the physician'. The cruelty of a fate which he had seen befall his cousin Minny Temple some 25 years previously is vividly present to him: 'She is like a creature dragged shrieking to the guillotine – to the shambles'; and almost as cruel is the speed with which, over the next few pages of the notebook, the notion of the living, dying individual is hunted down by the plot flung out in her pursuit. Her story rapidly becomes that of a rich girl connected somehow with a pair of lovers who want her money: conspired against, deceived and doomed before her death to recognise her error (Ntbks 169–73). Worse still, perhaps, for readers who take her plight to heart is to turn to the Preface written after the novel and feel that Minny, or Milly, has here been sacrificed to *style*. This happens to be among the most beautifully written, witty and evocative of the Prefaces, and one might scarcely notice that it has to do with a human tragedy. The terror-struck, debilitated 20-year-old of the notebooks has become 'the heir of all the ages'; her story 'one of those chances for good taste ... absolutely to be jumped at'; what happens to her is a 'show' which James regrets not having directed with more technical skill; and the cruelty of the pursuit, the pathos of the pursued, becomes a case of the lovers' story meeting

as with instinctive relief and recognition the possibilities shining out of Milly Theale. (AN 304)

Only some years later does James do something like justice both to the novel he had actually written and to the real depth of feeling we may suppose him to have had for Minny Temple, when in his autobiography he remembered her and what her death had meant for him personally. 'I was', he wrote, 'in the far-off after–time to seek to lay the ghost by wrapping it ... in the beauty and dignity of art.'[1] If Minny's premature extinction had a lurid aspect which fascinated and perhaps haunted him, he also saw in it a degradation of suffering only to be redeemed by some supreme artistic effort. Rewriting *The Portrait of a Lady*, which could also figure as a tribute to Minny, as *The Wings of the Dove*, James invested it with that mixture of personal pain and elegiac solemnity which characterises Ralph Touchett's deathbed farewell to Isabel Archer; but invested it, too, with that peculiar confidence in his heroine's capacity to survive which was also Ralph's – with the sense that the ghost might not be altogether laid, Minny not entirely wrapped up. He did for his own cousin what Ralph tried to do for Isabel.

This mark of consanguinity notwithstanding, and despite other points in common, the two novels are quite dissimilar in style and effect. The first describes, literally and figuratively, a long terrestrial journey into the sunset; the movement of the second, as its title suggests, is one of flight. Isabel's story could be described as having its ups and downs, and coming out more or less on the level, as human experience goes; Milly's story is one of vertiginous heights and drops. The cathedral dimensions of *The Portrait*, ample as they are, are on a human scale: Isabel sees her fate as a 'dead wall' and a prison-house; Milly's fate, from her first appearance perched on the rim of an Alpine crag, is figured as a yawning abyss, a dimension of the unknowable and indefinable.

Passions run higher in *The Wings of the Dove*: there are hints of the sublime in Milly's final bequest, and even in Kate Croy's intensity of wanting, besides which Caspar Goodwood's embrace or Ralph's leaving Isabel his fortune strike us almost as commonplace impulses. Yet this brave, bright world stands visibly, like Milly herself, on the brink of collapse. *The Wings of the Dove*, unlike *The Portrait of a Lady*, is a novel of great verbal and pictorial power, but its persuasive rhetoric and memorable images are disconcertingly offset by pedantic enquiry preoccupied with niggling detail, and the descents it depicts from good faith into bad, from belligerent courage to paralysed inertia, from grand houses to 'vulgar' back-streets are dizzying – and clearly intended to seem so. Nowhere did James more graphically juxtapose high life and low life, without making any simplistic relation between them: no more than in *The Princess Casamassima* or *The Spoils of Poynton* is grandeur necessarily equated with the good or, for that matter, a fine façade with a false interior. In *The Wings of the Dove* the effect of the juxtaposition is at any rate not, as it is in *Poynton*, that of a social survey, moving with documentary precision from Chippendale to stuffed parrot. Rather, this novel has (and one suspects that this was what James aimed at unsuccessfully in his account of Hyacinth) the charged atmosphere of Maisie's glittering fairytale that reached its pitch of exhilaration and terror in 'the highest push ... high, high, high' of the swing that suddenly fell back to earth. The stakes are set higher in *The Wings of the Dove* than in any other Jamesian fiction, except perhaps 'The Turn of the Screw'. For Milly they are literally those of life and death: 'She'll really live or she'll really not,' Kate Croy observes. 'She'll have it all or she'll miss it all'; and the pressure is on us, here as in *What Maisie Knew*, to believe that compromise is not possible; to feel – as Fleda Vetch, settling for a souvenir, evidently didn't feel – that if we can't have the grand style and the good faith and live on the highest level of experience, then we have 'missed it all'. Kate herself risks 'everything' on such a gamble – and loses.

James too takes risks in this novel, the greatest perhaps being the degree to which the latent energy of his subject-matter – the struggle not to die, the urgency of desire, the force of the will – is diverted, in the text, into the act of reading. I do not mean reading books (James's characters are always slightly embarrassed to be caught doing that), but reading people, the strained scrutiny of faces that hold the key to some elusive meaning; yet this activity might meta-phorically represent the strain the book imposes on the reader. That risk was one James thought well worth taking, for as he put it in his Preface, the 'luxury' afforded by engaging with a work of art is 'not greatest'

> when the work asks for as little attention as possible. It is greatest, it is delightfully, divinely great, when we feel the surface, like the thick ice of a skater's pond, bear without cracking the strongest pressure we throw on it. (AN 304–5)

This simile may well have been suggested to James by the glassy surfaces, the mirror-effects, the glides and circling movements that make *The Wings of the Dove* one of his most ambitious exercises in technique; and although in choosing his emotive subject James as it were ups the ante, making what happens to Milly seem worse than what happens to Isabel precisely because Milly is dying, the novel's layered density and refracting surface resist any facile interpreta-tion, demanding from the reader a different order of perception and imaginative involvement from that required by, for example, *Washington Square*. They force us to recognise the terms on which we must accept the 'larger life', rejecting simplification, sentimentality and second-rate copies – even if, like Milly in the gallery, we would rather look away.

2.

James first approaches Milly's 'case' through her relationship with her companion, Susan Stringham. Susie writes stories for magazines and considers herself a connoisseur of literature: she 'bristle[s] with discriminations' between bad writing and good. But literature pales when she encounters Milly Theale:

> all categories failed her – they ceased at least to signify – as soon as she found herself in presence of the real thing, the romantic life itself. (76)

One thing we may observe about the Milly thus assimilated to Susie's 'romantic life' is that she loses certain elements of 'real' life, such as hang so insistently about Hyacinth Robinson or, in this novel, Kate Croy. Susie hails Milly as the 'final flower' in a cluster of 'handsome dead cousins, lurid uncles, beautiful vanished aunts' and so on, but we gain no clear idea of her background and past history, what kind of upbringing she had, what she may have felt on the death of a parent. Handling, in her capacity as an author, exactly that sort of detail is, we may suppose, the life that Susie lays down for Milly ('she had now no life to lead'), only to pick it up again, pleasantly surprised, as 'court life without the hardships'.

But is Susie speaking now of material comforts? or of a state of mind, the luxury perhaps of abnegating critical responsibility? She has had an exclusive 'revelation', and her instinct, we are told, is 'to conceal the vision'. Unlike Henrietta Stackpole, a journalist of a very different breed, who continually questions and judges Isabel Archer, Susie has no desire to connect the real thing to the real world or to interpret the phenomenon that is Milly to a wider public: the touch of ordinary mortals, including Susie herself, can only be 'an ugly smutch on perfection'. The girl's isolation is regrettable, but inevitable: 'A princess could only be a princess.'

We share Susie's vision nevertheless, and at its most spectacular, when she spies Milly on the 'dizzy edge' of an Alpine promontory above 'gulfs of air', 'looking down on the kingdoms of the earth', in a 'state of uplifted and unlimited possession'. Susie's initial flutter of panic (is she likely to fall or even jump?) gives way to the settled conviction that Milly is not going to find in a 'a flying leap' any 'quick escape'; she is to take 'full in the face the whole assault of life'. It is as if Susie foresaw – exercising her famous discrimination in the interests of the fiction she would prefer – Milly's descent into a different type of story, one in which the metaphysical and melo-dramatic connotations of the abyss will sink to the cheap conventional currency of slang, and the 'kingdoms of the earth' be represented by the high society of the Old World that she and Milly have read about in novels; and as James's grand design moves between the planes of sacred and secular imagery, Susie follows it, albeit in a manner more suggestive of the random leap. Considering herself on the strength of her reading and by virtue of some Swiss schooling 'a woman of the world', she sees clearly the prime position that Milly with her 'abysmal' wealth will occupy in society. Milly will always remain, in her friend's view, distinct and apart, and no amount of contact with the world can alter her essence; but her essence, from being a divine sovereignty, suddenly becomes – here Susie takes a leap – her money:

> it prevailed even as the truth of truths that the girl couldn't get away from her wealth. ... that was what it was to be really rich. It had to be *the* thing you were. (87)

In *The Portrait of a Lady*, Ralph made Isabel rich to make her free: he saw romance inherent in her possibilities, not in the mystique of wealth itself.[2] In *The Wings of the Dove* the idea of that mystique is conspicuous because Susie actively promotes it, but this is only her way of accommodating her actual circumstances to her romantic imagination. This is why she presents Milly's wealth in terms of limitation rather than liberation. Ralph followed Isabel's course like that of some brilliant star into the unknown; but Susie's personal security depends absolutely on Milly's staying within her companion's orbit – on her being, and being recognised in society as, the fixed centre of the universe. Otherwise where would Susie be, emotionally, morally and socially? To be the mere hired companion of a stinking-rich foreigner wouldn't suit her book at all.

We have in Susie a refined version of that other childless widow, Maisie's Mrs Wix. Possessive and prone to fond fantasising as both are, they nevertheless exhibit a deep, uncomplicated devotion to their charge, a feeling which, like Henrietta's devotion to Isabel Archer, constitutes a more direct appeal to sentiment than the Jamesian novel as a whole admits: 'Milly looked at [Susie] as if she were almost venerably simple, but also as if this were what one loved her for.' The soft core of humanity Susie Stringham embodies somehow survives exposure to the faint mockery that she endures, as Henrietta and Mrs Wix did before her. That is her important contribution to *The Wings of the Dove*, as opposed to the 'divine' version of Milly that she promotes – which some critics have assumed to be James's.[3] It is suggested more than once that Susie keeps art and life in separate mental compartments.[4] The miracle of fiction made flesh that she sees in Milly is, as far as she is concerned, a one-way process; and this attitude means that she is never fully integrated into the more complex processes of James's fiction: the process whereby *we* see Milly become Susie's fiction, the process that transforms the story of Major and Mrs Monarch, who thought they were the real thing, literary archetypes made flesh, but of whom the painter could initially only produce a stiff, distorted picture, like the icon-portrait Susie makes of Milly.

Milly on the other hand proves adaptable to these processes, in what she says and does and even in how she thinks. She can see, for example, reading between the lines of Susie's fairy-story, that 'to treat her as a princess was a positive need of her companion's mind'; she understands how fictions are constructed, knowing what Maisie intuitively knew of human difficulties and the ways out that stories can provide. We shall see Milly drawn into James's narrative machine just as we see her drawn, in a conscious attempt to get away from Susie, to the National Gallery, which figures both as a refuge and a trap. Reflected in Milly's consciousness, the scene has an inconsequential, dream-like quality: she is humble and submerged, yet also in a royal ambience where, like a princess, she is both safe and at liberty to roam:

> the quiet chambers, nobly overwhelming, rich but slightly veiled, opened out round her and made her presently say, 'If I could lose myself *here*!' (205)

The 'chambers' might stand for James's novel (the description fits exactly): the sort of novel that would enfold Milly in the attributes of a heroine without denying her freedom of movement. But multiple exits are also multiple entrances: and the doorways that lead her from room to room might also be the windows in James's house of fiction (see above p. 37), vantage-points of the 'individual vision' and the 'individual will', lookout posts for those who want to fix Milly in *their* fictions, in images that deny her individuality. Why else should Milly, when there is nobody to catch her, wander 'keeping an eye on vistas and approaches, so that she shouldn't be flagrantly caught'? It is an oddly haunting passage, so suggestive of the Jamesian protagonist's search for a place to be right, and 'the case of escape'.[5]

3.

'I want to go straight to London' – the move by which Milly initiates her story – is one of very few straight moves made in a conversation with Susie at their mountain inn, talk that is ostensibly concerned with future plans but composed almost entirely of guarded allusion, incoherent effusion and verbal shots in the dark. 'I sometimes wonder——!' says Milly '... Shall I have it for long? That is if I *have* got it', claiming by 'it' to mean 'everything', while Susie wonders if it means pain. The real subject of the conversation comes up as the merest little bleep in Susie's consciousness, which registers 'talk of early dying'; but scarcely has the reader grasped the implications of this before Susie's voice-over has reverted to the 'light', 'quaint' note that is (so we are told) the secret of her success in the tasteful Boston magazines.

If *The Wings of the Dove* were only about how society handles death, or how friends seek to protect one another from the fear and horror of it (and on a certain level it *is* about these things), there would be no need for Milly to strike a different note. But it must also be about Milly's personal relation to her death: that is to say, if she is to be a heroine, is to have a story of her own, it can only develop in conjunction with that central, inescapable fact. It looks like a great opportunity for a heroine (death is dramatic, death is dignifying), but dying is a difficult part to sustain (for which reason it is usually played by secondary characters): it defines one too easily as an object of reverence or pity, a character in a thousand other fictions similar to Susie's. What can Milly do – 'shriek'? – like the girl of the notebooks, dragged to the guillotine? That, given the conventions of the Jamesian novel, would be like shrieking in the National Gallery. More importantly, what can Milly *be*? – since her death, unlike for example Hyacinth Robinson's, cannot be seen as the result of her having been, or done, anything.

Moving to London provides Milly with a hugely expanded context in which to become somebody (a context she explicitly recognises as the world of the English novel brought to life). Her entrée into society is taken care of by Maud Lowder, a friend from Susie's Swiss schooldays, now also a widow, but left with a great deal of money and a large house in Lancaster Gate where she receives the rich and titled. Susie, who isn't either, offers up to Maud, as a 'trophy', Milly instead. The pedestal on which Milly finds herself exacerbates her problem of self-definition: *everybody* is looking at her now. We observe her in the place of honour at Maud's dinner-table (behaving, incidentally, quite unlike the splendidly isolated princess of Susie's legend), enjoying placing her fellow-guests in hypothetical social and romantic relations, but also searching for her own image in the faces and responses of others.

In this new element, where everything seems both familiar and unfamiliar and where Milly has a distinct sense, as a fragile, valuable object ought not to have, of standing on the brink of something, she proceeds (as she did in the inn with Susie) not from any solid sense of what she is, but by a kind of radar, sending out signals in all directions, hoping to discern in the way they are reflected the true shape of things. Her telling Lord Mark, her neighbour at dinner, that Mrs Lowder regards her 'in the light of' an ideal and that 'That's all I've got to hold on by', characterises Milly's epistemological method as well as her precarious sense of identity and the danger she is actually on the brink of. Maud's being an idealist is merely a notion plucked out of nowhere, bounced off Lord Mark to see what impression it leaves: Maud will prove to be a pragmatist, a plot-maker adept at incorporating others into her stories. But Milly has as yet no idea that to be seen in a light – any light – carries that risk. She only knows that she doesn't see herself 'in the light of such an offering' as Susie's to Maud.

What really impresses Lord Mark is the idea that *he* might be seen in a light. But Milly's attention has left him, to dwell on the beauty and eminence of Maud's niece Kate. She wonders why she is so different from 'the handsome girl' and in this attempt to define herself in terms of Kate she marks the real beginning of both their stories.

Plot-making Susie sees Kate in the more utilitarian light of handmaiden to her princess; and Kate returns the compliment by treating Susie as casually as if Susie really were a servant. But the two young women do become friends; and through Kate Milly will encounter again a young English journalist she met and liked in America – Merton Densher, who hangs around Lancaster Gate as Kate's admirer, tolerated by Aunt Maud, but discounted as having nothing to offer her niece. This is the situation from which Susie, as she becomes increasingly anxious about Milly, eventually develops a saving fiction (one that is well adapted to the patterns of friendship forged, renewed and failed in which the reader can discern Susie's own true story). Milly is gravely ill, and has never been in love. Mr Densher, so unsuitable a match for Kate and (unlike Kate) so charming to Susie, must become Milly's prince, possibly her salvation. Milly will be happy – she will love and be loved – she will even, perhaps, live.

Susie will cling desperately to this 'one dream' in circumstances she finds increasingly disconcerting. It isn't just that life in a top person's novel is a colder, grander affair than she had bargained for (there is a poignant moment when she hankers 'rather yearningly' for the cosier domestic milieux of Thackeray); nor that Maud, like Milly, isn't as sound as she appears, but more concerned with action than principle. The trouble is that Susie sees the gulf between London and Boston is wider than she ever supposed, but can no longer make the reassuring distinction between the real life and real values of New England and the world of the novel represented by London, because she herself has got 'carried away' by the 'thrills' of London and lost the 'sustaining sense of it all as literary material': 'it' (the new social dimension) strikes her now as 'vast, obscure, lurid'.

'I want abysses,' Milly will tell her, in a tone which Susie appreciates as 'light' and 'quaint', and which gives a homely twist to her own wild forebodings; indeed, as Milly proceeds 'agreeably to embroider' her personal situation, talking of taking leave of Susie 'sweetly for ever' and of qualifying for 'a handsome cemetery', we may feel that she has caught Susie's note of quaintness and gentility too closely for our comfort. But what Milly is actually doing here is articulating a narrative technique based on euphemism, omission and indirection which, while it makes it hard to put a finger on the exact sense, also extends the area of the reader's reach. By holding back on the proper names of things, by groping in the blanks of her unfinished sentences, by occasionally hitting in her glancing sallies the note that *is* the right one, Milly helps to construct that dimension of the unspeakable, the unknowable, the indefinable which makes this novel the far from safe place Susie suspects it to be. The empty space that yawned beneath Milly's perch in the Alps might merely have marked a drop on a vertical axis (the sheer distance she could fall): but the image of the abyss, escaping from the snug confabulations where Milly uses it to denote thrilling intrigue, is soon assimilated to her ignorance of human nature, where she stands 'on the edge of a great darkness'. It becomes identified with all that she cannot have and doesn't know and doesn't want to know, finally expanding till a whole assembly of meanings the novel might be assumed to represent teeter on the brink of it. This is the abysmal mystery that Milly seems to invoke when, unexpectedly, her verbal 'embroidery' ends in a burst of rhetoric. It is as if she knew she had caught the 'note', as if she suddenly understood meanings that can't be seen or described but only apprehended:

> '...Since I've lived all these years as if I were dead, I shall die, no doubt, as if I were alive – which will happen to be as you want me. So you see,' she wound up, 'you'll never really know where I am. Except indeed when I'm gone; and then you'll only know where I'm not.' (143)

Susie is accustomed, like Milly herself, to read meaning conventionally in what people say and what they look like. What meaning can she hope to find in this paradox, this confident endorsement of the dubious relation between appearance and reality? Her reply comes after a pause: 'I'd die *for* you.' Straight as an arrow, it seems to strike at the heart of Milly's evasions; it seeks to reconnect, across the abyss, her inalterable, hallowed Milly with the earnest efforts, the fundamental decencies, of the 'smaller life'.

4.

'Nobody here does anything for nothing': that, Lord Mark tells Milly, is the ethos of Maud Lowder's London. Maud's wealth, unlike Milly's, is coupled to power and aimed at specific targets. It is easy to equate her with an impersonal social and financial system capable of destroying the finer aspirations of the human spirit. Yet the Maud whom Susie sees as a 'projectile of great size loaded and ready for use' is no Mona Brigstock, whose stream-lined function in *The Spoils of Poynton* is only to smash things; nor is she, like Mrs Newsome in *The Ambassadors*, remote from the contagion of fantasy-land. Maud operates very well in fact within the Jamesian narrative process – better than Susie, to whom she bears a coarse resemblance – because she sees people not as heroes and villains but as essentially ongoing investments, interesting in so far as they can be put to work to fulfil their potential (which will give the reader a different view of, notably, Merton Densher).

If her sister's remarkable daughter Kate makes a great match – with Lord Mark, say, who is uncle to a duke – Aunt Maud will leave her her fortune. Kate must be not merely rich but 'magnificent'. In pursuit of this dream, Maud issues her niece with an ultimatum. Kate's mother has recently died, separated from her mysteriously disgraced husband, Lionel Croy. Kate must break with her father completely: she is to make her home with Maud, not with Lionel and not with her elder sister Marian Condrip who, victim of another inglorious match, now lives widowed and with four children in middle-class squalor.

Kate, it is admitted, appreciates life's luxuries, and if she abandons Aunt Maud she loses the money she, and her family through her, might have had. But against her materialism and her strong sense of family responsibility work Kate's pride and her intention to marry the man she loves, Merton Densher. He wants urgently to marry her; she feels it dishonest to remain at Lancaster Gate under false pretences; but Lionel and Marian demand that she does. Kate's problem is not Milly's, to discover who she is, but simply to withstand *as* she is the extreme pressure of definitions imposed on her by others: a disposable asset, an object of desire, a line to pull in the Lowder loot.

The novel opens with Kate's incurious contemplation of her image in the mirror as she waits at Lionel's lodgings for him to come in. Aunt Maud's ultimatum has prompted her 'to save [herself] – to escape', and she offers to cast in her lot with his, to go – anywhere – with him. It's the point where a novel not written by James might end, in the reinstatement of true love and piety, with the prodigal falling on her father's neck. Lionel has 'kind safe eyes'; all he has to do, Kate urges, is to affirm: 'We'll have a faith and find a way.'

But Lionel is not what he seems – 'the English gentleman and the fortunate settled normal person'. His immaculate appearance hides a menacing manner that reminds us of Gilbert Osmond; but whereas we are soon told exactly what Osmond is and exactly how he attempts to destroy Isabel Archer, what's wrong with Kate's father, and what he's done, is something no one can name: at the centre of Lionel there is a great blank. And yet he has a powerful, parasitic hold on the story, not simply as a 'character' or, in Kate's phrase, 'an actual person, if there ever was one', but as something more frightening, which Kate also recognises: an indefinable horror who exists, like Peter Quint in 'The Turn of the Screw', by contriving somehow to be reflected in others; and not to their advantage, as Lionel's wife found out to her cost:

> He had positively been, in his way, by the force of his particular type, a terrible husband not to live with; his type reflecting so invidiously on the woman who found him distasteful. (7)

Lionel's great talent (it may also have been Quint's) is for making others appear to be in the wrong. Kate, he suggests, is sacrificing her father's well-being to the attentions of a cheap admirer – wicked if she will abandon him, and equally wicked if she remains with Aunt Maud. Caught between conflicting interests, Kate is misinterpreted on every side. The half of her mother's meagre legacy which she makes over to Marian – in a gesture which pleases nobody concerned – might stand for Kate's 'small stupid piety' that goes all too easily unremarked. Sent back by Lionel to Lancaster Gate, Kate reflects that:

> It wouldn't be the first time she had seen herself obliged to accept with smothered irony other people's interpretation of her conduct. She often ended by giving up to them – it seemed really the way to live – the version that met their convenience. (18)

Many readers will later find it convenient to accept the version of Kate that slots neatly into the novel they wish to read. It is as if Kate herself already sensed this when she remarks to her father, 'I wish there were some one here who might serve – for any contingency – as a witness ...' – a witness, that is, to her offer to come to him. How can something be true that isn't *seen* to be the truth? Always in Kate's mind is the thought of her dead mother, who seemed to exist only as a reflection of something distorted – as if she *became* the image of herself produced in a bent mirror.

Her sister, similarly, has become 'the plain prosaic result' of her husband the Reverend Condrip, left 'red and almost fat', 'less and less like any Croy'. With her father simply effaced from the concerns of the decent world, her brothers victims both of ignominious ends, Kate's whole family history is one of failure to maintain the right image. But these lamentable conclusions only serve to stiffen Kate's resolve that

She hadn't given up yet, and the broken sentence, if she was the last word, *would* end with a sort of meaning. (3)

Milly herself recognised Kate as 'the heroine of a strong story'; and if the story of Kate's attempt to rise out of obscurity, and of her love for Merton, has, for many readers, put Milly's story in the shade, Kate's own efforts are to thank for it. Milly's own tragic past, for example, known to us only through Susie's breathless allusions, cannot capture the imagination as does Kate's haunting first-person account of her father's disgrace, unnameable, unknowable, 'and yet it's a part of me'. It is Kate who – as if she *were* Milly's handmaiden – will most competently deploy the techniques Milly articulated: manipulating the power of the unnamed, leaving the blanks the reader most wants to see filled, forcing the reader to see the truth as reflected in her (the governess in 'The Turn of the Screw' achieves her effects in exactly the same way). Kate understands narrative and plot and, above all, language, and knows how to turn them to her advantage. She can say to Densher 'with extraordinary beauty', 'I engage myself to you for ever', a statement that actually reflects what is to him the most disturbing aspect of their situation (she pro-longs their engagement indefinitely); but it sounds, irresistibly, like a lifeline to some moral bedrock, to the 'sort of meaning' stories properly end in.

5.

Milly meanwhile, rising effortlessly on the social swell, finds herself at Matcham, a grand country house, where Lord Mark acts as her sponsor and guide. Why he takes her up so enthusiastically when she had started by trying to put him down is a question not, I think, entirely resolved by assuming him, as most critics have, to be stupid or self-seeking (i.e. after her money). When at Maud's dinner-table Milly first met Lord Mark, she had had the feeling of having 'been popped into the compartment' of his general experience of New Yorkers, and that 'she could neither escape nor prevail by her strangeness.' Milly, so struck on that occasion by the image Kate presented, urgently needing one for herself, one that wouldn't be ordinary, one that would 'prevail', had tried out on Lord Mark a couple of ways of being 'strange' (the image fostered by Susie). She played the American girl, a useful cover for the moderately aggressive personality we shall see further evidence of.[6] Meeting the 'potentially insolent nobleman' with democratic bluntness, as Isabel did Lord Warburton, she told him, 'There are things you don't know' and 'you've no imagination'. Yet Lord Mark appeared merely amused, and despite her determination to assert their differences, Milly noticed that their 'not mixing' induced them to talk 'almost intimately'.

That she found odd, and it isn't how Warburton talked with Isabel Archer. In fact Lord Mark's relation with Milly is more like Ralph Touchett's with Isabel in several key respects, one of which is his evident sensitivity to image. When Milly essayed an image of pathos (saying Kate was 'sorry for her'), Lord Mark tactfully let her see for herself that 'it had doubtless been a note of questionable taste.' He seems concerned that Milly should have the right image, and at Matcham he shows her an image worthy of her.

It appears she markedly resembles a portrait by Bronzino that is one of the great treasures of the house. As Lord Mark leads her off to see it through an assembly of aristocrats, Milly returns the 'bland stare' of their 'kind lingering eyes', consciously abandoning the effort of asserting her identity. No longer the inquisitorial observer of the dinner-party, for whom every bland stare like Lord Mark's was suspect, an affront to her individuality as well as a challenge to the imagination, Milly now decides that 'kind eyes were always kind eyes' (the parallels are striking with Kate's observation of her father's 'kind safe eyes' and her weary desire to offer other people 'the version [of her] that met their convenience'). Her progress as a passive object of scrutiny through the admiring throng seems to Milly 'the pink dawn of an apotheosis coming so curiously soon': she virtually is at this moment the princess of Susie's rose-tinted vision. And then Milly sees the picture:

> the face of a young woman, all splendidly drawn, down to the hands, and splendidly dressed; a face almost livid in hue, yet handsome in sadness and crowned with a mass of hair, rolled back and high, that must, before fading with time, have had a family resemblance to her own. The lady in question, at all events, with her slightly Michael-angelesque squareness, her eyes of other days, her full lips, her long neck, her recorded jewels, her brocaded and wasted reds, was a very great personage – only unaccompanied by a joy. And she was dead, dead, dead. (157)[7]

In the portrait, Milly faces the truth that she has never approached except through awkward circumlocution. She cannot name it even now:

> Milly recognised her exactly in words that had nothing to do with her. 'I shall never be better than this.' (157)

'This' is not the represented perfection of form; 'this' is where Milly feels that she is, resplendent and treasured at the pinnacle of society; 'this' is a line that Milly has reached, and her firm statement draws it, cutting off what she leaves behind her from what she sees in front of her: that the image of perfection is an image of arrested vitality, that the future is barren for the young woman in the 'wasted reds'.

Lord Mark makes a kindly joke to cover for Milly's sudden tears. Yet he insists on the resemblance, 'as if', Milly observes, 'it were important to his character as a serious man not to appear to have invented his plea'. She needs his being, as she sees it, 'nice', doesn't need his insistence: she has had her moment of recognition.

The very next day she keeps an appointment with Sir Luke Strett, a distinguished man of medicine, 'the great master of the knife'.[8] It is the first of two occasions when Kate, in the position of the reader, will demand to know the diagnosis and Milly will avoid telling her. Kate is fobbed off first with the reassurances of a bedtime story ('if I'll be a good girl and do exactly what he tells me he'll take care of me for ever and ever'), then with the dire innuendo of a romantic weepy ('I hope ... he didn't like me too much'). The lapse from the immmediate impact and unsentimentality of the Bronzino scene is disconcerting. It is hard to keep patience with Milly, and hard also to discern in the convoluted introspection wrapped round her dialogues with Kate and Sir Luke the rather remarkable way whereby she seeks to impose familiar structures on the dreadful blank ahead of her. The filial doctor–patient relationship itself fills in one of the empty spaces: Milly really wants at this point to be 'found out about' and depend on someone else for the way things are going to be; even to know that she is going to die will give her a shape to her 'queer little history' and a comforting sense of being placed:

> it was ridiculously true that her thus sitting there to see life put into the scales represented her first approach to the taste of orderly living. (168)

These are Milly's innermost thoughts; but under the pressure of social intercourse they are constrained, rather cruelly, into a nervous posturing. In her further consultations with Sir Luke she will be repeatedly doomed to some loss of dignity through self-advertisement, and capable, in her attempts to be both interesting and modest, of an excruciating coyness. 'I'm all that's left,' she tells Sir Luke, with reference to her obliterated family, continuing, 'to be fair all round', 'But they died of different things.' This is the poor little rich girl writ large, whose very relations in their suffering suffer from an embarrassment of choice! Milly's saving grace is that she sees something of this. The perception that she is behaving like 'an interviewed heroine or a freak of nature at a show' might be the narrator's, but might equally be hers; she observes that Sir Luke controls 'his impatience of her'. He will continue to treat her with the consummate tact of an expensive consultant, and James, equally tactfully, encourages the belief that theirs is a special, exclusive relationship. He does this, partly, by endowing Sir Luke with an oracular authority which places him, in the eyes of Susie and Densher at least, with Milly, above mere mortals. But through Milly's eyes we see that their special relationship might be just another comforting fiction, or safe story. She sees at any rate something in his 'kind, dim smile' that makes her ask a straight question: will she live? – and in his delphic advice that she should 'take the trouble to' she finds her own answer.

Drawn by Sir Luke's assured professionalism from its painful specific context, the question of 'living' loses for Milly its contours, becoming for her a 'grey immensity' like that of the city before her. And in an access of energy, inspired by the idea that she can live if she'll only try, she proceeds like 'a soldier on a march', wandering for miles through the streets of London, feeling for once the immediacy of that greater whole, yet intensely conscious of the peculiar figure she cuts there. Finally she reaches Regent's Park (it strikes her that 'this was the real thing') where, choosing a public bench, she pauses to survey the people on the grass around her: 'here doubtless were hundreds of others just in the same box'.

Milly draws these others in to share her discovery: 'They could live if they would.' But even as she does so, she lights on another aspect of the question: 'they would live if they could.' The first proposition – that you *might* live if you can just summon up the will – is bossily exhortatory, a carrot for the masses. The second proposition, which she recognises as a 'blessed old truth', seems to bring the mystery of free will into harmony with a divinely ordained certainty.[9] As Milly muses, finding the second proposition 'more appealing, insinuating, irresistible', and turns again to her fellow mortals, she observes that some of them have buried their faces in the grass, 'ignoring, burrowing'. The passage culminating in this scene doesn't, as is often suggested, link Milly to the rest of mankind. It exhibits, rather, the 'freak of nature' escaped from the show and on the loose; it represents a voyage of personal discovery that takes her far beyond the workaday notion of living by the doctor's orders. What the doctor said can be reinterpreted: all it takes is an expansion of the imagination, courage, energy, and a belief in one's own ascendancy. Milly's is an intensely private recognition, and sanctification, of an exclusive destiny: if she can, *she* will 'live'.

6.

The point to which Milly's wanderings return, literally and figuratively, is the enigma of Kate's relationship with Merton Densher. That this handsome pair have already appropriated to themselves the novel's boy-meets-girl romance is something that has long been obvious to the reader; and Milly's interest in them is uncomfortably stimulated by her sense that they have between them some sort of story, accessible to her only at one remove. She is like Maisie with her crush on Sir Claude and Mrs Beale, when she hadn't quite grasped the rules of the game or the extent to which she herself was disqualified to play. Milly is out of it; and her sense of exclusion grows sharper as she becomes increasingly aware that Kate, her confidante in other matters, is oddly silent on the topic of Densher.

Kate's habitual reticence – a conditioned as much as a calculated response – is the basis of the complicated game directed by herself and Aunt Maud against one another, and pursued throughout the central section of the novel. It is analogous to a game of cards in which Milly alone of the five players doesn't hold the key card (the knowledge that Kate loves Densher as much as he loves her), and it demands, like poker, the ability to read the closed countenances of the other players.

There is the risk, as I have suggested, that when the case is one of living or dying so much 'reading' may even strike the reader as faintly preposterous. The narrative game James is playing here, requiring of the reader considerable skills in drawing inferences and recognising the important moves, perhaps works better as a spectator-sport, when we more or less know what is going on but enjoy seeing it translated into lively conjecture like Maisie's or Fanny Assingham's in *The Golden Bowl*; or when the stakes aren't so high. Only Aunt Maud and Merton Densher, those least pre-occupied with death, seem really to enjoy the reading game, and that in Densher's case is because, slow to see the values of the cards, he is obliged to play it with Kate: 'The women one meets', he tells her, ' – what are they but books one has already read? You're a whole library of the unknown, the uncut.'

'We move in a labyrinth', as Susie perceives, and Milly for her part explores it with an 'appetite for motive' and a capacity for seeing round corners Susie considers to be worthy of her own New England heroines. But, like that other New England heroine Isabel Archer, Milly has too much confidence in her breadth of vision, when she should be reading in depth. She looks widely and not well (to Mrs Condrip, for instance); and as she peers round endless corners, lacking the insight into Kate's sexual passion which holds the clue to the puzzle, we begin to lose any sense akin to Densher's of penetrating deeper mysteries, and the resonance of the abyss becomes the mere flat echo of a series of dead ends.

But if James took that risk, he also saw and deployed the real nar-rative potential of the labyrinth: the fascination of observing from the unexpected angle, the fear of being observed, the shock of sudden confrontation, the terror of trying to get out and being trapped. On her return from Regent's Park, Milly from her balcony observes Kate as she arrives to learn the result of the second visit to Sir Luke. She has a 'strange sense' of seeing Kate from Densher's point of view, which has 'more than one' effect. First, she is able to infer from the very look of her friend – a look Kate then 'lost' on the way upstairs – the nature of her 'connexion' with Densher. It is as if she suddenly recognised Kate's desirability as the point of the read-ing game, and Kate's inscrutability as the way to play it. Second, having seen Kate 'in a light', momentarily exposed as Milly now feels herself exposed among her knowing friends, Milly suddenly realises the necessity of concealing from the others the weakness of her hand – the physical and emotional vulnerability which they could use to their advantage. Lying to Kate about the doctor's diag-nosis, she enters the game of deception, albeit 'with no conscious-ness of fraud, only as with a sudden flare of the famous "willpower" … her medical adviser had mainly thrown her back on.'

Unfortunately, however, her interest in Densher is the one thing she hasn't skill enough to conceal; it gives her away to Aunt Maud, who now singles her out as a decoy to lure Densher away from Kate. Milly becomes the hunted innocent, and, knowing now the idea of the game, she knows when she loses her cards. A sense of desperation takes hold of her: she's helpless, cornered, people will try to pin her down, they will say: 'There's something the matter with you!' The tension culminates in Milly's perception of Kate as a panther, and in the sudden violence of her response to Milly's appeasement: 'Oh you may very well loathe me yet!'

This is the unexpected encounter with the bad-faced stranger, the real 'beast in the jungle', the happening springing out of a thicket of non-events that validates all that has, or rather hasn't, gone before.[10] It is a crisis as sharp as any in James's fiction, a moment when something profoundly nasty in the depths of the novel rises to Kate's lips, yet emerges, after so much obfuscation, with the ring of piercing honesty. And while her threat signals those developments the reader has been waiting for, Kate's 'explanation' of it ('Because you're a dove') gives Milly the sign *she* has been waiting for, signalling her escape route:

> It was moreover, for the girl, like an inspiration: she found herself accepting as the right one, while she caught her breath with relief, the name so given her. She met it on the instant as she would have met revealed truth; it lighted up the strange dusk in which she lately had walked. *That* was what was the matter with her. She was a dove. Oh *wasn't* she! (202)

Milly has been assigned a role which seems to take care of her (in both senses), but which she will transform to a position of power, as Catherine Sloper, in acting like a 'good daughter', gained the upper hand over her father; and as Maisie, behaving as the child who 'knew', found a place in the adults' world. No longer a sitting duck, Milly the dove begins to mislead Aunt Maud: which gives her at once a sense of 'the success she could have as a dove'. It's a little triumph for her, though it leaves her exhausted and is followed by her retreat to the National Gallery. There, when she turns from the lady-copyists, she will see for the first time Kate and Densher together: it is they, not Milly, who are 'flagrantly caught', they who are ill at ease when they find that they can no longer read Milly.

But it is also the point where Milly is most alone, and most evidently in need of finding her own story. It mustn't be one in which her youth, beauty and virtue are there merely to guarantee an untimely death, or one that fixes her in helpless immobility. Right from the start, Susie of the unavowed flat-earth mentality found it odd that the centre of her universe, the ailing princess, should move, should indeed 'stir the stream like a leviathan', so that Susie 'floated off with the sense of rocking violently at her side'. The tide turned for Milly when she saw the Bronzino, the image of stasis. Those were

> the moments that had exactly made the high-water-mark of her security, the moments during which her tears themselves, those she had been ashamed of, were the sign of her consciously rounding her protective promontory, quitting the blue gulf of comparative ignorance and reaching her view of the troubled sea. (321)

When she recalls these moments, she is in the city of seafarers, the city built on sand.

7.

Milly's position was already undermined before she left London, where despite having learnt the art of subversion she was 'successfully deceived'; and now, in Venice, it stands on the verge of collapse. Densher, who accompanies the party thither, comes, Milly thinks, in hopeless attachment to Kate, but in the eyes of the other women his role is to be Milly's suitor. Eventually, Kate's plot becomes clear: Densher will woo Milly, marry her and in due course inherit her money. Densher agrees to do as Kate dictates, but only if she will come to his *quartiere*, his anonymous little rooms, and go to bed with him. Slowly – for the novel takes a long time to recover momentum – the baffling game of deception is overtaken by the narratively more powerful current of coercion as both Kate and Densher are dragged where they don't want to go – she to the compromising compromise of unwedded, underfinanced bliss, he to 'make up to a sick girl'.

While the others rush about in gondolas Milly, quietly and not very visibly dying, remains in the upper rooms of her palazzo. This 'ark of her deluge' will be the last resting place of the dove, and

Lord Mark, who comes on some pretext to see her there, finds her clinging to it, in physical exhaustion, as if to the security of ancient legends:

> 'Oh the impossible romance——!' The romance for her ... would be to sit there for ever, through all her time, as in a fortress; and the idea became an image of never going down, of remaining aloft in the divine dustless air ... 'Ah not to go down – never, never to go down!' she strangely sighed to her friend.
>
> 'But why shouldn't you,' he asked, 'with that tremendous old staircase in your court? There ought of course always to be people at top and bottom, in Veronese costumes, to watch you do it.'(323)

His concern brings Milly to the edge of breakdown. With overwhelming relief, she feels she will be able to tell him – 'doubtless' because she cares for him so little – what she cannot tell the others, and particularly not Merton Densher: that she doesn't 'go down' because she is very badly ill. Then suddenly, thinking Lord Mark is about to propose, the thought flashes into her head: '*She* mightn't last, but her money would' – an ugly motive for marriage, though it 'didn't sit, the ugly motive, in Lord Mark's cool English eyes'.

He strikes her, in fact, as 'the one safe sympathiser', her 'one easy relation' – which Milly finds 'strange'. Her intercourse with Lord Mark is invariably marked by the words 'odd', 'singular', and 'strange', because he never quite fits the compartments of Milly's mind. What he says *sounds* plain enough: 'you want to be adored. ... You're not loved enough. ... believe in me'; but Milly finds it too plain for the expression of 'a force that should sweep them both away'. Her instinctive response to Lord Mark's friendliness and warmth is overlaid by her determination to perceive him in the role of mate, and to reject him. He isn't, as she rather smugly puts it to herself, 'good for what she called her reality'.

Both here and in her interviews with Merton Densher, the question arises (as it does with Fleda Vetch in her various retreats) whether Milly is interpreting her admirers quite correctly – whether her 'case' isn't simply one of an impaired capacity for social relationships. One aspect at any rate of Milly's reality is indisputable, one which might well have had that effect. And it is this aspect – her illness and loneliness – which, whatever his motives, Lord Mark seems rather firmly to have grasped. One might also note that his remarks about her descending the steps, like his remarks about the

Bronzino, show that he has – as Densher doesn't – a very clear apprehension of Milly as a physical entity. He saw the Bronzino as a picture of the real girl he knew; it was Milly who saw it as a symbol. And now, when she seems in danger of being subsumed into the generality of myth, the idea of the princess in the tower (that he doesn't see her as an individual has always been an obstacle to her relationship with Densher), Lord Mark proposes a new, 'walkabout' image for Milly, one that would bring her down out of her isolation and a potentially sterile symbolism into a more direct and natural relation with life. He offers her, furthermore, the opportunity to be in her dealings with him who she really is ('really' in the sense that Henrietta Stackpole or Mrs Gereth or Maisie would understand it; for in their world anything as oblique and metaphysical as a symbol would be out of place, while Lord Mark – it is one of his oddities – would not).

Those who take Lord Mark in this scene to be merely obtuse or self-serving appear not to see the parallels here with the relationship between Ralph Touchett and Isabel Archer, both in what is offered and the manner in which it is rejected. It's not of course Milly's fault, any more than it is Isabel's, that she doesn't find her admirer physically attractive; but we don't see her quite face that fact. What Milly *feels* is that he responds 'the pleasant, human way, without depths of darkness' to the straightest thing she ever says: 'I think I should like to die here.' But what she subsequently formulates (and the attempt to substitute formula for feeling is pure Isabel) is that Lord Mark is simply too frivolous to suffer with her in 'the chill of the losing game'. And, with a sense of kindly superiority, Milly urges the man who isn't *her* idea of the real thing that he should try for Kate instead.

Lord Mark's response is to suggest that Kate is as much in love with Densher as Densher is with Kate. He does so, incidentally, very much more tentatively and tactfully than Ralph Touchett put to Isabel the general view of Osmond, but Milly is, like Isabel, upset and angry and declares him 'wholly mistaken'. Earlier, she had had similarly to explain to Sir Luke that Kate 'didn't like' Densher, aiming to forge a conspiratorial intimacy with the sophisticated doctor, and just at the point where Susie – discovering Kate *did* – would join the conspiracy to deceive Milly. Now, as Lord Mark retreats, Milly informs him Densher is on his way up; and in the following chapter she, who has never been anywhere in Venice, will invite herself to Densher's *quartiere*, for tea. It strikes Densher, in his

anticipation of Kate's visit there, 'quite as a hateful idea'. There
could scarcely be for a heroine a worse light to be seen in.

The view shared with Susie by certain critics that Milly ultimately
dies from contact with evil[11] makes too little of the consideration
that evil anywhere most easily takes hold in that combination of
self-absorption, inexperience and elective ignorance which Milly
exhibits all along, and particularly in this first encounter with Lord
Mark in Venice, when she imputes to him an ugly motive that may
possibly be his but is most certainly Densher's. Milly gets it wrong
precisely when she thinks she is getting it right – which is not quite
the mode of experience we associate with blessed innocents; so that
the alternative view, that she dies when she sees herself finally
thwarted and humiliated, fits the case much better – at the cost,
however, of bringing it to the brink of the bathos implied in
Samuels's summary – that Milly 'dies of disappointment at losing
her man'.[12] Either way of looking at it makes too much of her death
(Samuels's trivialisation only works because of that 'dies of'): the
death that makes Milly a stereotypical emblem of virtue – or merely
pathetic. There must, surely, be more to James's novel, and to
Milly's life, than this.

8.

The loss of Milly's dignity and of her grasp on the plot is not
retrieved in *The Wings of the Dove* by any passage corresponding to
that in *The Portrait of a Lady* where Isabel, sitting up over the fire,
comprehensively surveys her position, recognises the extent to
which she is the victim of her errors, and in doing so establishes an
autonomous narrative territory within that novel. The marked
absence in the closing chapters of *The Wings of the Dove* of any such
survey on Milly's part poignantly suggests a Milly who is past
caring about novels. The burden of sustaining the story as its
heroine appears to be disintegrating and fading out, like the burden
of dealing with the pressures (moral, psychological, financial,
sexual) which any novel of adult life should properly reflect, is left
to Kate – as everything, always, by Densher and by her family, is left
to Kate.[13]

Milly had gone to see Kate's sister once, prompted by a Dickensian
ghoulishness to inspect the middle classes brought low, and had
returned 'indescribably' disconcerted by the insinuating nastiness of

Mrs Condrip, who attempted to engage her as an ally against Densher. Mrs Condrip, poverty and what it does to the soul are things Milly absolutely doesn't want to know about; and if we appreciate that she is vulnerable because she is ignorant, we must also appreciate that Kate is hard because she is not. One way of looking at Kate is from this deterministic point of view: 'she is what she must be, determined by her circumstances and her endowments.'[14] But while that description might cover, for example, Hyacinth Robinson (especially if we assume his qualities are inherited), it doesn't cover the complexity most readers find in Kate. This isn't altogether a question of personality and personal dilemma – the kind of terms *The Princess Casamassima* deals in. Kate is not a complex 'character' in the sense that the Princess is. What's behind the moves the Princess makes? Does she really *like* Hyacinth or Paul? Kate's motivation, whom she likes and dislikes, the mixture of pity and envy she feels for Milly – all these things are clear to the reader (if not always to the others). Kate is a simple or comprehensible character of whom James makes complex use; not, like the Princess, a superficial adornment to the real story, but as James pointed out in the Preface one of his 'registers or "reflectors"'(AN 300), in other words one of his 'true agents', those of whom it is most apt to say that 'The worker in one connexion was the worked in another' (for this, Kate's description of society, is singularly applicable to James's fiction). To write her off simply as wicked, or the sort of person who couldn't help it, is to ignore two fundamental aspects of her function in *The Wings of the Dove*: what she does for Milly and what she does for the novel's 'sense of life'.[15] It is in her relation to them that we should seek to understand Kate; although 'understand' implies a kind of loyalty that James's 'true agents' can never rely on.

Milly, like Densher and Aunt Maud, is deeply impressed by Kate's glamour and her self-command, but also by her less superficial qualities of 'straightness', 'fineness', intelligence and spirit. We can see too that something savage in Kate covertly seduces Milly and Densher, an attraction which has its counterpart in Maud's sympathy for their feebleness. Feeling not quite up to it themselves, both Milly and Densher explicitly identify Kate with 'life'; and thereby endorse a conception of 'life' that, whatever else it may mean, means not being like Mrs Condrip, whining ineffectually amid 'the lingering odour of boiled food'.[16]

This will surprise nobody familiar with James, though he will always have detractors who take exception to it as somehow immoral, suspecting him of a tendency merely to wave a stained antimacassar where they would want to see some firmer stuffing bolster his case against the materially disadvantaged. James in fact made no such case (as *The Princess Casamassima*, for instance, amply demonstrates): he simply has a clarity of vision which doesn't sentimentally spare the weaknesses of the weak; he leaves it open to us to see that their (relative) poverty induces her family to exploit Kate, just as the fear of it will lead Kate to exploit others; and to see also that if Milly, unlike Marian Condrip, disregards Kate's 'social uses' it is because *she* can afford to.

The reader is, however, positively encouraged to see Kate in terms of aesthetic value by Milly and Densher's persistent perception of her as a picture, one that a grand frame – a palace, a park, a piazza – will show to best advantage, but who isn't diminished by a cheap one. Seeing Kate all too obviously out of place in her sister's ugly little house is to suggest to Densher the noble premises where she *would* fit: nobody ever sees a Kate who, brought as low materially as her sister, might actually resemble the petty, greedy, dispirited and dispiriting Marian. In fact, dazzled by the picture of her in the grand frame, averting their eyes from the other, Densher and Milly can't ever quite get a fix on where Kate herself really is;[17] at Matcham, even as she notices how appropriate her friend's glamour is to that particular frame, Milly observes that Kate has

> the extraordinary and attaching property of appearing at a given moment to show as a beautiful stranger, to cut her connexions and lose her identity, letting the imagination for the time make what it would of them ... (150)

Fascinating, elusive and inscrutable, and wielding a mesmerising authority even when the evasions that underlie it are evident, Kate is the figure that Milly and Densher see in the carpet, a vivid streak leaping out of a dense weave of character and situation that seems to designate ultimate meaning. And by expertly manipulating the responses of the reader who is looking for that figure – by never being quite where or what we expect, by refusing to say straight out what her meaning, or plot, is, by substituting blanks for confidently awaited revelations – Kate carries the story forward when it threatens to sag. It is through Kate that the reader, like Densher, feels pressurised into accepting the bold statement, the eloquent gesture, as the prime constituents of reality. Her 'coming to'

Densher contrives to appear exactly such a statement or gesture, self-sufficient and inclusive, entirely detached from its logical or natural consequences: that Densher is to proceed from bed with Kate to bed with Milly, or that Kate herself might become pregnant. Any lead trailing off into these unaesthetic physical realities, into the 'smaller life' as represented by the 'greasy' Condrip children, is among the connections that Kate simply cuts.

What Kate embodies is that high style which in *The Wings of the Dove* struggles to establish an ascendancy over moral, deterministic and sentimental interpretations of the novel's meaning – interpretations that might trap her in the same frame as her sister. She looks in fact very much like the 'larger life' that Milly is looking for in the picture gallery, and which the 'smaller' life – Marian Condrip, the lady-copyists – would like to reflect. The small protagonist of *What Maisie Knew*, whose efforts to copy her mother, Ida, give an odd twist to sentimental, deterministic and moral interpretations of *that* novel, might find her ideal parent in Kate, who has a sense of family responsibility as well as Ida's sex-appeal, and Ida's ability to shape her own story.

Milly, as Maisie might have done, puts it to Sir Luke that by 'life' he means 'mainly gentlemen' – a gloss which the doctor tactfully amends, just as Sir Claude finally detaches Maisie from any notion that life, or her particular story, necessarily involves sitting on gentlemen's knees. What Sir Luke says he means by 'life' is as unspecific as all his remedies; but enough to make Milly see that it's Kate who has what she wants, and Kate through whom she can get it: 'It's in her that life is splendid; and a part of that is even that she's devoted to me.' This reference to Kate's 'devotion' is likely to strike the reader as another blunder, or else as just another fiction invented to compensate for a defective reality; for isn't Kate Milly's adversary, don't they represent the polarisation of good and evil, of ignorance and knowledge? Yet Milly is not entirely wrong to trust in Kate, any more than Maisie was in holding to those dubious articles of faith, her mother and Sir Claude; for Kate *is* in a sense devoted to Milly.

'It was a pretty part of the intercourse of these two young ladies that each thought the other more remarkable than herself.' The faint irony detectable here doesn't necessarily imply that Kate's admiration is insincere (though Milly wonders if it is). It suggests rather that the international theme – the confrontation of innocence and sophistication – also has a cosier personal dimension in which individuals are attracted to one another precisely because of differences in style and character. Kate is not as emotionally disengaged from Milly as her manner sometimes suggests. In fact, virtually all that we know of Kate's inner life after the Americans arrive is the increasing hold Milly has on her imagination. She is fascinated by the phenomenon of 'an angel with a thumping bank-account' – by the size of Milly's fortune and the eccentric disregard of it that Susie too has observed. What Kate also observes, however, as Susie does not, is how her feeling for Milly is affected by these things. She expects to hate her, but is charmed by her sweetness and generosity. And it's because she is obsessed by the idea of Milly as powerful and free, by her all-encompassing *reach*, that Kate is so quick to see Milly's reach isn't quite going to make it. She will have it all or she will miss it all, Kate explains to Densher, and 'Now I don't think she'll have it all.' By 'all' she means life, love, *and* money, and Densher sees in her feeling for Milly a disturbing mixture of 'noble compassion' and self-interest; but for Kate it is a happy blend, never more happily expressed than when she called Milly 'a dove'. The dove is to be caught and caged, but also to be petted and protected – most of all, from the things she herself doesn't want to know. One might make the point that Kate is watchful first, and protective second; but if her close observation of Milly enables her to seize her advantage, it makes her also witness to Milly's covert courage and pride as she tries not to let go of life. While the two elder women make the most, in their own terms, of Milly's approaching doom,[18] Kate is the 'wondering pitying sister' who watches in silence, instinctively understanding that Milly's doom is too awful for words: 'to recognize [it] was to bring down the avalanche.'

The narrator has just made the point clear:

> It may be declared for Kate, at all events, that her sincerity about her friend, through this time, was deep, her compassionate imagination strong; and that these things gave her a virtue, a good conscience, a credibility for herself, so to speak, that were later to be precious to her. (318)

In this perhaps slightly clumsy intervention, he represents the witness *Kate* had wanted, at the very beginning, in her father's house, to testify to her good faith.

9.

Kate, as James's agent or 'reflector', is, as he explained in his Preface, 'turned on' '"for all she is worth"', and 'largely at Venice', where he describes the drama as 'brought to a head' by the scene of the party held in the palazzo to mark the arrival, on holiday, of Sir Luke Strett (AN 300–1). It is Milly's first public appearance for some time, and almost her last appearance in the novel, and Susie rises to the occasion. 'She's ever so much better,' she tells Merton Densher; then, in a paroxysm of enthusiasm, 'It's a Veronese picture ... one of the courts of heaven, the court of a reigning seraph ... this is beyond any book' – remarks which point to the crucial dependence of what follows on a virtuoso handling of visual effects.

Densher recalls an earlier occasion at Lancaster Gate when Milly had not appeared but Kate had made a 'wonderful entrance'. Yet Kate seems to him now strangely 'wanting in lustre': tonight Milly, 'let loose among them in a wonderful white dress', is stealing the show, inspired, as Densher sees it, by 'some supreme idea', which he recognises as that of 'the American girl'. This is a role we have seen Milly adopt before, and always to conceal some difficulty in communication. Kate comes up with a better role, nudging Densher to take a closer look at Milly's priceless pearls:

'She's a dove ... and one somehow doesn't think of doves as bejewelled. Yet they suit her down to the ground'

– and Densher, noticing an intensity in her response, becomes aware that Kate is

exceptionally under the impression of that element of wealth in [Milly] which was a power, which was a great power, and which was dove-like only so far as one remembered that doves have wings and wondrous flights, have them as well as tender tints and soft sounds. (373)

Milly's pearls, he remarks loyally, would look good on Kate too.

'Oh yes, I see myself!'
As she saw herself, suddenly, he saw her – she would have been splendid ... (374)

It is a revelation and a turning-point that balances Milly's earlier confrontation with the picture at Matcham. Densher is struck by the realisation that Kate is simply not made to be the wife of a poor man, and this will weaken his resistance to her directives when shortly afterwards she makes her plan clear to him. One doubts if he sees unblinkingly where those directives are bound to lead: to Kate arrayed in the pearls of Densher's defunct benefactress. But the reader can see: and see too that, like the moon reflecting the sun, Kate would be merely the lustreless, lifeless image of Milly; that the friend who had seemed to Susie in Lancaster Gate like 'a figure in a picture stepping as if by magic out of its frame' is framed by James now, as the 'pale sister' whom Milly had recognised in Bronzino's portrait – splendid indeed, like the Bronzino bejewelled and glorious; but, like the Bronzino, transfixed and dead.

Has Kate ever actually envisaged Milly's death? Has she her cold-blooded plan in mind when she adds: 'She isn't better. She's worse'? Densher at any rate is disconcerted, as Kate continues, by the kindness in her voice: 'To-night she does want to live. ... It's wonderful. It's beautiful.' Her words catch the echo of Susie's effusions, but have a deeper resonance, for they are based on a closer reading of Milly's reality. Suddenly it sounds as if Kate were the author, understanding, loving, and believing in her own creation; suddenly Milly looks like a work of art struggling to come alive, and Kate's note of authority, Kate's sharp eye, has effected the transformation – and, like Mrs Monarch in 'The Real Thing', at the cost to herself of being recognised as the poor copy.

10.

Densher's imagination is explicitly noted at this point as being still obsessed with Kate. He himself has culture, sensitivity and intelligence, but Kate shows him a standard of style and a quality of spirit that he feels a constant obligation to live up to. It is because of Kate that Densher is anxious not to read 'the romance of his existence in a cheap edition'.

If this sounds like the kind of thing her father, Lionel Croy, might say, Densher too sees Kate as an asset, compensating for 'his weakness, as he called it, for life'. She is also an anchor (to whom he demands, repeatedly, to be tied) against that tendency to drift which the reader recognises as Densher's principal weakness. James contrives to give the impression that Densher doesn't actually *do* much for his newspaper; his life seems to consist always of being sent hither and thither, and being recalled. In all this he very much resembles a younger version of Lambert Strether in *The Ambassadors*. Both are men whose romantic impulses are held in check by a strong respect for facts and principles of conduct, and an anxiety to get things straight that sharply distinguishes them from those two twisters Lionel Croy and Chad Newsome. They view their respective missions – to capture Kate and to rescue Chad – as regularising a situation that is out of line with a society in which they both need to promote their authoritative masculine status. Yet both are men with an imagination shaped by a literary cast of mind who are much less concerned with their readership at home than with some masterplot that they feel in the air about them. Are they being written into it? Or are they being simply written off? Densher is as preoccupied with Aunt Maud and, later, with Susie as Strether is with the American expatriates in Paris; and this is mainly because his self-esteem depends so much on whether they think *he* has a place in the story.

This is what Densher would above all like to get straight, although his natural instinct for straightness also prompts him to point out the unlikelihood of Milly's not suspecting what's really going on between him and Kate, thereby drawing attention to her generous capacity for self-deception (or to a basic implausibilty in the plot, an awkwardness that only Densher, who is always putting his foot in it, could be allowed to get away with); but finding that such bald observations too often strike the wrong note with Kate and with Milly, Densher, who is afraid of boring the one and being bored by the other, learns to make the best of the game of appearances: 'He was in a wondrous silken web, and it *was* amusing.' And though he will never enjoy it as much as Strether, who stops asking awkward questions altogether, he acquiesces in the false situation Kate and Milly have between them established, hanging on in Venice to be kind to Milly and to further Kate's plan.

If Strether's position in Paris will become equivocal in the eyes of Woollett, Massachusetts, Densher's position now is obviously much more so, and according to much more general standards. But there is a less obvious, more interesting distinction to be made here, which has to do with a tendency among critics to see them both as 'consecrating by their appreciation';[19] that is, as distilling, concentrating and transmitting the impressions they receive in their capacity of 'lucid reflector', with the effect of enhancing the splendour of Madame de Vionnet and of Milly. It is true that Densher goes through the outward forms of some such consecration at the end of the book. But throughout the greater part of it he has, unlike Strether, a little plot of his own on the side which relegates Milly to an inferior narrative. Densher was always aware of the 'poetry' of 'poor pale exquisite Milly' in her 'grand old palace' (the poetry of Madame de Vionnet, examined dispassionately, amounts to not much more); but while Strether succeeds in making us feel that Madame de Vionnet *vaut bien* an unvirtuous attachment, Densher's courtship of Milly is a case of not quite finding her unattractive, not quite spoiling her fabrications while not quite bringing off his own, of not 'really bringing to a point, on Milly's side, anything whatever'. It is bound to seem tepid and flat compared with his pursuit of Kate, driven by desire, requiring opportunities to be seized and risks to be run, with a very specific end in view but giving him meanwhile in the very sense of scheming a sharp foretaste of mastery. Densher is only sensitive to Milly's personal needs and feels her 'reality' after he has brought Kate to the point that matters and his passion, with the pressure off, expands into a 'spirit of generosity', a lagoon, so to speak, of dilute benignity, unmoved by currents that run deeper.

This is as good a place as any in the novel to fish about for some clear idea of what might be morally right, since it has plainly become detached from Merton Densher. What the writer must look for, however, is not the real in the sense of ideal, but the workable thing, what he can get out of his subject in terms of psychological and narrative effect. Densher is the vehicle through whom James returns once more to the difficulty of distinguishing beautiful behaviour from wicked intentions, the puzzle of the beneficial effects that can arise on a flawed basis. He is one of James's ubiquitous 'bewildered' intelligences (AN 63–4) who see too many sides of a given question; he assumes a precarious stance between the sensual experience of release and expansion and the more rational fear of cutting loose from the safety of established norms. James, surely, isn't concerned with Densher's ultimate moral value but with the spectacle of his struggle with nervous and psychological strain, his sense of 'walking ... on a high ridge ... where the proprieties reduced themselves to his keeping his head', his anxiety about what other men would think of him caught in 'a circle of petticoats', his justifications of the way he 'so decently' sought to spare Milly: the ordeal, in short, of his self-consciousness.

If in some respects Densher seems to be encroaching here on territory which Milly herself already represents, his efforts to see himself and be seen in the right light are typical of a different sort of performance in James, of which the narrator of 'The Aspern Papers' and the governess in 'The Turn of the Screw' offer notable examples. This may slightly confuse the reader who, given that the interest has been squarely shifted to Densher at this stage, may reasonably wonder whether he is to be taken as the type of the lucid reflector or of the unreliable narrator. The answer is that he is both, in the same sort of combination James had essayed with Fleda Vetch in *The Spoils of Poynton*. There, as here, James takes a risk with it, but not one so great as to lead us to conclude that he doesn't know what he is doing – still less, that his evident 'appreciation' of the deeply compromised Densher somehow indicates his own sense of morality as having come adrift.[20] It isn't that Densher betrays James, but rather that James betrays him.

Densher's case demonstrates, as with Strether, something else that clearly fascinated James: that losing one's integrity doesn't necessarily happen in a flash; it can also be a long insidious process of little failures to act, little failures to respond.[21] And when Densher decides in Venice that solutions 'consisted mainly and pleasantly of further indecisions', he adds himself to the list of Jamesian characters – Hyacinth, Fleda, Strether, Maggie Verver – who exhibit a passivity that may be more or less culpable, but on whom the story indiscriminately takes its revenge.

If the mark of the victim is his otiose fictions, the sign of the story is melodrama or coincidence.[22] Densher recognises that the 'shock' has come on the day when Milly's servants block his access to the palazzo with blank politeness and the unexpected apparition of Lord Mark meets his gaze with a blank stare from behind the glass of a café in the piazza. Wandering through the storm that has suddenly broken, trying to make a pattern of chaos, Densher traces it to the figure of Lord Mark. 'The weather had changed ... *because* of Lord Mark. It was because of him, *a fortiori*, that the palace was closed'; Lord Mark's return looked 'sharp, striking, ugly *to him* ... he didn't need, for seeing it as evil ... to know more about it than he had *so easily and so wonderfully* picked up' (italics in the second quotation mine). James makes obvious here the illogicality, the subjectivity and the dangerous complacency of this hypothesising: all symptoms of unreliable story-telling, which are exacerbated in Susie's subsequent descent on Densher's *quartiere*.

This visit marks an important stage in Susie's developing relation with Densher. There have been faintly portentous hints from far back of an alliance between the two journalists, and that 'something was preparing that would draw them closer'. She comes now to tell him that, after seeing Lord Mark, Milly has turned her face to the wall and lost the will to live. The scene of these disclosures is extraordinarily atmospheric, combining the dankly domestic feel of Susie's 'wet waterproof' with a sense of global doom, and it offers Susie and Densher a chance neither has hitherto had, to do something impressive with it. There is indeed a touch of the heroic in Susie's assault on Densher's sensibilities, which leaves him open to Milly's pain. But then they make a hash of it. Each as anxious as the other to deflect attention from Densher's guilt, they return to the question of Lord Mark; and they elaborate what may not be a fiction but which catches the note (the note, precisely, of 'The Turn of the Screw') of a story unhinged from reality. Lord Mark is a 'horrid little beast'; his action was 'mere base revenge ... deviltry ... duplicity' – the behaviour of a thwarted fortune-hunter – 'The hound!'

Here Densher has gone too far; for the image projected on to Lord Mark is his own, which he himself had seen, on the palace steps, reflected in Eugenio's eyes – that of a fortune-hunting gigolo. The reader hears Densher's accusation as hollow, bouncing off walls that don't absorb the sound, just as Merton, shocked and sickened at himself, becomes aware that the one unassailable fact of Milly's dying, 'the great smudge of mortality across the picture, the shadow of pain and horror', finds 'in no quarter a surface of spirit or of speech that consented to reflect it'. Something of what we may imagine Milly to be going through is, perhaps, reflected in Densher's shifts and subterfuges, in the decay of his sense of himself, and the darkness of his big scene. But that would be to read the romance of *her* existence in a cheap edition.

11.

The Venice part of the novel closes as Milly finally, through Sir Luke, summons Densher to her presence. But when the page turns, he is back in London. It is left to the reader to reconstruct a picture of their meeting from his fractured account of it and from the events that follow. Kate's plot has injured Milly, and Densher is appalled at his complicity. These are wholly expected developments, heralding a death and a parting – items James could have dealt with in four or five pages (as he did for example in *Roderick Hudson*). The protracted and difficult dénouement of *The Wings of the Dove* takes us through the painful process of separation undergone by Densher and Kate, but it also shows how differently they are disposed to handle the materials of James's story, and what can still be done for Milly's. Presented in a socio-religious context of five o'clock teas and of the Brompton Oratory, it is really a struggle for command of the story, a battleground on which it is hard to fix where Kate stands – in the field of life or in the frame of art? – for Milly's life, or for her death? More perceptibly, it is a process in which we see Kate's lustre fade and watch her gradual decline towards an extinction that will leave Milly in the ascendant.

Kate might be directing a film, with the story yet to run to the end of its reel. But for Densher it is as if the picture had become a still, in which he sees himself placed in relation to Milly and to Kate in the light of what he and Kate have done, and in which the ethical issues involved, like the people in the photograph, must be fixed in black and white. And Lord Mark is stuck, obstinately, in Densher's viewfinder: 'He told her, the scoundrel, that you and I are secretly engaged.' The issue of Lord Mark's culpability is one that Densher will continue to pursue, as if the thread of logic he finds in it might lead him out of the moral labyrinth. Thus it was wrong of Lord Mark to tell Milly the truth – but he, Densher, didn't have to, because 'she never asked me for it.' This is the sort of casuistry that has earned him the description of 'moral moron'.[23]

Kate on the other hand has no use for parcelling out the blame (her casual acceptance of it is a marvel of narrative and spiritual economy, compared with Densher's). Consistently she turns the enquiry back to the still living, loving and lovable – if not to the suffering – Milly.

> 'She never wanted the truth ... She wanted *you*. She would have taken from you what you could give her and been glad of it, even if she had known it false ....' (451)

In so saying (and she impresses us that this *is* the truth), Kate draws Milly away from Densher's bloodless abstractions, into her own world, a world of wanting, of human frailty and desire, of the lie that Kate wanted Milly told 'to save her life!', of the love that she claims (accurately, as it proves) Milly has inspired in Densher. It is a world that allows of course for *her* wanting the money, and in which the sort of clarification Densher is intent on appears simply irrelevant; so that while he becomes increasingly irritated, he is also left looking faintly silly on the arid plane of theory, like Lambert Strether, who rejected Maria Gostrey for an idea, left at the end of *The Ambassadors*, high but dry.[24]

Was his final encounter with Milly 'really almost happy?' Kate puts the question because the success of her plan depends on a reconciliation, but we too want to know the answer out of natural curiosity; and when Densher remains fastidiously evasive, we may wonder whether James is primarily concerned to enshroud Milly's dying in a respectful hush, or merely to assert his power over the reader, as Densher by stalling keeps Kate hanging on his lips. We are conscious at any rate of an ugly tension between the lovers and corresponding strain in the narrative as he tries to suppress the story through silence and she tries to revive it in speech. Kate's mastery of the spoken word and confidence that she can manipulate it to her own ends have never been more in evidence, and more evident to Densher, than in these closing scenes. But her facility is a double-edged weapon, and Kate takes risks with it; and now, when she attempts 'with a beautiful authority' to wrap up Milly's story, she strikes a seriously false note. Milly, she insists, has '*been* loved'; she has 'realised her passion', she 'has had *all* she wanted'. The reader recognises this exorbitant claim as a mere flourish of pink ribbon round the crude summing-up that follows:

'She won't have loved you for nothing.' It made him wince, but she insisted. 'And you won't have loved *me*.' (456)

If Kate's pursuit of her own story carries her well over the boundaries of taste, Densher's cover-up of his part in it leads him to adopt the supine posture of Milly's 'stricken suitor'. In this role, which removes him from the competition for Kate's hand (and in which he makes, unlike the bereaved Mrs Condrip, no demands on her purse), Aunt Maud takes him at last to her bosom. Maud feels for Milly too, clearly sharing James's sentiment, expressed in the Preface, that to be 'balked of your inheritance' is particularly hard when your inheritance is so big (AN 292). Her disinterested sympathy at least makes it possible for Densher to speak to Aunt Maud (as he cannot to Kate) of Milly – dragged from life like a victim to the scaffold, 'grimly, awfully silent'. That soundless, nightmare image is the only one we will have of what reality has become for Milly. The beam of Densher's imaginative sympathy, unlike Kate's, glances off the dying girl only to provide a comforting glow in which he can take a rest from proper narrative responsibility. We learn that he left Venice determined to think of Milly as already dead, for he recognises her terror of death's approach as '*the* horrible thing to know'; however, 'in so naming it, he found the strangest of reliefs', and to relieve Aunt Maud of the horrors he has told her he outlines the 'wonderful scene' of his 'sublime' last meeting with Milly ('all gaiety and gilt') – 'sublime' being the note he knows 'exquisite London gossip' wants.

There is another aspect to all this which Densher cannot put into words:

> something had happened to him too beautiful and too sacred to describe. He had been, to his recovered sense, forgiven, dedicated, blest … (463)

This is the 'essence' of his experience. Yet we may reasonably be wary of assuming that because his 'something' is both beyond description and vouchsafed exclusively to the reader it necessarily indicates a priceless insight, to the effect that Milly's is a saintly goodness and that Densher is redeemed by recognising, or 'appreciating' it. Densher after all can't share his sense of being forgiven with Aunt Maud because she doesn't know – Susie hasn't told her – that he has anything to be forgiven *for*. Can we really make anything of this (the only) clue to what has passed between him and Milly, except what we already know, that Milly is a person of tender impulses and finds it hard, with Densher, to articulate what she feels? Densher's seeing himself in the light of Milly's aura doesn't preclude our seeing him through Aunt Maud's eyes as 'haunted and harmless', or, less indulgently, seeing that he is drifting into the role of heartbroken lover as the safest refuge within the worldly novel where you have to pay for what you get and sleepless nights are just retribution for unprincipled deeds; or seeing him simply (Aunt Maud encourages this way of thinking) as a narrative investment who hasn't fulfilled his potential.

What turns Densher in his course is a renewed sense of ignominy at being stuck in the wrong role. He acts at last in 'high passion',

urging Kate once more to marry him, before Milly dies and there
can be any question of an inheritance:

> 'Our marriage will – fundamentally, somehow, don't you see? –
> right everything that's wrong ... we shall only wonder at our past
> fear. It will seem an ugly madness. It will seem a bad dream.'
> (467)

But, as indeed can happen in a bad dream, and happens elsewhere
in James, the person who looks like Kate has turned into somebody
else, a kind of harpy who dismisses moral scruples and crudely
reasserts her sexual hold over her lover, who is 'nearly sickened' by
the knowledge of her motives. And yet his notion of marriage – this
imposing of a pattern that will somehow make things 'right' –
doesn't impress the reader any more than it does Kate. It may carry
a distant echo of Caspar Goodwood's last appeal to Isabel Archer,
but a door closed long ago in James (in *The American*?) on Caspar's
uncomplicated vision of justice and freedom of action. Where in
Densher's tidy solution – where for that matter in the pages of
domestic bickering that precede it – is Milly's lonely end? What of
her suffering and pain?

We appear to have lost Milly herself among an amalgam of
themes familiar from James's other novels – the pursuit of an heiress, betrayal by close friends, the exploitation of decency, all of them
variations on the manipulation of innocence which we also see
reworked in James's tales, and which can strike us there, like the late
theme where the dead come to supplant the living, as faintly creepy
or maudlin, or induce a distinct moral queasiness.[25] When Densher
meets Aunt Maud on Christmas morning and hears at last the news
from Venice that 'Our dear dove ... has folded her wonderful
wings', well may the reader, sickened with the lot of them, wonder
whether Milly has gone through her dying only to dissolve like a
cachou on Maud Lowder's tongue.

12.

Growing stale and distasteful, the story is revived by a decisive
move on the part of Kate, which, while it reinforces her connection
with the 'smaller life', also establishes the extent to which she
transcends it. Just when we supposed her sitting tight, waiting for

the money, she abruptly quits Lancaster Gate to be with her sister, on whom their father has calamitously descended. Seeing her in Marian's ugly little parlour, Densher is once more impressed by the sense of her sorrows and of her fineness: he thinks he himself would be less of a misfit there than she.

And if Kate has inherited her father's talent for making others appear shabby, Densher seems to have caught from Marian the air of the victim. For he returns to the question of Lord Mark, attempting to find out whether, after failing with Milly, he had asked Kate to marry him. Did she encourage him or not?[26] What strikes the reader isn't that Kate denies the imputation of bad faith (she would, wouldn't she?), but that Densher won't let the matter rest; and over his attempts at organised logic, the rational tone of his 'My dear girl' and his 'certainly you may ask' hangs a cloud of paranoid obsession, a miasma of petty grievance – pure Condrip. Like Kate earlier, Densher is now victimised by his own language, and his laborious detective-work seems merely a paint-by-numbers re-creation of the great Venetian scenes James has already given us.

'What has the brute to do with us anyway?' cries Densher, desperate in the knowledge that he's being a bore about Lord Mark. James himself may seem to be in danger of succumbing to a fascination with the theme of betrayal and the psychology of obsession; yet he redirects our attention here to the enigma of Lord Mark and the extent that he *has* had to do with Milly. Their last encounter, like whatever it was that Lionel Croy did, is one of the gaps in the story deliberately left to invite speculation, and most critics have followed Densher into the breach, calling Lord Mark a villain, cruel, brutal, sinister and so on. It seems to me rather that Lord Mark emulates, in small specific ways, what Kate does for Milly on a grander scale. That is, if he does her an injury, he also promotes her humanity and her dignity. It is Kate who has observed a side to Lord Mark no one else seems to see:

'... *The* thing's his genius ... I don't know at least ... what else to call it when a man's able to make himself without effort, without violence, without machinery of any sort, so intensely felt. He has somehow an effect without his being in any traceable way a cause.' (260)

Allowing effects without causes is not the way newspaper reporters are trained to look at events. Densher 'establishes connexions' the moment he makes out Lord Mark behind the glass of Florian's café and later, through the London fog, in Maud Lowder's brougham. But such barriers to perception are virtually the sign of Lord Mark, like the double eyeglass he always wears through which Milly peered at Maud's dinner-table, for a first glimpse of the world. And although the reader may choose to think that Milly dies from coming into contact with the world's wickedness, to share Densher's view of Lord Mark as the conduit making that connection is to ignore that Lord Mark is on the contrary more consistently represented as a screen – or a shield. It was he who protected Milly in those moments at Matcham and in Venice when she faced most squarely up to her grim reality; it was he whom after their first meeting Milly perceived as having 'had some way of his own, quite unlike anyone else's, of assuring her of his consideration'. And in a curious way that can't be related to his intentions, whatever they may have been, the effect that Lord Mark has on Milly is salutary. It was his tacit disapproval that stopped her taking refuge in the role of the American girl or the pitiable invalid; and although the image he offered her (in clumsy emulation of Ralph Touchett) was not auspicious, the Bronzino portrait had the right result of inciting Milly to seek a better one. We don't know (and it scarcely matters) how or why he broke the bad news to her in Venice, but his having done so means that he has prevented Milly from making a fool of herself; that any action she subsequently takes has the weight and the dignity of full knowledge behind it (the Countess Gemini does the same for Isabel Archer).

Milly *has* taken action. Densher has had, on Christmas Eve, a 'communication' which he recognises as coming from Milly, announcing (so he suspects and Kate assumes) that Milly has made him rich; and he hands it – 'something I feel as sacred' – over to Kate as a symbol of his good faith and of his love for her. Kate tosses the letter, unopened, into the fire; and with it flares up, briefly but vividly, the latent, the ultimate issue: whose bid for Densher – Milly's or Kate's – is going to win?

Densher 'tests' Kate again (his term) by sending her, again unopened, a subsequent letter from Milly's lawyers which must contain details of the legacy. He offers her a choice. He will marry her, and renounce the money (they will simply return the letter unread); or, she can have the money without him. It seems so clear an exposition of spiritual versus mercenary values, it exerts so strong a pressure towards the neatest of endings and satisfactory retribution for Kate, that many readers appear to have failed to notice that she doesn't in fact accept the terms of the bargain. Kate has always resisted coercion; but her attitude now also implies something else: that she sees the futility of civilised sorting-out sessions over cups of tea; that she senses how behind the formalities of the post-mortem something indefinable and uncontrollable has got the story in its grip. It is Milly, operating from beyond the tomb on a level far above that of Merton's clumsy quid pro quo. She is playing now with stakes in moral superiority and in hard cash and, by forgiving Densher *and* giving him the money, she is sweeping the board on both counts.

Kate sees that Densher has in the wake of that last meeting finally fallen in love with Milly: 'she died for you then that you might understand her. From that hour you *did*. And I do now. She did it *for* us.' Her solemn note sets a seal on Milly's story that is very different from her earlier, prettified version, and which concludes it as Ralph on his deathbed concluded Isabel's, redeeming it from utter futility. Milly's life is over, but if she hasn't known love, she has at least inspired it. It is a story that clearly encompasses the destruction of another love, and if these were Kate's last words we could close the book feeling (as Aunt Maud does) sentimentally replete and satisfied that the familiar system of balances and checks embodied in such safe stories is well under control. But now, in the very act of tenderly wrapping her up, Kate lets loose the creature she herself created:

> 'I used to call her, in my stupidity – for want of anything better – a dove. Well she stretched out her wings and it was to *that* they reached. They cover us.' (508)

'Stupidity', as used by the Jamesian heroine in jeopardy, means not that she can't see but that she doesn't want to see. Kate and Densher had seen well enough, as Milly circled in her Venetian ballroom, the connections between her wealth 'which was a great power' and her reach and 'doves [who] have wings and wondrous flights';[27] so that we now see how this, Kate's final comment on her rival, invokes that other Milly who went to the doctor's surgery to be taken care of only to soar out of it as Milly militant, Milly dynamic, reinterpreting the prescription to 'live' in the interests of her own ascendancy – and in whom we can see Kate's comment reinterpreted, to sinister effect. 'They cover us': the wings that protect also cast a shadow. Is

Milly now the sweet innocent scarcely conscious of her wealth, or is she the inscrutable power through whom that wealth is being deployed to drive the lovers apart for ever?[28]

We cannot know, of course, in what spirit Milly made her last bequest. But however we interpret the final image of the dove, we have seen Milly retrieved by Kate from its more commonplace associations – just as Lord Mark on the more mundane level of the dinner-party circuit tried to prevent her from appearing banal and sentimental. We have heard Kate describe the phenomenon of having an effect 'without being in any way a traceable cause', which she observed in Lord Mark perhaps because she had already seen it in her father Lionel; we have heard her evoke in Lionel someone who has done something awful that finds no place in the book, and who for that reason reaches beyond its limitations, like the Milly we can never definitively read, because Kate has burnt the letter; we have seen in Lionel someone else who is determined to 'live', whose grip on the story depends on the bond with Kate, and whose genius consists in making everyone that comes near him appear in an invidious light. Where once we saw the 'dove' as a fake, a role that Milly adopted from expediency, and saw Milly herself as suppressed and marginalised, now we see – thanks to Kate – Milly restored to the centre of the picture, Milly as the string on which the pearls are strung, as Hugh Vereker said of the figure in his carpet, yet also, mysteriously, an absence: the figure visible only in what it has done.

It isn't for Kate to become what her mother became, the mere crooked reflection of somebody else. Not yet conceding the game to Milly, not yet spiritually bankrupt, she puts down her last stake. She had engaged herself to Densher 'for ever', and when he can't return her pledge, can't deny his feeling for Milly, Kate acknowledges the end. She rejects a marriage offering only a bogus security, a union that seeks to blot out the undiminished reality of a third person. Her parting from Densher thus curiously re-enacts Isabel Archer's final parting from Caspar Goodwood under the aegis of Ralph, and it also casts an ominous light forward on to the embrace that will conclude *The Golden Bowl* with Maggie's inability to look her husband in the face, because Charlotte is not dead to *her*. Kate's perspective is different, though, from Densher's or Isabel's or Maggie Verver's. It originates in an infinitely older, wearier world, and it isn't complicated by the search for the self. Kate's task – the artist's primary task – is not to know what she is, but to say what she sees, and her vision has a kind of primeval clarity. When she steps out of the picture, it isn't into Isabel's obscurity, where the sense of an ending escapes us. Kate's darkness signifies final and certain emptiness, and she has seen it in her father's 'kind safe eyes', just as Milly, probing Sir Luke's 'cheerful blankness', couldn't find there what she was looking for, the safety of retreat. So Kate is lost to us, while Milly like Isabel remains at large, in the darkness of the abyss where haunting fictions breed.

Epilogue

'Her memory's your love. You *want* no other.' Merton Densher (trailing as always in the rear) is left, according to Kate's fiat, satisfied with what he's got ('it will do', she says, for him); and left, according to a conventional reading, redeemed by the power of Milly's love. But if this is so, it's a story we read nowhere, and that, especially in journalist's terms, is no story at all. His sense of Milly as 'something too beautiful and sacred to describe' simply shuts her away with the rest of his spiritual heritage, that is, with his dead mother, of whom all we know is that her son 'held her image sacred', and that she 'copied, patient lady, famous pictures in great museums' – like the ladies in the National Gallery whom Milly sought refuge among, unable directly to face the real pictures, or 'the larger life'.

Densher, similarly seeking sanctuary, takes refuge in a church: the Brompton Oratory, 'to make him right, would do'. But will it 'do' for us to find there, in the ineffable mystery of the Cross, the beauty and virtue of self-sacrifice, the ultimate significance of it all? Susie had promised Milly, 'I'd die *for* you'; and the words find an echo in Kate's 'She did it *for* us.' Kate had seen the narrative as a 'broken sentence': is it now complete? We might recognise a pattern here, one that constitutes a firm guideline going straight from one end of the story to the other, linking Susie and Densher in the Christian masterplot. Only, if we look back to where the idea of the pattern or figure, and of an ultimate significance, is most conspicuously equated with the holy of holies, the point *didn't* seem to be that the only thing worth having is veiled from our sight, or that the revelation of it redeemed anybody, or that if one person fails to see it, everything depends on the next person, who will. It's in the light of that last consideration that we must take Densher's 'presentiment of the juncture at which the understanding of everyone else [but Susie] would fail, and this little person's alone survive'. We may choose to go back to the sort of novel Susie might have written, where Milly and Densher are good and Kate and Lord Mark are bad, and find our security there; but the point of 'The Figure in the Carpet' is that the figure alone survives all attempts to understand exactly what it is.[1]

219

Milly herself, in the last days in Venice, had dismissed Susie's chances of survival: 'she could see Susie, in the event of her death, in no character at all.' Hers is the confidence of an author here as regards what the story is about and her companion's *ad hoc* place in it. (One might compare how at the end of *The Ambassadors* Strether dismisses Maria Gostrey.)[2] Can Susie exist – Milly puts it to us – in any aspect other than that of being 'insistently, exclusively concerned in her mere makeshift duration'?

What gives weight to Milly's view of the matter is the extent to which *The Wings of the Dove* as a whole bears out James's dictum in his Preface that 'the poet's [or novelist's] essential concern' is not the 'act of dying' but 'the act of living' (AN 289–90). His novel is not essentially concerned (as Kate to begin with is) with the fact of Milly's demise. This is not to deny that it in several ways promotes the idea of sacred sacrifice – in its religious imagery, in Kate's casual turns of phrase that hint at a violent subtext, in Densher's reiterated association of cutting and knives with 'the great master of the knife' Sir Luke. But what we actually see, on those pages where Milly acts and thinks and speaks, are her strenuous, if hit-or-miss, attempts to adapt, to appropriate, to latch on to whatever will give her the visibility and audibility of a heroine: could she be like Kate? could she get Kate's man? can she catch the note of the novel itself?

Milly is seen by others as too good for this world, as a conveniently placed innocent, as an isolated, vulnerable individual, as the adjunct to a drama presented in cruder terms than her own. (It was the same for Maisie.) To remain the focus of these variously angled mirrors without suffering damaging distortion requires the ability to keep moving, keep adapting. This is how Milly, like Maisie, literally 'makes shift' to ensure her 'duration', and it is not a case of passively 'being' anything , least of all an emblem of sacrifice, but a dynamic process – a case of discovering for herself some more original relation to the novel than that of the poor-little-rich-girl; which is what James has Milly realise at the very point where Sir Luke has just indicated that deadly prognosis. Leaving his consulting rooms, she senses that:

The beauty of the bloom had gone from the small old sense of safety – that was distinct: she had left it behind her there for ever. But the beauty of the idea of a great adventure, a big dim experiment or struggle, in which she might more responsibly than ever before take a hand, had been offered her instead. (177)

This is the call to which James's truest agents respond, the recognition that distinguishes Milly, 'stir[ring] the stream like a leviathan', from Densher and Susie with their efforts to keep things at all times on an even keel, and from others like them who prefer the status quo, the stable point of view, the picture to stay squarely in its frame, the cage door to be shut on the dove – or the panther; like Pinnie unwilling to open the prison gate, pinning little Hyacinth firmly into the costume of a lord. 'The great adventure' is the swoop of Maisie's swing, the flight that Hyacinth, trapped in the orbit of Rosy's imagination, could never achieve; its spirit is in the 'puff' of Fleda Vetch that Mrs Gereth launched, its denial is Fleda's refusal to 'let herself go'. The great adventure is for those who like Strether and Maisie don't want the return-ticket that will return Fleda to the safety of Ricks; who mean to steer the story in a new direction, who want to become Chad at the tiller of the boat or Ida who always catches her trains.

The point of it all isn't just what escaping does for a character called Strether or Maisie or Milly. Milly taking up arms or taking flight, like Maisie mimicking her mother, stands for movement and metamorphosis: the force that has altered the contours of James's fiction, the energy made visible in the sudden flash of some reflected image, the dynamic that has brought us a long way from *Washington Square* and *The Portrait of a Lady*. The familiar features of good and evil that we recognised there, even when Catherine and Isabel didn't, are blunted; the moral, social and ideological structures that propped up the façades of old New York and fenced about the garden of Isabel's soul are no longer clearly discernible. Only in the narrative structure of Isabel's story were there gaps, which have now opened so wide as to bring us to the edge of the abyss, Milly's 'great darkness', the threatened epistemological void into which the old monolithic truths are fast disappearing, and where anyone who doesn't adapt fast enough (lady into dove) might be lost altogether.

If there does remain a conception of the real thing, an indicator of where the real James has got to, Susie is very near it, I think, when her discriminating eye instantly recognises in Milly something marvellous, never seen before, but also hinting at impermanence (would she ever see it again?) and eluding definition (*was* it 'the real thing'?). But in her subsequent fixation on a specific love and loss, Susie finds her place, with Densher, in the ranks of James's idealists, or idealists *manqués*, whose idea of ultimate significance resides in some symbol of integrity, of wholeness, or source of illumination that holds them in awe – Hyacinth's flawless Princess, Fleda's Poynton, Sir Claude's 'beautiful' Maisie, Strether's Madame de Vionnet, Maggie Verver's 'golden fruit that had shone from afar', figured by the gleaming bowl she acquires from the *antiquario*. The value of these objects of reverence lies, of course, partly in the dazzled eye of the beholder, in whom it is always associated, consciously or unconsciously, with the loss of security in some form: for Hyacinth, this was his 'rightful' heritage; for Fleda, Poynton before Waterbath invaded; for Sir Claude, the nursery cosiness of his cameraderie with Maisie; for Strether the family group he was once part of; for Merton Densher, the impeccable decency of his courtesy calls on Milly; for Susie Stringham and Maggie Verver, the exclusiveness of a cherished relationship. Yet in all this yearning for safety, or the sort of impermeable enclosure graphically designated by the supposedly uncracked bowl, there is also an abnegation of responsibility, and in particular of interpretive responsibility, an unwillingness to recognise complicated or threatening situations, or unsafe stories.

One cornerstone of safe stories, and of security in general, is the idea of a sacrifice such as Milly might be taken to represent (Fanny Assingham's version of *The Golden Bowl*, a story she is very anxious to keep safe, posits that Maggie the good will 'die first' before acknowledging that her husband and her best friend, Charlotte, are lovers); and sacrifice, as I observed at the beginning of this book, is never far from 'the real thing'. Indeed, to be so designated is virtually, in James, to wear the badge of doom: Major and Mrs Monarch had 'bowed their heads' to the inevitability of theirs; little Jeanne in *The Ambassadors* is offered up on the Parisian marriage market; Charlotte is transported to America; Maisie's Paris is never reached; the figure in the carpet is never found. And time after time we see what might be taken for the real thing, something exemplarily fine, like Fleda Vetch, or solid, like Catherine Sloper, at the mercy of a cynical world; and we see Isabel Archer and Hyacinth Robinson, easily recognisable in their contradictions as 'real', forced into an emblematic role, sacrificed in the flower of their expanding personalities to the exigencies of an art form, confined to a particular frame.

It may be that James, like Fanny Assingham or Mrs Wix, saw catastrophe looming on every side: he claimed, after all, to have 'the imagination of disaster'. But this is never translated to his fiction in the form of a crass pessimism, still less to establish an inevitable relation between absolutes, such as the 'good' always going to the 'bad'.[3] James's fictions do not investigate the *nature* of the ideal as providing a clue to its evanescence (what his protagonist assumes by the term 'the real thing' is always taken for granted); but register, rather, the impact of its disintegration, adulteration or failure to materialise on the recording consciousness, where the story takes shape. He is not concerned with Charlotte's inscrutable being, but with accumulating perceptions of her ability to make things different; not concerned with what 'Paris' might leave to be desired, but with the way in which Maisie and Strether build their cities of dreams on so gappy a basis; concerned, ultimately, not with the loss of the meaningful, but with the reconstruction of meaning, and it is in this area that his sacrifices pay off.[4]

It must strike us, then, as a little too easy, too glib, to conclude that the real thing that marks the authentic James is, quite simply, that which is always lost, some kind of impossibly dear unattainable ideal. That would be to find the sort of simplistic answer epitomised in Fanny Assingham's summary way with the golden bowl that she sweeps off the chimney-piece, which is to say, 'there's the point, in neat pieces easily picked up' – Fanny being of course the last person to abrogate her interpretive responsibility, but the first to dodge the messy truth when it seems likely to emerge.[5] It is only accidentally that her action reveals the flaw in the bowl which explains why it and why Maggie's perfect marriage in fact came impossibly cheap. But Fanny if she were a competent soothsayer would know that the 'truth' always lies precisely in this incidental, accidental way between life and art, essence and style: between what the bits and pieces actually look like and what we make them 'say'.

The real thing then – if it exists – must be sought somewhere in that meeting-ground of art and life. There, on the one side, are those realities touching the human body and the human psyche and the human purse that James never lets go of; and on the other, those moments of revelation created by the story-teller's skill, and stamped with his authority. Maggie, face to face with her husband and the evidence of his adultery, finds herself torn between a very real sense or 'conviction' of her wrong, and a more enticing prevision of the narrative process, the 'action', whereby it might be made to come right: 'conviction budged no inch ... but action began to hover like some lighter and larger, but easier form ... '. She feels 'the sudden split between conviction and action. They had ceased ... to be connected.' James's protagonists, James's readers, stand in the same treacherous place, or space.

For because art and life are fighting it out over the same area, generating in their tug-of-war stresses and strains that render the whole area prone to collapse, no territory in James can ever be guaranteed entirely safe. The lesson of 'The Real Thing' is that the rigorous standards of art, the basis of the painter's security, of his integrity and self-respect, can't always cope in the context of life. Compromises have to be made; and the messiness of living – the petty concerns, the illusions, the bad luck associated with Major and Mrs Monarch – everywhere infiltrates art in the guise of the trivial detail, the little blurs, the random element, which conspire to produce the effect of life. Yet the Monarchs, without the painter to see them whole, would simply have disintegrated and ceased to signify – would have been, from the point of view of art, as good as dead.

It is the pressures accumulating in an unstable system that, reading *The Wings of the Dove*, we feel as sudden shifts of perspective, or as a more insidious coercion. The artist's ideal of permanence, coherence and significance, which demands that we think (like Kate) in terms of having it all or losing it all and that we risk everything for it, is pitted against the exigencies of the smaller life, the lesser ambitions of those who like Susie and Densher and the lady-copyists must manage by painstakingly muddling through. That context asks us to acknowledge, almost with sympathy, Kate and Densher's recognition, as 'real' people desperate to stay together somehow, of the 'possibilities' in Milly (that she might be sacrificed to their security); but the intenser vision of the artist forces us also to acknowledge, almost with misgiving, James's more sophisticated conception of those possibilities which will take Milly from the smaller to the larger life, where she won't be, as she dreads being, pointless and ephemeral like a bad copy. And if, under pressure, we accommodate our experience of the actual world to the artist's picture, as Mrs Monarch did in 'The Real Thing', we have to look beyond the frame of the smaller life, where we know it to be true because we feel it that Kate is 'bad' (we would hate to be deceived by our best friend) and Milly sacrificed to the vicious world as a scapegoat for us all, to see in the frame of the larger life (where we feel it must be true, because we see it) that Kate is good: good because she embodies the talent and the striving of the artist, but also because she creates in Milly something that isn't just a collection of bits that (like Major Monarch and his trousers) don't add up. Only in the second frame, that of the larger life, is justice done to them all – to Kate, Milly and James – as, in 'The Real Thing', justice is eventually done to the Monarchs and the painter and his models; but to see it so – to cross the divide – demands that input of imaginative energy in default of which all such transpositions are copies; it requires, as it does of the painter, all our ability to see and feel, and that we abandon his stringent distinction between the real and the apparent.

Life interacts with art in James always to produce these conflicts and reconciliations, a pulling in opposite directions which is also a kind of exchange of charge between the imagination seeking to impose an ideal form and a more primitive vitality, the will to survive in any shape or form. This is the interaction we catch a glint of in the phrase 'the real thing', with its connotations both of authority and of a more evasive and manipulative enthusiasm (it is generally used in James by those – Hyacinth, Maisie, Susie, Strether – who most urgently need to be regarded as connoisseurs); and this is the interaction which James evokes in the Preface to *The Wings of the Dove*, where he relishes the dazzle and solidity of the perfect artefact – the skater's pond that resists the cracks – and at the same time pays implicit tribute to the counter-resistance of the human element, as represented by Milly's struggle: 'The process of life [that] gives way fighting, and often may so shine out on the lost ground as in no other connexion.'

James has another, more celebrated image for the real and the ideal and the space between them:

> The balloon of experience is ... tied to the earth, and under that necessity we swing, thanks to a rope of remarkable length, in the more or less commodious car of the imagination; but it is by the rope we know where we are, and from the moment that cable is cut we are at large and unrelated ... The art of the romancer is, 'for the fun of it', insidiously to cut the cable, to cut it without our detecting him. (AN 33–4)

The real thing that is the sign of the authentic James has to do with that moment of disconnection, of disengagement, with the release of latent energy and expansion of the frame of reference that the figure of the balloon in free flight implies. James's fictional system is one in which cracks, doors, gaps, reflections are increasingly suggestive of infinite spaces, infinite possibilities; so that as we enter it in pursuit of *our* idea of ultimate meaning, we rely increasingly on our rope, our guideline, to 'know where we are'. But then, deflected perhaps by some mirror-image or finding in some loophole a line of least resistance, the live wire of our imagination escapes into the shifting frames: and there occurs, at some random point of contact, the epistemological jolt that we associate with sighting the real thing: we know it when we see it! But there's no ultimate meaning here; for we see it only in context, and it looks different every time. The system is set up to short-circuit in this way; the rope is there to be cut.

'We shall never be again as we were!' It was Kate Croy who seemed to 'cut connexions'; and as her final comment brings *The Wings of the Dove* to a close we too might perceive her, as Densher does, altered beyond recognition, the past irrevocably broken with. In that sense her last words do indeed possess the 'sort of meaning' in which Kate always felt that her 'broken sentence' must end. But the real thing reveals itself in the sense that the sentence does break: that somewhere between Susie's 'I'd die *for* you' and Kate's 'She did it *for* us', the rope of the story is cut which so securely connected the real to the ideal, Susie's invocation of unselfish love to Milly's death as the emblem of it. For if, as part of that safe story, Kate 'dies' *from* Milly – destroyed, that is, as by the direct action of Milly's goodness zinging along the cable, the cable snaps to the effect that Kate also dies *for* Milly: that is, she transfers to her the energy and the potential, the drive and mystery, with which *she* had charged the story; and Milly, like the balloon, takes off.

The ascent of the dove – a 'succession of flights and drops', to borrow a phrase from James[6] – describes a bumpy but persistent evolutionary trajectory. Lifting Milly out of those limitations (sickness, mortality, the point of view that fixes rather than interprets) which made *The Princess Casamassima* a place of contracting horizons, it launches her as the American girl, the free spirit; but Milly sails the ether as the free spirit who has, unlike Fleda Vetch, known how to gain control of James's narrative vehicle, as the American girl who has contrived to capitalise on the ephemeral charm and the faults of untutored innocence and yet come through looking, like Maisie, 'exquisite' and 'sacred'. It is Milly in whom Catherine Sloper's inarticulate dignity that blocked the fictions of others becomes the most pregnant of silences; Milly whom the narrative buries to see her re-emerge as Maggie in *The Golden Bowl*, where the heroine-victim turned heroine-triumphant will proceed to become the heroine-artist: someone who *sees* her rival the bad heroine die 'for' her, only to re-create her by recognising in 'her variety, her power', her 'mastery of the greater style', an inexhaustible capacity to hold us in thrall.[7] Milly is Catherine's mass converted to an explosive literary potential: she stands for the *story*'s life after death, embodied in that critical state where the story has most to gain because it had most to lose.[8] This is the Milly who has battened on to Kate's 'sort of ending' to make it her own, and given Kate's last, weary acknowledgement of movement and metamorphosis a more confident and a creepier twist. For, as she herself predicts, Milly will die as if she were alive, and Susie will never really know where she is, but only where she's not.

Susie is perhaps furthest from the real thing when she turns her back on Milly precariously poised on the Alpine ledge, satisfied that she is what and where Susie wants her to be, the lamb of God 'looking down on the kingdoms of the earth', who isn't, just yet, for the high jump. Milly is after all on the edge of the abyss, where Susie herself will see obscurity engulf things which, besides Milly, she desperately wants to hang on to: the pious hope, for instance, that intentions connect directly to events; the belief that her own 'what do we see in it?' matters more than Maud's 'what can we get out of it?'; the notion that the authors of being, father-protectors, doctor-deliverers (the Austin Slopers, the masters of the knife) are ever to be relied on.

For as Susie tiptoes away, James is already closing in, knife in hand, on the 'possibilities shining out of Milly Theale'. To sacrifice her for the sake of *all* our safe stories? Or to cut her loose? – to release, that is, the protean, infinitely adaptable, self-regenerating entity which has lodged itself in Kate's story, just as her father's hidden tale of self-destruction lodged itself in Kate: unnameable, unknowable, 'and yet it's a part of me.' Of James's intentions we can never be sure; but we suspect that the germ or the gene of the story will always outlive our saving fictions, because it is, like Lionel Croy, a parasite on our vitality, compelling us time after time to accommodate it, to adapt to its mutations our imaginative vision.

Notes

Places and dates of publication are those of the editions used.

Introduction

1. First, Mrs Monarch adjusts Miss Churm's hairdo to look more stylish; then she and her husband start on the housework which is Oreste's regular job. Both actions are done with a grace and spontaneity which accords with Henry James Sr's idea of the 'aesthetic man or Artist': 'I mean the man of whatsoever function, who in fulfilling it obeys his own inspiration or taste, uncontrolled either by his physical necessities or social obligations ... Beauty reveals herself to him only as he obeys his spontaneous taste or attraction' (*Moralism and Christianity*, 1850, quoted in Richard Poirier, *A World Elsewhere: The place of style in American literature*, London, 1967, p. 23).

2. 'Any point of view is interesting that is a direct impression of life': letter from James to the Deerfield summer school (HF 46; HJL iii. 257); 'the affair of the painter is not the immediate, it is the reflected field of life' (Preface to *The Princess Casamassima*, AN 65); see also Preface to *The Wings of the Dove*, AN 306.

3. That James could be, like Major Monarch, 'anecdotically unconscious' of his surroundings is well attested. See e.g. the reminiscences of Stephen Spender, Edward Marsh, A. G. Bradley and F. M. Hueffer in *The Legend of the Master*, ed. Simon Nowell-Smith (Oxford and New York, 1985), pp. 67–70.

4. e.g. S. Gorley Putt calls 'The Figure in the Carpet' 'almost auto-erotic' (*The Fiction of Henry James: A reader's guide*, Harmondsworth, 1968, p. 205) – an aberration in a critic who usually has a clear sense of what James is about and, clearer still, of what he is *not* about.

5. Is what the narrator really wants Gwendolen herself? What does she marry *for*?, etc. See Terence Cave, *Recognitions: A study in poetics* (Oxford, 1988), pp. 264–9.

6. The plot of 'The Figure in the Carpet' (marry the girl and get the goods) recognisably grows out of 'The Aspern Papers' (1888), in which we are also aware of suppressed elements of sex and violence. But unlike in 'The Aspern Papers', in 'The Figure in the Carpet' the idea of a hidden treasure – the essence of the story – arises virtually accidentally, like a chance mutation. Vereker's almost incidental reference to a 'little trick' (9.282) burgeons and is elaborated with startling speed, becoming finally 'all gold and gems' (9.300).

7. 'The Figure in the Carpet' deliberately, I am sure, and perhaps counter-productively, gears anxieties about the idea of the 'story' to overdrive: the more excited we are by the promise of a grand design, the more likely we are to be panicked into missing the story alto-

228

gether. This is effectively the theme of James's 'The Beast in the Jungle' (1903).

8. Yvor Winters, 'Maule's Curse', in *In Defense of Reason* (London, 1960), p. 306. The broad discussion of James that follows it in itself belies Winters's premise.

9. Ruth Bernard Yeazell, *Language and Knowledge in the Late Novels of Henry James* (Chicago, 1976), p. 14; cf. Millicent Bell, *Meaning in Henry James* (Cambridge, Mass., and London, 1991), p. xi.

10. Introduction to *The Golden Bowl*, The World's Classics (Oxford, 1983), pp. i–xxxi.

1. Washington Square

1. Even as he completed it and saw it serialised, *Washington Square* was diminished in James's mind by the excitement of producing a 'larger', 'better' novel, *The Portrait of a Lady* (see HJL ii. 265, 277, 308, 314–15). It is not clear nonetheless why he left the former out of the New York Edition, a venture undertaken mainly to make money, incorporating most of his fiction, revised and with specially written Prefaces ('I have tried to read over *Washington Square* and I *can't*, and I fear it must go!' – HJL iv.37). It may be that, given the close fit between his compact subject and perfected early style of treatment, James could get no purchase on this novel, find no loose ends to play around with.

2. A remarkable parallel to the refuge Catherine finds in silence is reflected in the diary of the more articulate Alice James, who wrote of her young womanhood: 'I had to peg away pretty hard between 12 and 24, "killing myself" as some one calls it – absorbing into the bone that the better part is to clothe oneself in neutral tints, walk by still waters and possess one's soul in silence' (*The Diary of Alice James*, ed. Leon Edel, London, 1965, entry of Feb. 1892, p. 95). On Alice's rather different circumstances (her father, who never had a chance to stop her marrying, told her he wouldn't stop her killing herself), see Jean Strouse, *Alice James: A biography* (London, 1981). James first read his sister's diary in 1894, after her (natural) death.

2. The Portrait of a Lady

1. See Graham Greene, Introduction to *The Portrait of a Lady*, The World's Classics (Oxford, 1981), p. vii.

2. Unsigned review, *Blackwood's Magazine*, March 1882, repr. in *Henry James: The Critical Heritage*, ed. Roger Gard (London, 1968), p. 101.

3. On the relation of *The Portrait of a Lady* to other nineteenth-century (American) fictions see William Veeder, *Henry James: The lessons of the Master* (Chicago and London, 1975); and Alfred Habegger, *Henry James and the 'Woman Business'* (Cambridge, 1989), especially Chs 3, 4 and 5. For *The Portrait*'s thematic links with James's earlier fictions, see Philip Horne, *Henry James and Revision* (Oxford, 1990), pp. 197–205.

4.   A tremendous 'ado' has been made about Minny's place in James's life and work, much of it presupposing too simple a relationship between the writer's source and his end-product; in other cases, that the relationship was unutterably devious. For a view that restores the balance, see Horne, *James and Revision*, pp. 184–91.

5.   The Prefaces, essentially, show how what James called the 'wind-blown germ' of the story (its starting-point, or donnée) is converted into a strenuous *doing*, a struggle to impose control, 'economy', 'neatness' on the energy, the elasticity, the 'explosive principle', of the writer's raw material. In the Prefaces, the protagonist tends to become a relatively pale shade of the character the reader remembers; the self-effacing author, on the contrary, is vividly present, whether as the hunter stalking his subject, the writer suffering 'the cold editorial shoulder', or as 'the designer left wholly alone, amid a chattering unperceiving world'. But the real hero of the Prefaces is 'the inveterate romance of the labour' (see AN 43, 172, 278, 254–7, 314–15, 286, 326, 311, 288–9, 295, 228, 287).

6.   Cf. James's response to criticism of the figure of Miss Birdseye in *The Bostonians*, which he claimed wasn't a portrait of a real person, but 'If I have made my old woman *live* it is my misfortune ...': the irony of his tone indicating he appreciated the unintended compliment (HJL iii. 69).

7.   On Isabel's Emersonian attitudes, see Richard Poirier, *The Comic Sense of Henry James: A study of the early novels* (London, 1960), especially pp. 219–21 and 246; also Joel Porte, Introduction to *New Essays on 'The Portrait of a Lady'* (Cambridge, 1990), pp. 2–3 and pp. 27–8, n. 1, where there is a useful summary of critical comment.

8.   Poirier, *Comic Sense*, pp. 187–9.

9.   See William Veeder, 'The Feminine Orphan and the Emergent Master: self-realization in Henry James' (*Henry James Review* 12:1, Winter 1991), p. 29. It is Isabel who, as I will suggest, encourages Osmond to see her as an art-object. Ralph's remarks, cited by Veeder, about this or that person 'doing' things to Isabel are jocular (and his mother's objection to them is a joke against Mrs Touchett, who is not responsive to other people's jokes).

10.   For two extended and valuable discussions of Isabel's relation to traditional plots and to the role of the heroine, see Rachel Brownstein, 'The Portrait of a Lady' in *Becoming a Heroine* (Harmondsworth, 1984), especially pp. 239–50; and Millicent Bell, 'Isabel Archer and the Affronting of Plot' in *Meaning in Henry James*, pp. 80–122.

11.   Dorothea Krook, *The Ordeal of Consciousness in Henry James* (Cambridge, 1967), p. 58.

12.   In *The Golden Bowl*, Charlotte Stant comes to London for the marriage of her friend Maggie Verver. She goes shopping with Maggie's fiancé, Prince Amerigo, for a wedding present. The *antiquario* (dealer) who tries to sell her the golden bowl, understanding what they say to each other in Italian, picks up that they have had and may still have a clandestine relationship. Charlotte intuits that 'he was pleased with us, he was struck, he had ideas about us... we're beautiful, aren't we? – and he knows' (*The Golden Bowl*, p. 80). That is the hidden story that

Maggie must discover. She does so when the *antiquario* later sells *her* the bowl, and tells her what he knows.
13. Poirier, *Comic Sense*, p. 224.
14. Poirier, *Comic Sense*, p. 243.
15. In letters written in the late 1870s and early 1880s to a bereaved and lonely friend, Grace Norton, James strikes precisely the note of Ralph's farewell and the novel's ending: the belief in endurance, the sense of life going on, the consolations that are not religious. On 28 July 1883 he wrote: 'Sorrow comes in great waves ... – but it rolls over us, and though it may almost smother us it leaves us on the spot and we know that if it is strong we are stronger, inasmuch as it passes and we remain. It wears us, uses us, but we wear it and use it in return; and it is blind, whereas we after a manner see' (HJL ii. 424–5; see also ii. 144, and cf. letter to Enid Wharton, iv. 495).
16. Poirier, *Comic Sense*, p. 245.
17. Poirier, *Comic Sense*, pp. 243–55.
18. Krook, *Ordeal of Consciousness*, p. 366.
19. I leave out of account here certain feminist interpretations which criticise Isabel for not acting like a woman of the twentieth century and fail to recognise that since James was not in this novel primarily concerned with female emancipation or the morality of divorce, he was not looking for solutions framed in such terms. Cf. *The Bostonians* and *What Maisie Knew*, novels more directly concerned with these issues, in which it is possible to read the ending as a direct comment on subjection in marriage and broken homes respectively (the wife will be unhappy, the child is taken away).
20. Poirier, *Comic Sense*, p. 245. I find this comment curiously uncharacteristic of a critic whose account of *The Portrait of a Lady* – the most searching I have read – has made the point, in connection with her flight from Caspar, that Isabel is not a real person, and so persuasively relates her to James's designs and intentions as to make one nervous about using a phrase like 'she is' at all. Emphasising the supremacy of the deathbed scene, and explaining Isabel's behaviour from the Emersonian point of view, Poirier seems as impatient as Isabel of Caspar's presence in the novel (and less alarmed by it).
21. The lesbian element in Olive Chancellor's relations with Verena was one James could not openly raise in the 1880s. But in any case sex or types of sexuality is not the important issue in James compared with, to quote Adrian Poole, 'the whole issue of desire. The forms of the world [James's] people inhabit dictate a few narrow possibilities for its expression, legitimising some and proscribing others; yet desire is multiple, diverse, not narrowly "sexual" in kind, not merely different forms of a single essential drive.' (*Henry James*, Harvester New Readings, London, 1991, pp. 85–6).
22. William Veeder ('The Feminine Orphan', pp. 20–54) explains the novel's ending in terms of the psychobiographical structure that he imposes on James's fictions, and which emphasises the regressive movement in the conflict between safety and freedom I have touched on above. He outlines the following connections: James himself – Isabel

(and Ralph) – not-being-a-man – isolation (social and psychological) – negation – death-drive – freedom-in-death (what Isabel might be seeking at the end and James implies by leaving her *'en l'air'*). This is a rough summary of a subtle argument, though I would prefer to leave out of it James's psyche, which is at best a dark horse to the coach of the story.

23. Millicent Bell makes a neat analogy between Isabel's sexual relation to Caspar and her relation to the narrative, putting the emphasis where it belongs, on the latter: 'Isabel both desires and fears a story as much as she both desires and fears sexual union; both threaten the pure potentiality of the unaroused personality, which only subsists in itself' (*Meaning in Henry James*, p. 117).

24. James's comment on his projected ending to *The Portrait*, anticipating the reader's dissatisfaction, was: 'The *whole* of anything is never told; you can only take what groups together' (Ntbks 18). Cf. his much-quoted dictum in the Preface to *Roderick Hudson*: 'Really, universally, relations stop nowhere, and the exquisite problem of the artist is eternally but to draw, by an exquisite geometry of his own, the circle within which they shall happily *appear* to do so' (AN 5).

25. This passage was altered in revision, as Philip Horne has pointed out, with the effect of increasing its pathos. A photograph of the alteration, reproduced by Horne, shows that James first put the more emotive 'safety' for 'security' (see *James and Revision*, p. 224 and frontispiece).

26. See particularly in this connection 'The Story of a Masterpiece' (1868); 'The Liar' (1888); 'The Private Life' (1892); 'The Special Type' (1900); *The Wings of the Dove* (1902); 'The Jolly Corner' (1908); *The Sense of the Past* (incomplete, 1917).

3. *The Princess Casamassima*

1. Lionel Trilling, *The Liberal Imagination* (London, 1951), pp. 61–3.

2. The germ of *The Princess Casamassima* – the conception of a sensitive illegitimate nobleman who loses both his faith in the radical cause and the woman he loves – is, as frequently observed, to be found in Turgenev's *Virgin Soil* (1877). That, however, remains a skeletal novel of ideas, with characters artificially created to animate it; whereas the structural building-block of *The Princess*, as of *Fathers and Sons*, is the intensely felt individual experience; compare in the two novels the reassuring warmth of domestic intimacies, the strained father–son relations, the *femme fatale* fascinated by the man of the people, the prickly male friendship (notably as expressed in the confrontations between Arkady and Bazarov in Chapter 21 of *Fathers and Sons* and between Hyacinth and Paul in Chapter 35).

3. The realism of this novel invokes the genetic heritage as it is never invoked in *The Portrait of a Lady* (would Isabel 'really' fail to see in Pansy any physical trace of Madame Merle?). It is, however, his mother, not Lord Frederick, whom Hyacinth is said closely to resemble in looks; and in character he resembles the Mr Vetch who is described as

'a lonely, disappointed, embittered, cynical little man', with 'the nerves and sensibilities of a gentleman'. The difficult, sympathetically observed relation between surrogate father and son strongly emphasises nurture at the expense of nature.

4. Trilling, *Liberal Imagination*, p. 75.
5. 'H.B' in *Critic*, Dec. 1886, repr. in *The Critical Heritage*, ed. Gard, p. 179.
6. For conflicting views on the accuracy of James's picture of anarchism, see Trilling, *Liberal Imagination*, pp. 68–74, and Irving Howe, *Politics and the Novel* (New York, 1957), pp. 145–56.
7. Cf. James's comment in his Preface to *The Princess*: 'My vision of the aspects I more or less fortunately rendered *was*, exactly, my knowledge. If I made my appearances live, what was this but the utmost one could do with them?' (AN 77).
8. Julia Wordsworth in the *Contemporary Review*, Dec. 1886, repr. in *The Critical Heritage*, ed. Gard, p. 174.
9. Mark Seltzer has drawn interesting parallels between systems of policing and supervision operative in nineteenth-century London and the relationship between seeing and power in *The Princess Casamassima* (*Henry James and the Art of Power*, Ithaca and London, 1984, pp. 25–57). He usefully emphasises the novel's theatricality, though without making a clear distinction between watching what people are doing (surveillance) and looking at what they represent (theatre) – a distinction implicit in the novel's *modus operandi*.
10. 'My scheme called for the suggested nearness (to all our apparently ordered life) of some sinister anarchic underworld, heaving in its pain, its power and its hate; a presentation not of sharp particulars, but of loose appearances, vague motions and sounds and symptoms, just perceptible presences and general looming possibilities. ...... the value I wished most to render and the effect I wished most to produce were precisely those of our not knowing, of society's no! knowing, but only guessing and suspecting and trying to ignore, what "goes on" irreconcileably, subversively, beneath the vast smug surface' (Preface to *The Princess Casamassima*, AN 76, 77–8). These sentences come closer to describing, for example, *The Golden Bowl* than the novel in question. By the time he wrote them, James had learnt to evoke the fascination and threat of 'the thing behind' to much greater effect.
11. Adrian Poole (*Henry James*, pp. 63–4) has pointed out that this passage, bolstering Hyacinth's sexuality, was added in the New York Edition revision.
12. 'If a pistol is hung on the wall in the first act, it must go off in the fourth': remark attributed to Chekhov by I. Gurlyand (*Chekhov v vospominaniyakh sovremennikov*, Moscow, 1962, p. 754).
13. As John Colmer has pointed out, it is not the case that Hyacinth has been abandoned by his friends, as he thinks (see *Coleridge to Catch-22*, London, 1978, p. 103). And to see him die the victim of heartless womankind, as Cargill suggests James intended, is a sentimental simplification (Oscar Cargill, *The Novels of Henry James*, London, 1971, p. 163). Hyacinth has had many weeks and warnings to get used to the idea that the Princess is fickle; as for Millicent, her *rapprochement* with

Sholto was precisely what he anticipated when he was in Paris. The emphasis, when he sees her with Sholto and the Princess with Paul, in both cases is on the proportions a trivial incident assumes in his eyes (cf. Strether by the river). To speak as Trilling does (*Liberal Imagination*, p. 76) of the 'great scene of lust in the department store' is similarly to overload it from a very personal point of view.

14.   *Chatterton* (1856) by Henry Wallis hangs in the Tate Gallery, London.

4.   *The Spoils of Poynton*

1.   The so-called 'aesthetic premise' difficulty some readers have with *Poynton* (are beautiful furnishings worth all the fuss?) is not a problem in James's text, though it is one his text can be manipulated to address. It should not be confused with Cargill's interesting if untenable theory (*Novels of Henry James*, pp. 227–30) that Fleda's aesthetic evaluation of the spoils is at fault, which attempts not to deplete but to add something to the novel. It is sometimes argued that Fleda herself, its real subject, is spiritually above mere things. Even if that were true, neither Poynton nor Ricks represents mere things: they are both evidence and symbol of artistic creation and re-creation.

2.   For these assessments, see respectively Kenneth Graham, *Henry James: The drama of fulfilment* (Oxford, 1975), pp. 136–7; Nina Baym, 'Fleda Vetch and the plot of 'The Spoils of Poynton', *PMLA* 84 (Jan. 1969), p. 106; Robert C. McLean, 'The subjective adventure of Fleda Vetch', in *Henry James*, Modern Judgements, ed. Tony Tanner (London, 1968), pp. 204–21 passim.

3.   For an account of these discrepancies, see Matthiessen and Murdock's notes to the drafts for *Poynton* (Ntbks, pp. 138, 210, 219–20, 251, 254); also Baym (see preceding note). Apart from incidents that don't materialise, the main differences between James's ideas about it and the novel we have are: the deposition of Mrs Gereth from her central role of wronged mother by Fleda, who is first a figure of action, later a complex psychological one; James's deciding to begin with that Owen 'doesn't in the least take to Fleda' (Ntbks 137), then that he does; Mona's narrative function, which is given most weight in the Preface; and the absence in the Preface of any mention of Owen at all.

4.   McLean's article (see note 2 above) was the first detailed account of Fleda's narratorial unreliability, though he strains a point here and there and is less convincing on Owen's capacities.

5.   The 'she' whom the squabble is said to show in such a bad light is ambiguous. If Owen were really speaking (and only the closest reading of the text reveals that he isn't), it could mean his mother. The novel is scattered with similar truncated little hints of alternative interpretations – rather like the 'scrap book art' of Waterbath which threatens to deface the integrated picture of Poynton.

6.   It is simplistic to assume, as McLean and others have, that Fleda is 'considerably repelled by sex' (McLean, p. 206). On the contrary, it is

Owen's sexuality, emphasised by repeated references to his physique, which explains an attraction some critics profess not to understand. What does frighten and at the same time fascinates Fleda is the idea of sex overstepping the boundaries of social propriety. The telegraphist in 'In the Cage' is similarly fascinated; and that story is certainly not concerned with sexual fears (what attracts her to her Mr Mudge is precisely his uncouth virility – 10.166–7), but, like *Poynton*, with the crash of illusions.

7. In suggesting that Ricks represents 'female self-reliance even to the point of spinsterhood', Bell (*Meaning in Henry James*, p. 221) gives a positive twist to Fleda's choice of Ricks which I cannot see validated by James's text. The maiden-aunt, 'battered', and even 'exterminated' by the 'masterful' Mrs Gereth, is not a good role-model: even Mona is a better one, for getting Owen on *her* terms.

8. Modern commentators play into Mrs Gereth's hands when they continue to refer to her place of exile as a 'cottage', as she does, plangently, though the term could once be applied to small country houses in the classic style, which Ricks, from James's description, clearly is.

9. James has been accused of 'almost excessive stagecraft' in suggesting here 'that the kind of love Owen wants is maternal love' (Patrick Quinn, 'Morals and Motives in *The Spoils of Poynton*', *Sewanee Review* 62 (1954), p. 571). I think this is to take the question of James's intentions here and of Owen's psychological needs rather too seriously.

10. James stresses, perhaps exaggerates, the point in his Preface: 'Every one, every thing in the story is … sterile *but* the so thriftily constructed Mona, able at any moment to bear the whole of her dead weight at once on any given inch of a resisting surface' (AN 131–2). Mona's streamlined narrative function might be compared with that of the Princess Casamassima, whom Hyacinth deemed 'a grand natural force', but whose romantic trimmings disguise an essentially light-weight contribution to that novel, and who obscures in it that interplay between decisive action and sexual attraction on which the tension of *The Spoils of Poynton* depends. Unlike the Princess, Mona keeps largely out of the limelight, like one of the 'things' at Poynton, subjugated to an overall effect.

11. The leech-like Fleda's surname, in James's first drafts, was 'Veetch' (Ntbks 198).

12. Leon Edel suggests (*The Life of Henry James*, revised edn, Harmondsworth, 1977, II. 225) that the fire is a metaphor for the 'destruction' (failure) of James's play *Guy Domville* (1894). To Bellringer's equally dubious suggestion ('*The Spoils of Poynton*: James's unintended involvement', *Essays in Criticism* 16, p. 197) that only Mona is dealt justice by the blaze because only Mona is interested in owning Poynton, I would answer that Mona presumably gets the insurance; she also has Owen, and, like Gwendolen marrying Drayton Deane in 'The Figure in the Carpet', another story with sexual undercurrents, she may have married Owen 'for something else' (see 9. 314).

5.   What Maisie Knew

1. Cf. Kenneth Graham's illuminating comments on the presentation of Mrs Wix in *Indirections of the Novel: James, Conrad and Forster* (Cambridge, 1988), pp. 61–4.

2. Edward Wasiolek usefully emphasised Maisie's self-assertiveness in his article 'Maisie: Pure or Corrupt?' (*College English* 22, Dec. 1960, 167–72), which also makes the point that 'purity' vs 'impurity' is too crude a dialectic to employ here. He still yields too much ground to those critics who focus too exclusively on the erotic element in *What Maisie Knew*. Maisie's being glad to see Sir Claude afraid of her doesn't necessarily, as Wasiolek suggests, imply a new, sexual basis to their relationship. Sir Claude may associate fear with sex, but Maisie, as demonstrated in her attitude to her mother, associates it with love.

3. To elevate, or relegate, her to symbolic status is exactly the kind of sending upstairs, out of the action, that Maisie with every fibre of her being resists. The implication in the Preface that she exerts a direct moral influence on her elders may have been deliberately intended by James to placate those readers he goes on to mention who found the child's situation 'disgusting'. Maisie *qua* 'torch of virtue' at any rate takes very much second place in the Preface to the 'little wonder-working agent' whose narrative function James discusses at length. The phrase for example 'the death of her childhood' is used there not in an emotive context, but simply to denote the end of the relevant phase of Maisie's information-processing (AN 146-7).

4. Tolstoy's handling of the naïve viewpoint in the opera scene, loaded with his own sense of significance, positively creaks and groans in comparison with James: 'it was so pretentiously false and unnatural that [Natasha] first felt ashamed at the actors and then amused at them' (*War and Peace*, trans. Louise and Aylmer Maude, The World's Classics, Oxford, 1983, i. 598–9). Cf. John Bayley, *Tolstoy and the Novel*, London, 1966, pp. 160–1).

5. This perception is one indication that Maisie never sees her relations with Sir Claude in sexual terms. What she does dimly see by now is that if he weren't her stepmother's lover he would be better placed to act the responsible stepfather and give her a home (p. 154). Playing the part of paramour is only Maisie's make-believe; but that home life might have room for true love is on the contrary, and thanks to Maisie, one of the story's real discoveries.

6. That is one reason why their alliance strikes us as more credible than that between Fleda and Owen, as Elizabeth Allen has pointed out (*A Woman's Place in the Novels of Henry James*, London, 1984, p. 128).

7. One might compare the attempts of Merton Densher in *The Wings of the Dove* (pp. 490, 499) and of Amerigo in *the Golden Bowl* (pp. 339, 567) to obliterate problems in physical embraces. It is the woman in each case who seeks a solution.

8. 'I have the imagination of disaster – and see life indeed as ferocious and terrible': James to Arthur Benson, 26 June 1896 (*Henry James:*

Letters to A. C. Benson and Auguste Monod, ed. E. F. Benson, London, 1930, p. 35). The younger James put it more prosaically: '[I have] an unlimited capacity for imagining and apprehending that things are going, or will go, badly' (letter to Grace Norton, 29 Oct. 1883, HJL iii. 12).

9. Cargill, one of those who maintain unconvincingly that Maisie ultimately offers herself to Sir Claude, cites her reference to the Virgin 'with no sense of irreverence' as a mark of irreligiosity (*Novels of Henry James*, p. 258). I see it as a good example of Maisie's practical sense (the statue, as we know, is an obvious landmark); and of how the words James puts in his characters' mouths can expand and complicate the frame of reference in ways they don't dream of, and deliver us from oversimplistic interpretations. (The Virgin in question remains after all immaculate, conspicuous for her filial rather than marital connections.)

10. Sir Claude of course is 'really' not a knight but a baronet, not as yet having achieved the distinction Mrs Wix envisages for him.

11. F. R. Leavis, 'A Disagreement', in Marius Bewley, *The Complex Fate: Hawthorne, Henry James and some other American writers* (London, 1952), p. 131. His defence of Mrs Wix is, however, provoked by Bewley's exaggeration of her sexual interest in Sir Claude.

6. *The Wings of the Dove*

1. 'Notes of a Son and Brother' in *Henry James: Autobiography*, ed. F. W. Dupee (Princeton, NJ, 1983), p. 544.

2. The conception of great wealth as intrinsically romantic is not as central to James's world-view as is sometimes supposed. It fails to get off the ground in *The Princess Casamassima*; it proves distinctly leaky in *The Golden Bowl*; it collapses altogether in *The Ivory Tower* (incomplete, 1917). For some ramifications of this conception in American literature and an astringent view of the part it plays in Susie's evaluation of 'the real thing', see John Goode, 'The pervasive mystery of style: *The Wings of the Dove*', in *The Air of Reality: New essays on Henry James*, ed. John Goode (London, 1972), pp. 257–66.

3. See Charles Thomas Samuels, *The Ambiguity of Henry James*, Urbana, Ill., 1971, p. 68: 'James clearly wished the reader to think Milly divine'. Also F. O. Matthiessen, *Henry James: The major phase* (New York and Oxford, 1963), p. 59, and Joseph Ward (*The Search for Form: Studies in the structure of James's fiction* (Chapel Hill, NC, 1967), pp. 188–9.

4. Milly and Densher see Kate as a picture in a frame, while Susie, characteristically, sees Kate as stepping *out* of the frame (p. 122), in order to minister to her Milly. See also pp. 131–2, 248.

5. James describes in his autobiography 'the most appalling yet admirable nightmare of my life', in which he pursues and is pursued by some 'awful agent, creature or presence' through the Galérie d'Apollon in the Louvre (see 'A Small Boy and Others', in *Autobiography*, pp. 196–7).

6. Ward (*The Search for Form*, p. 194) both makes a point of Milly's aggression and connects it with her legacy to the lovers. See below, n. 28, on the dove-destroyer.

7. The portrait described is generally recognised as Bronzino's *Lucrezia Panciatichi*, at present in the Uffizi Gallery, Florence.

8. 'the great master of the knife' is Densher's phrase (p. 367), and, like other images he connects with Sir Luke ('Ah fifty thousand knives!', p. 256, 'a vision that cut like a knife', p. 434), echoes the note of violence struck in the novel by casual metaphorical references to hurting, killing, sacrifice, execution, beasts and birds of prey, etc.

9. Interpretations of 'if they would/ if they could' differ. To me, the reversal of the terms does not imply synonymity, but a shift in meaning articulated by 'would', deriving from (1) 'to wish' and (2) 'to be'.

10. In *The Golden Bowl* (p. 471) Maggie finds 'the horror of the thing hideously *behind* [the conspiracy to deceive her] … had met her like some bad-faced stranger surprised in one of the thick-carpeted corridors of a house of quiet.' In 'The Beast in the Jungle', the terrifying event which John Marcher spends his life waiting for never happens (at least not in the way he anticipates).

11. See Krook, *Ordeal of Consciousness*, p. 200. The view of Milly as an emblem of goodness whose death affirms that evil has touched her corresponds to the 'straight' view of 'The Turn of the Screw' (taking the governess's story on her own terms), which establishes Miles as a 'good' soul, whose death is the result of evil being driven out of him. Just as this version of the story suppresses what James is at pains to show us – the children's unpredictability, the housekeeper's doubts, the curious attitudes of the governess herself, so the analogous version of *The Wings of the Dove* leaves out of account what we clearly see, Milly's very human failings, her continual accommodations to 'civilised' life, her connivance in the idea of plot.

12. Samuels, *Ambiguity of Henry James*, p. 7.

13. A major difference between Kate and Densher is that though he also bears these pressures, he doesn't, except for sex, *deal* with them (the essence of Densher is to be dealt with).

14. Bell, *Meaning in Henry James*, p. 299.

15. Yeazell (*Language and Knowledge*, p. 83) gets it exactly: 'to decide that Kate Croy is simply a hypocrite and a liar is to ignore her power as an artist – her power to reshape the world according to the demands of her imagination.'

16. Kenneth Graham, in 'The Sense of Life in *The Wings of the Dove*' (where he doesn't in my view do full justice to Kate) gives a necessary emphasis to the importance of context in reading James: 'Any suggested interpretation, like the meaning of the word "life", requires immediately to be, as it were, dropped back into the pot again – to "prove" itself locally by its ability to be absorbed into the texture of the scene in question' (*The Drama of Fulfilment*, p. 164).

17. See e.g. pp. 43, 109, 136, 278.

18. Susie promotes the sentimental aspect of Milly's dying, Maud empha-
    sises her emotional economy: '"I might be crying now," she said, "if I
    weren't writing letters"' (p. 294).
19. See Krook, p. 198.
20. See Leo Bersani, 'The Narrator as Center in *The Wings of the Dove*',
    Modern Fiction Studies 6:2 Summer 1961, p. 140: 'James himself appar-
    ently does not see that Densher's staying in tribute to Milly's hospital-
    ity is nonetheless also staying to betray her.' Bersani shows that the
    narrator's point of view is in places indistinguishable from Densher's,
    and argues that the latter is assimilated to an idealised vision of Milly
    that is James's own and in which the real moral issues are obscured. I
    think he makes too little of the irony directed at Densher in the
    Venetian scenes; nor need we assume that the narrator's point of view
    coincides with James's or is responsible for the moral message. The
    space given Densher might be accounted an artistic weakness, but the
    moral of the book remains, for James, uncommonly clear: if you act
    unethically, you will be the loser.
21. The theme of the man who can't make up his mind is exemplified early
    on in 'Daisy Miller''s Winterbourne (1878), and again in Vanderbank in
    The Awkward Age (1899). In the subsequent fictions *The Ambassadors*
    (1902), 'The Beast in the Jungle' (1903) and 'Crapy Cornelia' (1909),
    there is a perceptible shift of emphasis from the fate of the woman who
    puts up with him to the protagonist's self-absorption.
22. On melodrama and coincidence in relation to James see respectively
    Peter Brooks, *The Melodramatic Imagination: Balzac, Henry James,
    melodrama, and the mode of excess* (New Haven, Conn., 1976), passim;
    and Cave, *Recognitions*, especially pp. 250 ff.
23. Samuels, *Ambiguity of Henry James*, p. 70.
24. Cf. the similar pressures working in *The Ambassadors* against
    Strether's desire to get things straight: the lies that everyone tells,
    Madame de Vionnet's trying to make him fall a little in love with her.
25. Cf. in the tales points of similarity in theme and/or tone to *The Wings
    of the Dove*: the exploitation of an innocent party by a pair of lovers in
    'The Special Type' (1900); the temporising morality of the male pro-
    tagonist in 'The Aspern Papers' (1888); the worship of the dead in
    'The Altar of the Dead' (1895) and in the maudlin 'Maud-Evelyn'
    (1900).
26. Whether Kate encouraged Lord Mark has a bearing on his possible
    reasons for telling Milly the truth; he could have done it out of cool
    self-interest: if Kate *might* have him, he must ensure Densher remains
    penniless and can't have her; or out of rank dog-in-the-manger spite:
    if Kate won't have him, no one else must have her. The case exempli-
    fies the complicated deductions James expects his reader to follow.
27. Goode ('The pervasive mystery of style', p. 283) suggests that only
    Densher, not Kate, sees the connection between the dove's wealth and
    its 'wondrous flights'; but the passage in question (see above, p. 204)
    surely implies that it is the intensity of *Kate's* vision which communi-
    cates itself to him.

28. Relatively few critics (they include Frederick Crews, Ward, Samuels, Yeazell) have touched on the idea of the dove-destroyer. Yet it's an interpretation that the novel's ominous resonances seem to invite. (James refers in the Preface to the 'dark wing' of the 'portents' he deployed.) The imagery of Psalm 55 ('Oh that I had wings like a dove! ...') denotes flight from 'horror' and 'the terrors of death', but as Goode points out ('The pervasive mystery', p. 267) in Psalm 68 'the dove's wings are used as a metaphor of triumph over humiliation.' I am struck too by Yeazell's suggestion (*Language and Knowledge*, pp. 136–7, n. 15) that the idea of a dead woman's jealous revenge is one James would have come across in George Eliot's *Daniel Deronda* (1876). Of course, it is possible to construct the psychology of a Milly who simply wanted to make the lovers happy together (although her ignorance of human relationships didn't preclude – indeed contributed to – her capacity for jealousy). There is no doubt James originally envisaged Milly's act as one of pure benevolence (Ntbks 172). But, as he says in the Preface, 'one's plan, alas, is one thing and one's result another' (AN 296).

Epilogue

1. Densher's position at the end of *The Wings of the Dove*, like that of the narrator in 'The Figure in the Carpet', is perilously similar to Marian's, left by the death of the Reverend Condrip 'crumpled and useless, with nothing in her but what he accounted for'. It will be noted that Marian doesn't seem to have got much out of the Christian connection either.

2. The name 'Stringham', among other things, suggests that James regarded Susie as a *ficelle* (French, 'string', or figuratively 'narrative device'), the category 'not of the true agent' to which he also assigned Maria Gostrey (see AN 55).

3. In *The Awkward Age*, the spectacular plunge into sin, after her marriage, of the virginal Aggie ('the real thing') might seem to have that kind of inevitability about it. Yet we are not called on here to look for an absolute moral difference between Aggie and her counterpart Nanda, who don't ask to be related along such an axis because they are being used by James in unrelated functions: Aggie as an emblem, Nanda as a recording consciousness. Mr Longdon as he considers the two girls knows that he is concerned with 'surfaces'; so that his comparison of the pink-beribboned pet lamb Aggie with Nanda who, suspecting her 'doom', catches the 'far-borne scent, in the flowery fields, of blood' (p. 159), is an invitation merely to see the idea of bloom and doom as a chiaroscuro effect, crimson and pink, worked into James's novel as part of its overall pattern of domesticated violence. It gives the carpet a characteristic appearance, but it can't be the figure in it, because the figure isn't so ubiquitously visible.

4. No story invites reconstruction as urgently as 'The Turn of the Screw'. The governess, faced with the facts that Miles is dead and she was

responsible for him, constructs a meaning that makes sense of them. (Her construction is based on the premise that the good has gone to the bad, for *she* deals in absolutes; on this, see Bell, *Meaning in Henry James*, especially pp. 229–37.) But we find our own meanings in the spaces where our observation ought to dovetail with her interpretation but doesn't. Hundreds of stories must have been constructed in this way out of James's, though most will resemble the governess's in so far as they involve mystery, terror, the fear of losing something (the children? the meaning? self-esteem?). In this sense the sacrifice of the boy represents James's biggest pay-off: if Miles weren't dead, the governess wouldn't have, or perhaps want, to tell the story at all; and our own recuperative efforts would be less intense.

5. *The Golden Bowl*, pp. 429–33: Fanny seems about to offer Maggie an interpretation ('A crack? Then your whole idea has a crack'), but then when the bowl is smashed tries, in an act of epistemological vandalism, to obliterate meaning entirely ('Whatever you meant by it … has ceased to exist.'). The different meaning that Maggie picks up seems partly to reside in the violence of the action itself, uppermost in her mind as she tries to piece the shards together: 'She *knew*, and her broken bowl was proof that she knew …' (cf. the governess's assumption that Miles's death *means* he is 'dispossessed'). The idea that violence can masquerade as epistemological certainty has its relevance to a conception of 'the real thing', as something that hits us in the eye, but might not be there at a second glance.

6. I quote from 'The Turn of the Screw' (10.23), where the governess perceives her story's initial (and continuing) course as a 'succession of flights and drops'. Her ballooning aspirations resemble those floated in *The Wings of the Dove* (I will be a heroine, take control, my narrative will end in meaning); and her sudden lapses of certainty and belief in herself, shared by the reader, are similar to Milly's.

7. 'She's wonderful and beautiful and I feel somehow as if she were dying. Not really, not physically … but dying for us – for you and me – and making us feel it by the very fact of there being so much of her left' – says Maggie to the husband whom she has retrieved from Charlotte (*The Golden Bowl*, p. 550, and see pp. 564–5, 567).

8. James took, in *The Wings of the Dove*, certain gambles: by raising the sentimental stakes, by letting his heroine die before the end, by allowing his anti-heroine to dominate the narrative, by letting the story languish only to re-energize it at the last minute. In *The Golden Bowl*, his next and his last completed novel, the destabilising element of the have-it-all–lose-it-all, risk-taking mind-set is quarantined in Charlotte, and the result a sense of restored equilibrium. Actual death is no longer an issue; sentiment is subdued by a stronger infusion of worldly considerations; control of the narrative point of view is more evenly distributed, and denied to the anti-heroine; narrative energy is not wasted but recycled, action regularly provoking further action; and Maggie's re-creation of Charlotte, when like Kate she finally has, and is, lost, contributes to our last impression – which is also Maggie's – of a precarious balance achieved between loss and gain.

Further Reading

The following brief list is supplementary to the items mentioned in the notes.

Anesko, Michael, *Friction with the Market: Henry James and the profession of authorship*, New York and Oxford, 1986.

Beach, Joseph Warren, *The Method of Henry James*, Philadelphia, 1954.

Bersani, Leo, 'The Jamesian Lie', in *A Future for Astyanax: Character and desire in literature*, Boston and Toronto, 1976.

Bradbury, Nicola, *Henry James: The later novels*, Oxford, 1979.

Brooke-Rose, Christine, 'The Squirm of the True', in *A Rhetoric of the Unreal*, Cambridge, 1981.

Chatman, Seymour, *The Later Style of Henry James*, Oxford, 1972.

Crews, Frederick C., *The Tragedy of Manners: Moral drama in the later novels of Henry James*, New Haven, 1957.

Falconer, Graham, 'Flaubert, James and the problem of undecidability', *Comparative Literature* 39 (1987), 1–18.

Fetterley, Judith, *The Resisting Reader: A feminist approach to American fiction*, Bloomington, Ind., and London, 1977.

Henry James: Literary Criticism, Library of America, ed. Leon Edel and Mark Wilson, 2 vols, New York and Cambridge, 1984.

Hocks, Richard A., *Henry James: A study of the short fiction*, New York, 1990.

Holland, Laurence Bedwell, *The Expense of Vision: Essays in the craft of Henry James*, Princeton, NJ, 1964, revised edn 1982.

Jones, Vivien, *James the Critic*, London, 1985.

Kaplan, Fred, *Henry James. The Imagination of Genius: A biography*, London, 1992.

Kaston, Carren, *Imagination and Desire in the Novels of Henry James*, New Brunswick, NJ, 1984.

Kimball, Jean, 'The Abyss and *The Wings of the Dove*', in *Henry James, Modern Judgements*, ed. Tony Tanner, London, 1968.

Lewis, R. W. B., *The Jameses: A family narrative*, London, 1991.

Lodge, David, 'Strether by the River', in *Language of Fiction: Essays in criticism and verbal analysis of the English novel*, London and Henley and New York, pp. 189–278.

McWhirter, David, 'In the "Other House" of Fiction', in *New Essays on 'Daisy Miller' and 'The Turn of the Screw'*, ed. Vivien Pollak, Cambridge, 1993.

Mitchell, Juliet, '*What Maisie Knew*: Portrait of the artist as a young girl', in *The Air of Reality*, ed. John Goode, London, 1972.

Ozick, Cynthia, *What Henry James Knew and other Essays on Writers*, London, 1993.

Pearson, Gabriel, 'The novel to end all novels: *The Golden Bowl*', in *The Air of Reality*, ed. John Goode, London, 1972.

Perosa, Sergio, *Henry James and the Experimental Novel*, Charlottesville, Va., 1978.

Rahv, Philip, 'Attitudes towards Henry James', in *The Question of Henry James: A collection of critical essays*, ed. F. W. Dupee, New York, 1945.

Rowe, John Carlos, *The Theoretical Dimensions of Henry James*, London, 1984.

Tanner, Tony, *The Reign of Wonder: Naivety and reality in American literature*, Cambridge, 1965.

Thurber, James, 'Onward and Upward with the Arts: The Wings of Henry James ', *New Yorker*, 7 Nov. 1959, pp. 188–97.

Willen, Gerald (ed.), *A Casebook on Henry James's 'The Turn of the Screw'*, New York, 1960.

Woolf, Judith, *Henry James: The major novels*, Cambridge, 1991.

Index

FORSYTH LIBRARY
FORT HAYS STATE UNIVERSITY